The Chinese Idea of a University

The Chinese Idea of a University

Phoenix Reborn

Rui Yang

HKU
PRESS
香港大學出版社

Hong Kong University Press
The University of Hong Kong
Pokfulam Road
Hong Kong
https://hkupress.hku.hk

© 2022 Hong Kong University Press

ISBN 978-988-8754-29-8 (*Hardback*)

British Library Cataloguing-in-Publication Data
A catalogue record for this book is available from the British Library.

10 9 8 7 6 5 4 3 2 1

Printed and bound by Sunshine (Caimei) Printing Co., Ltd. in Hong Kong, China

Contents

Acknowledgments   vii

Introduction   1
   Theoretical Grounding   2
   The Empirical Core   4
   Structure of This Book   6

1. Evolution, Features, and Spread of the Chinese Tradition in Higher
   Learning   10
   Schools in Traditional China   13
   Dong Zhongshu's Legacy in Higher Education   18
   Historical Roots of Chinese Higher Education   20
   The External Influence of China's Higher Learning Traditions   24
      Korea   25
      Vietnam   27
      Japan   28

2. Perceptions of Foreign Universities in the Nineteenth Century and the
   Birth of China's Modern Higher Education Institutions   31
   A Century of Humiliation and Transformation   32
   Early Conception of a University   35
   The Oldest Universities in Modern History   40
   Missionary Colleges and Universities   44
   State-Run Universities from 1898 to 1948   47
   Private Higher Institutions   51

3. The Chinese Idea of a University in Academic Discussions   53
   The Chinese University in the English Literature   54
   Debates on Ideas of Modern Universities in Mainland China   58
   Contributions from Hong Kong and Taiwan   62

4. Increasingly Alike: Formal Resemblance   65
   Institutional Infrastructure   66
   Social and Financial Resources   75

Research and Innovation   81
Teaching and Learning   85
Evidence from the Fieldwork   91

5. Similar but Different: Substantive Mix   99
Monitoring Competing Imperatives   101
Managing Local-Global Relations   104
Bringing Back Cultural Traditions   107
Fostering a Bicultural Intellectual Mind   110
Reactivating the Chinese Idea of a University   113

Conclusion   119
Bibliography   129
Index   147

Acknowledgments

I acknowledge with gratitude the General Research Fund project entitled "Integrating Chinese and Western Higher Education Traditions: A Comparative Policy Analysis of the Quest for World-class Universities in Mainland China, Hong Kong, Taiwan and Singapore" (751313H) supported by the Research Grants Council, Hong Kong Special Administrative Region. The grant allowed me to carry out the research for this book.

I want to thank all my participants for their trust and generous input. As senior members of major universities, they were kind to spend time to share with me their passion and insights as well as their excitement and frustrations.

I owe a special debt of gratitude to Professor Ruth Hayhoe of the University of Toronto and to Professor Simon Marginson of Oxford University. They not only carefully read and commented on my manuscript but have also shared their ideas and knowledge with me on related themes over the years.

I would also like to thank Peter Daniell and Kenneth Yung of Hong Kong University Press.

Introduction

I started writing this book in Hong Kong amid the global outbreak of COVID-19 in 2020. The pandemic was rampant both in Hong Kong and on the Chinese mainland. In Chinese astrology, 2020 is a Metal Rat year. From the traditional Chinese calendar, it is Geng Zi (庚子, the thirty-seventh year of the sixty-year cycle), a calamitous year of a complex series of natural catastrophes. In history, it brings crises: in 1840, the First Opium War with Britain; in 1900, the Boxer Rebellion; and in 1960, the Great Famine that followed the Great Leap Forward, during which an estimated thirty to forty million Chinese died of starvation. However, it is also a year of transformation and growth, symbolizing great change and the ending of past stagnation. As a year and cycle of new beginnings, it helps to nourish any changes that take place in 2020. By the time the final manuscript of this book is submitted to Hong Kong University Press, it will be well after the year 2020. I therefore selected Phoenix Reborn as the subtitle of this book, hoping for a pleasant future of higher education development in Chinese societies.

Another more important reason for me to choose the subtitle is the symbolic meaning of the destruction, renewal, and multi-sourcing origin of the legendary phoenix that expresses the sense I have made of the Chinese idea of a university. In mythology, the symbolism of the majestic phoenix dies and is reborn from the ashes to start a new and long life. From the pile of ashes, a new phoenix arises, young and powerful. The mythical phoenix has been incorporated into many religions, signifying renewal, resurrection, creation, and fresh beginnings. In East Asia, it represents Chinese virtues: goodness, duty, propriety, kindness, and reliability. As this book reveals, the Chinese higher learning tradition is deeply and historically rooted. It differs greatly from that in the West in both epistemology and structure. Modern universities in Chinese societies, however, are patterned after the Western model, after their tradition experienced a baptism of blood and fire in the nineteenth century. Integrating both traditions would open further space for them to explore their own academic model.

Theoretical Grounding

Recent decades have witnessed remarkable higher education development in Chinese societies, including mainland China, Hong Kong, Taiwan, and Singapore. While the achievements have been widely acknowledged, what lies ahead is much less agreed on. Higher education development in these societies has reached a critical yet uncertain stage. It is important to challenge some long-held notions of doom and gloom about Asia's higher education development based fundamentally on their traditional culture as "twisted roots."[1] However, a closer scrutiny would find that the increasingly appealing note of optimism about higher education development in the societies is not always well founded. There has been insufficient theorization to effectively come to terms with their newly gained experience, especially how it differs from Western experiences, and in what direction it would lead the higher education systems. As these societies, mainland China in particular, are rapidly becoming rising players in global higher education, an examination of the Chinese idea of a university is highly timely and is both theoretically and practically significant.

This book conceptualizes the cultural foundations of modern university development in Chinese societies. Its focus, however, is not centered on the uniqueness of such societies. Instead, it aims to prove that one purpose could be fulfilled via many paths and that most of the characteristics that the university had could be found in other institutions of higher learning. Citing the practices of four selected Chinese societies, it argues that it is possible to combine Chinese and Western ideas of a university. The impasse between them, often suggested by researchers both within and outside these societies, is not well based. The modern research university that developed in the nineteenth and twentieth centuries differs greatly from the medieval university. Against a backdrop of increasingly intensified globalization, the university today is a global institution rooted deeply in its own national traditions. This is not to suggest Chinese societies could simply emulate Western practices. Rather, this volume calls for bringing history and culture back into the studies of universities.

Echoing a growing awareness of multiple university identities and calls for alternatives to the West's global higher education hegemony,[2] the Chinese idea of a

---

1. Altbach coined the term to illustrate the cultural conflicts in the development of modern universities in Asia. See Philip G. Altbach, "Twisted Roots: The Western Impact on Asian Higher Education," *Higher Education* 18, no. 1 (1989): 9–29.
2. Scholars have argued that universities in Africa, Asia, and Latin America were often established according to European models. The 'Eurocentric' higher education in those societies has hampered universities in releasing endogenous creativity and seeking their cultural roots, causing tensions between the orientation toward indigenous values and problems on the one hand and addressing global problems on the other. See Simon Marginson, "The West's Global HE Hegemony—Nothing Lasts Forever," *University World News*, March 28, 2014; Adebayo Akomolafe and Ijeoma Dike, "Decolonizing Education: Enunciating the Emancipatory Promise of Non-Western Alternatives to Higher Education" (paper presented at the XII International Seminar on Globalization of Higher Education: Challenges

university comes into people's view as research universities develop and mature in Chinese societies. Higher education development in these societies is fundamentally about the relations between Chinese and Western cultural values. Whether or not the societies can fulfill their long-desired integration between the two value systems is the true meaning of and biggest challenge for their higher education development. The strikingly different traditional cultural roots and heritages have led to continuous conflicts between indigenous and Western higher education values. Although the establishment of modern universities in Chinese societies has been based almost exclusively on Western values, there exists an informal yet powerful system supported by traditional culture. The formally institutionalized Western-style higher education system and the informal Chinese value system often do not support each other. Instead, constant tensions between them reduce the efficiency of university operation. Since modern times, operating Western-style universities in the Confucian context has never been easy for these societies. Due to their divergent historical trajectories, they have adopted different approaches to encountering the West, giving particular meaning to comparisons between them.

However, this has proven much harder than expected. The Western academic model has not been tolerant of alternatives. The definitive feature of autonomy and academic freedom in their strict sense does not exist in the Chinese higher education tradition. In contrast to the healthy tension between truth and power in the West, as Bové has illustrated,[3] Chinese higher education traditionally relies heavily on its relations with the ruling elites. Ever since Dong Zhongshu (179–104 BCE), such a legacy of strong alliance between education and politics has survived dramatic social and cultural changes remarkably and remains deeply rooted among Chinese people. As former president of Yale University Richard Levin has acknowledged,[4] the concept of world-class university is still defined by the strongest American and British universities. China's rich intellectual and higher education legacy becomes a major barrier to the development of its modern universities. Researchers see such an obstacle: Hayhoe contends that there was no institution in the Chinese tradition that could be called a university, while Altbach has long predicted that a kind of "glass ceiling" would be reached for Chinese universities.[5]

& Opportunities, New Delhi, India, January 4–5, 2011); Berte van Wyk and Philip Higgs, "The Call for an African University: A Critical Reflection," *Higher Education Policy* 20, no. 1 (2007): 61–71; Torsten Husén, "The Idea of the University: Changing Roles, Current Crisis and Future Challenges," *Prospects* 21, no. 2 (1991): 171–188.

3. Paul A. Bové, *Edward Said and the Work of the Critic: Speaking Truth to Power* (Durham, NC: Duke University Press, 2000).

4. Richard Levin, "Top of the Class: The Rise of Asia's Universities," *Foreign Affairs* 89, no. 3 (2010): 63–75.

5. See Ruth Hayhoe, *China's Universities 1895–1995: A Century of Cultural Conflict* (New York: Garland, 1996), 10; Philip G. Altbach, "The Asian Higher Education Century?" *International Higher Education* 59, Spring (2010): 4.

Despite fast-growing confidence in the universities in Chinese societies, few have been able to theorize how these universities have developed differently from those in the West. Puzzlement remains regarding their significant features, such as the close alignments in Chinese societies between universities and government goals, and a resulting level of government support that few Western universities are seeing nowadays. Identity-building is doomed to be an arduous task for the universities. Reflecting the general discourse on university development, what has been lacking in the debates is empirically based studies that take cultural values and their actual impact seriously. The deep-rooted cultural heritages have led to continuous conflicts with the dominant Western values that underlie successful operation of modern universities. Meanwhile, both extraordinary achievements and enormous difficulties in the university development in Chinese societies are sufficiently substantial to challenge existing understandings. People wonder about how to come to terms with the current and future university development in these societies and their implications, especially for other non-Western societies.

The Empirical Core

This book attempts to link the historical to the present against a backdrop of an enormous impact of Western academic models and institutions from the beginning of modern universities in Chinese societies all the way to the contemporary period. Its empirical core derived from a General Research Fund project entitled "Integrating Chinese and Western Higher Education Traditions: A Comparative Policy Analysis of the Quest for World-Class Universities in Chinese Mainland, Hong Kong, Taiwan and Singapore" funded by the Research Grants Council, Hong Kong Special Administrative Region, during 2015–2017. Focusing on the quest for world-class universities in mainland China, Hong Kong, Taiwan, and Singapore, it was a comparative investigation consisting of eight universities as cases in the four societies.[6] The cases included Peking University (BJ) and Tsinghua University (QH) in mainland China; The University of Hong Kong (HKU) and The Hong Kong University of Science and Technology (HKUST) in Hong Kong; National Taiwan University (TU) and National Tsing Hua University (THU) in Taiwan; and National University of Singapore (NUS) and Nanyang Technological University (NTU) in Singapore.

The cases were chosen to be representative of comprehensive and technological types of universities in the four selected societies. Cross-case analyses were undertaken to identify common themes and major differences within and between them, to build an understanding of rapidly evolving policies on higher education

---

6.   A case study approach was adopted due to my recognition of both the complexity and the context, informed by Punch. See Keith F. Punch, *Introduction to Research Methods in Education* (London: Sage, 2009).

in the context of globalization. The sampling was purposive, involving the selection of particular societies, particular universities, and particular participants within individual institutions. The societies were chosen based on the following reasons. First, they are mainly of Chinese settlement and share to a great extent Chinese cultural identity that influences both social elites and masses in new, popular, or other varied forms.[7] Second, they have been under considerable Western influences with different historical trajectories. Hong Kong, Taiwan, and Singapore all have a history of colonization. Although mainland China was never a colony, Western models have had immense prestige there. Third, their rapidly improved economic situation allows and even requires them to begin to change their frame of reference in higher education policy.[8]

Within each case study institution, participants were drawn from both administrators and ordinary academics. Initial approach was made to the administration through professional and personal contacts in each society. Administrators were then asked to identify other participants for the study by snowball sampling.[9] In each university, both administrators (the president, other senior executive leaders, and administrators working in international programs) and academic staff members from various faculties of the humanities and social sciences, natural sciences, and engineering were invited to participate. Institutional participants were selected to obtain a range of seniority from assistant to chair/full professor levels and to include both men and women. Many held academic and administrative leadership positions at that time. All participants were required to have at least five years' experience in the university, in order to obtain a sense of the changes in each institution over the time under study.

Document analysis and in-depth semi-structured interviews were used to gather data. For each university, a series of high-level policy documents from institutional mission and/or vision statements, strategic plans, to leaders' speeches were collected, reviewed, and interrogated, to analyze the context for policy on building world-class universities.[10] They were also used to examine the localized context (historical, geographic, social, economic, and cultural dimensions) and specific

---

7. For a detailed discussion of how Confucian values spread throughout the region in premodern times and how these values were transformed in an age of modernization, see Gilbert Rozman, ed., *The East Asian Region: Confucian Heritage and Its Modern Adaptation* (Princeton, NJ: Princeton University Press, 1991).
8. By creating institutions of global status on their own soil, these societies embrace international norms in the top layer of their universities. For a theoretical analysis of such mechanisms, see Simon Marginson, "Dynamics of National and Global Competition in Higher Education," *Higher Education* 52, no. 1 (2006): 1–39.
9. See Keith F. Punch and Alis Oancea, *Introduction to Research Methods in Education* (Thousand Oaks, CA: Sage, 2014), 212.
10. In the study, documents were seen as a rich source of data for education and social research. See Max Travers, Qualitative Research through Case Study (London: Sage, 2001). The conduct of document analysis followed the instructions in the methodological literature on social research, in particular, Zina O'Leary, *The Essential Guide to Doing Research* (London: Sage, 2004).

policies on becoming world-class in each case study university, prior to the collection of interview data. In-depth semi-structured interviews were scheduled flexibly to encourage participants to talk as much as they pleased on different issues as they arose, "core" questions asked at each case to make comparisons and contrasts for triangulation purposes between different localized sites. They were conducted in either Mandarin or English, depending on the interviewee's preference, and lasted normally for an hour, the shortest for thirty-two minutes and the longest one hour and forty minutes. All interviews were taped and later transcribed (translated and transcribed in the case of those in Mandarin).

There were two stages of analyzing the data set. Stage one identified important themes in answering the research questions, following the approaches suggested by Miles, Huberman, and Saldaña.[11] Stage two used the themes for cross-case comparisons. Documents at both societal and institutional levels were collected and analyzed to identify key features of the policy on the world-class university for the society and universities. Collection of the empirical data occurred in May 2014 in Beijing, May 2015 in Taipei, and July 2015 in Singapore and Hong Kong. A total of seventy-one interviews were carried out, nineteen in Beijing, fifteen in Hong Kong, seventeen in Singapore, and twenty in Taiwan. Analysis of interview data was then conducted, followed by the triangulation of data from documents with interview data within and between the cases.

Structure of This Book

Set in a global context, this book consists of five chapters between this introductory chapter that provides readers with a narrative of the book project and a conclusion that summarizes the principal findings and major arguments. Based on a strong belief that cultural traditions play a critical role in the development of modern universities in Chinese societies, Chapter 1 traces the origin of China's higher education, chronicles its later development, and analyzes its major features, often in comparison with the European tradition. The chapter also looks at the cross-border spread of the Chinese tradition to neighboring societies in East Asia and Southeast Asia. Since China's past—imperial or otherwise—strongly shapes its views of the world, of itself, and of its place in the world, the chapter argues that it is time for Chinese policy and intellectual elites to engage in deep introspection on this historical matter.

Chapter 2 is devoted to the perceptions of foreign universities in the nineteenth century and the birth of China's modern higher education institutions. In a context of Chinese-Western civilizational conflicts in the nineteenth century, China's traditional idea of higher learning faced unprecedented challenges from the European

---

11. Matthew B. Miles, A. Michael Huberman, and Johnny Saldaña, *Qualitative Data Analysis: A Methods Source Book* (London: Sage, 2014).

university and experienced a baptism of blood and fire. This chapter first documents Chinese people's early perceptions of the universities in the West and Japan during the second half of the nineteenth century. It then elucidates how China's pioneering thinkers, including intellectuals, officials, and industrialists, explored a Chinese path to modern universities that combines both indigenous and Western traditions. It reveals that the establishment of a Chinese idea of a university predated China's modern universities that did not result from Chinese history. Patterned after Harvard and Yale Universities, Imperial Tientsin University (天津北洋西學學堂, later Beiyang University), established in 1895, was China's first perfectly justifiable modern university to acquire Western knowledge in a comprehensive and systematic manner. The chapter further expounds the great significance of the early endeavors in the histories of Chinese societies.

Chapter 3 critically appraises the literature on the Chinese idea of a university in both English and Chinese languages. Since the nineteenth century, Chinese societies, as latecomers to modernization, have prioritized Western learning. Following European and North American patterns, modern universities were created to serve this purpose, with little linkage to their indigenous cultural traditions. However, operating in Confucian sociocultural contexts, they have been constantly struggling with their cultural identity. This chapter sorts out the scholarly and professional pursuit of this theme internationally in a systematic way. It starts with Philip Altbach's well-known assessment of the tremendous Western impact on Asian higher education development in the 1980s.[12] It then moves across Chinese societies to reassess the discussions of higher learning ideas in both East and West,[13] traditional ideals of a Chinese university,[14] the Confucian model of higher education in East Asia, and the present debates over the new Chinese model for higher education.[15]

---

12. Altbach, "Twisted Roots."

13. Among those who have contributed to such discussions, the most prominent is Professor Ruth Hayhoe, who has written extensively and profoundly on Chinese higher education and educational relations between East Asia and the West. Her theoretical thrust is particularly in the ways in which cultural values and epistemologies from Eastern civilizations may provide a resource for new thinking in global higher education development. See, for example, *China's Universities 1895–1995*; and Ruth Hayhoe, "Ideas of Higher Learning East and West: Conflicting Values in the Development of the Chinese University," *Minerva* 32, no. 4 (1994): 361–382.

14. There has been a burgeoning body of literature on this theme, published especially in Chinese within the Chinese mainland. Few of such works, however, are well based on a sound understanding of the Western idea of a university. In comparison, a collection of Professor Ambrose King's random thoughts on fifteen divergent themes largely related to the origin, ideal, and development of modern universities, particularly in Chinese societies, has been widely read in Chinese societies. With many brilliant expositions, it covers a wide range of topics on humanism, science, and culture, including general education, the international nature of a university, modernity, globalization, and general educational issues in Chinese societies. See Yeo-chi Ambrose King 金耀基, *Daxue zhi Linian* 大學之理念 [The Idea of a University] (Beijing: Joint Publishing, 2001).

15. Such debates have become heated in a context of a rising Chinese power, due to substantial contributions by writers such as Simon Marginson. See Simon Marginson, "Higher Education in East Asia and Singapore: Rise of the Confucian model," *Higher Education* 61, no. 5 (2011): 587–611; and "'Ideas of a

Starting from Chapter 4, the line of sight turns relatively from the historical to the contemporary and from theory to practice with much incorporation of empirical evidence. With an eye on achievements, Chapter 4 delineates a lively scenario of the impressive progress the societies have made in higher education. The achievement becomes even more remarkable when compared with many other non-Western societies. It demonstrates that a Western-style modern higher education system has been well established throughout these societies. The massification of higher education has provided people with wide access to tertiary institutions. With a strong emphasis on Research and Development (R&D), the research conducted in these universities has also been growing rapidly. Through mainly a lens of the centrality of governance, this chapter details how the universities and systems in the societies have become increasingly similar to their counterparts in North America and Europe, at systemic, institutional, and individual levels.

Reporting findings from the empirical data collected at premier universities in Beijing, Hong Kong, Singapore, and Taipei, Chapter 5 substantializes contemporary higher education development in Chinese societies. Viewing the experience as a cultural experiment, it unveils the products of the higher education systems with a bicultural intellectual mind that positions their flagship universities well to combine Chinese and Western ideas of a university in everyday operation. The integration opens space for ways to enrich the idea of a university and calls for a reconceptualized view of modern university development in Chinese societies. Through exploring how they have, and have not, achieved establishing world-class universities on their soil, and how their experience could contribute to the betterment of the idea of a university, the efforts and achievements by Chinese societies indicate that the idea of a university means both challenges and opportunities for them and that a university rooted in Chinese educational heritages does not have to reject Western knowledge while providing services to their communities.

The concluding chapter discusses the historical legacy of the Chinese idea of a university and its modern implications. It points out emphatically that the experience of Chinese societies in their development of higher education is essentially an experiment of interplay between different cultural traditions. It is a process in which higher education plays its most significant role and at the same time is much shaped by it. In a context of global dominance by the Western academic model, the development of modern universities in Chinese societies involves necessarily responding to the overweening power of the West. Since this has indeed been a fundamental challenge to all non-Western societies, the experiment of the Chinese idea of a university is therefore historically unprecedented and globally significant.

University' for the Global Era" (keynote speech delivered at Positioning University in the Globalized World: Changing Governance and Coping Strategies in Asia, Centre of Asian Studies, The University of Hong Kong, December 10, 2008).

Instead of providing an alternative to the Western model, it adds to the idea of a university as an asset that belongs to the entire human society.

All four selected Chinese societies have been struggling with encountering the West for at least one and a half centuries. They have also made great progress in higher education recently. Both their success and failure are substantial enough to challenge the existing interpretations in the literature. Yet, the experiences have been poorly theorized, mainly due to the unsuitability of the lens borrowed uncritically from the West to observe higher education development in the societies. While their experiences differ strikingly from that in the West, they have been measured by the same yardstick. Through incorporating the most recent progress made by the four societies, this book critiques the literature and delves deeply into the theorization of higher education development, especially in non-Western societies. It hopes to demonstrate how researchers studying higher education in Chinese societies, from outside and within, can avoid being bogged down in a quagmire of a tradition-modernity contrast in their interpretation of what is happening to the higher education systems. It also intends to reveal how to overcome an overreliance of the current conceptualization of higher education development in those societies on Western theoretical constructions and calls for new perspectives that give weight to the impact of traditional Chinese ways of cultural thinking on contemporary practices.

1

Evolution, Features, and Spread of the Chinese Tradition in Higher Learning

China's history of schooling can be traced to the sixteenth century BCE, during the late Xia dynasty (2070–1600 BCE). Some argue that the ancient Chinese education system was established during the Yu period (2257–2208 BCE), and the earliest higher learning institutions appeared during the Eastern Zhou dynasty (771–221 BCE). According to the description of Confucian scholars (儒林傳) in Volume 88 of the *Book of Han* (漢書), formal schooling emerged in China during the Xia dynasty. A national government school system had been established by the Western Zhou period (1046–771 BCE).[1] Confucius (551–479 BCE) left an indelible mark on Chinese education,[2] similar to that of Socrates in the

---

1. The oldest Chinese word for "school," *Xiang* (庠), means a building for livestock with two facing walls, where elderly people reared sheep, pigs, or cattle and at the same time were entrusted with the duty to watch children and instruct them. In primitive society, knowledge was passed on orally by elders to their children. As hieroglyphic writings emerged around 3,000 years ago, professional institutions emerged to transmit knowledge. They were called *Chengjun* (成均), the predecessors of schools. Formal schools were established during the Xia dynasty (2070–1600 BCE). They were called *Xiao* (校) during the Xia dynasty, *Xu* (序) during the Shang dynasty (1600–1046 BCE) and *Xiang* (庠) during the early Zhou dynasty (1046–221 BCE). See Guo Qijia 郭齊家, *Zhongguo gudai xuexiao* 中國古代學校 [Schools in ancient China] (Beijing: Commercial Press, 1998).

2. It should be noted that the evolution of China's intellectual landscape has been featured by different social and political ideas, especially Confucianism, Daoism and Buddhism. As Chen Yinke (1890–1969) observed, "From the Jin dynasty until the present day, Chinese thought may be represented by the Three Teachings of Confucianism, Buddhism, and Daoism. This may appear to be no more than popular talk, but check it against the facts of past history, test it against the sensibilities of today, and one will find that this proposition about Three Teachings is indisputable." See Chen Yinke 陳寅恪, "Feng Youlan Zhongguo zhexueshi xiace shencha baogao" 馮友蘭中國哲學史下冊審查報告 [Report on my inspection of vol. 2 of Feng Youlan's history of Chinese philosophy], in *Chen Yinke Ji* 陳寅恪集 [The works of Chen Yinke], vol. 2 (Beijing: Sanlian shudian, 2001), 285. Over time, the blending of Buddhism, Daoism, and Confucianism resulted in the development of specific schools of thought that viewed these three teachings as one. See Timothy Brook, "Rethinking Syncretism: The Unity of the Three Teachings and their Joint Worship in Late-Imperial China," *Journal of Chinese Religions* 21, no. 1 (1993): 13–44; Daniel J. Paracka Jr., "China's Three Teachings and the Relationship of Heaven, Earth and Humanity," *Worldviews* 16, no. 1 (2012): 73–98. However, the central emphasis on Confucianism in official ideology and intellectual discourse led to fragmentary and insufficient documentation of the impact of other schools of thought and a lack of understanding of how these traditions interacted and counteracted. Although many people feel strongly about such profound influence, few have articulated it in a clear and systematic manner.

West.[3] China is also the earliest country to select officials through education to serve bureaucracy and state-building.[4] Its long history of schooling is featured particularly by a unification of education and politics. Education has always and arguably only been designed to serve political needs. Throughout history, Chinese education was never separate from politics.[5] Highly aware of the significance of education for their dominion, Chinese rulers were keen to buy educators' support, and they succeeded. A related feature of Chinese traditional schooling is its overwhelming focus on Confucian ethics,[6] which was, again, fundamentally for ruling purposes. Traditional schooling was designed to serve the aristocracy only.[7] The ties between the past and the present have remained powerful.[8]

Chinese people are proud of China's long history as a strong and vibrant culture and as a highly influential political and social entity. The cultural influence of China, one of the oldest countries in the world, goes beyond its territorial boundaries.

---

3. Confucius was the first professional teacher. His teachings formed the foundation of much of subsequent Chinese speculation on education. See Jingpan Chen, *Confucius as a Teacher: Philosophy of Confucius with Special Reference to Its Educational Implications* (Beijing: China Foreign Languages Press, 1990). The similarity to Socrates was expressed in a classic chronicle of Chinese philosophical thought from the third millennium to the twentieth century by Feng Youlan (Fung Yu-lan 馮友蘭, 1895–1990). The book was intended for the general public in the West. In it Feng presented and examined the history of Chinese philosophy from a viewpoint that was very much influenced by the Western philosophical fashion prevalent at the time. The book later became the standard work in its field and had a huge effect in reigniting an interest in Chinese thought. See Yu-lan Fung, *A Short History of Chinese Philosophy* (New York: Macmillan, 1948).

4. Beginning from the time of the Xia dynasty, it was traditional for ancient kings and emperors to select well-educated officials to assist them in administering their kingdoms.

5. Indeed, some would argue that calls for educational independence never emerged. See Sun Hongan 孫宏安, "Zhongguo gudai jiaoyu tedian" 中國古代教育特點 [Features of ancient Chinese education], *Journal of Liaoning Normal University* 遼寧師範大學學報 4 (1996): 26–29.

6. Having a 5,000-year timeline history, the category of China's classical cultural tradition is complex and entails very different elements. As a main resource for cultural *Bildung* and combined with the system of autocratic monarchy, Confucianism attained the status of a national ideology after the establishment of the Han dynasty. Its institutionalization allowed it to be the dominant school of ethical and moral thought in traditional Chinese culture for more than two thousand years. Confucian texts were key to the orthodox state ideology of the Chinese dynasties. Confucianism has been the core value of Chinese society and permeates every aspect of Chinese society: the politics, economy, philosophy, social psychology, social customs, ways of thinking, and ways of living. See Ming-huei Lee, *Confucianism: Its Roots and Global Significance* (Honolulu, HI: University of Hawai'i Press, 2017); Yu Ying-shih 余英時, "Zhongguo wenhua yu xiandai bianqian" 中國文化與現代變遷 [Chinese culture and its modern changes] (Taipei: Sanmin shuju, 1992).

7. See Huang Ji 黃濟, "Zhongguo gudai jiaoyu zhexue sixiang de fazhan licheng ji zhuyao tedian" 中國古代教育哲學思想的發展歷程及主要特點 [Educational philosophy in ancient China: Developmental stages and characteristics], *Journal of Beijing Normal University* 北京師範大學學報 6 (1994): 28–34.

8. The late John Cleverley pointed this out in the mid-1980s, but only briefly. See John Cleverley, *Schooling of China: Tradition and Modernity in Chinese Education* (Sydney: Allen & Unwin, 1985). Until now and generally, for all the attention focused on China's recent growth story, relatively little is understood outside China about its education system. There is a dearth of research on the empirical linkage between China's traditions and present socioeconomic practices. Therefore, it is no surprise that few scholars have been able to theorize about China's recent remarkable achievements in education.

Indeed, it is almost impossible to overstate the level of the impact on surrounding countries. A large geographical region, especially in East and Southeast Asia, is heavily influenced by Chinese culture, most notably in Japan, Korea, and Vietnam. The spread of Buddhism from India via the Silk Road into traditional China and then outward to Northeast Asia and Southeast Asia,[9] along with Confucian ideologies and mode of thinking, has provided a unifying foundation. Japan, Korea, and Vietnam all used Chinese characters for writing their language for centuries, and Japan still does. Japanese culture is substantially derived from Tang dynasty (618–907) China. Korea's was fundamentally shaped by Chinese culture. In Vietnam, the government was not only a protectorate of the Chinese emperor for much of the last two thousand years, but many aspects of Vietnamese culture, from food and social customs, to government and philosophy, have come almost exclusively from China.

Education has always been the most valued key component of Chinese culture. During China's long past, practices of education varied enormously from dynasty to dynasty and between periods of strength and weakness. However, some of China's most distinctive and enduring traditions in education were developed quite early, including in particular a highly sophisticated set of scholarly values. They survived dramatic social and cultural changes remarkably and have remained deeply rooted among Chinese people. As part of historical and cultural traditions, they have also exerted a profound impact on how education is practiced and reformed in China's neighboring countries although these societies have all developed their own modern education systems. To a great extent the traditional Chinese idea of a university could also be seen as the East (and to a relatively less extent Southeast) Asian pattern. It compares markedly with the traditions in the West. Such an educational legacy forms an integral and significant part of human wisdom in education and has strong implications for reform and development in other parts of the world. It deserves much attention both theoretically and practically.

More specifically in the field of higher education research, Clark Kerr famously counted that, of seventy-five institutions founded before 1520, "which are [still] doing much the same things in much the same places, in much the same ways and under the same names," about sixty are universities, putting some universities in such company as the Roman Catholic Church, the Bank of Siena, or the Royal Mint.[10] This does not mean universities have remained the same. Indeed, since their establishment in Europe in the twelfth century, the core missions and roles of a university have changed dramatically. Universities have become more and more

---

9. See Richard Foltz, *Religions of the Silk Road: Premodern Patterns of Globalization* (New York: Palgrave Macmillan, 2010), 37–58.
10. Clark Kerr, "The Internal and External Threats to the University of the Twenty-First Century (with Comments)," *Minerva* 30, no. 2 (1992): 150.

national institutions and serve many purposes in contemporary society.[11] In the case of China, the history of the educational institutions called university today is longer, and the changes have been far more drastic. Without a good grasp of the nature of Chinese traditional higher education and institutions, it is almost impossible to truly understand modern Chinese higher education.

Schools in Traditional China

Ancient Chinese universities were part of China's imperial school system. It is necessary to understand traditional China's school system before any investigation into ancient Chinese universities. Ever since China's initial encounters with the West, schooling has been a significant part of China's nation-building throughout the twentieth century. As part of the new administration implemented by the late Qing dynasty (1644–1912), Emperor Guangxu issued China's first modern school system (壬寅學制) in 1902 and its modified form (癸卯學制) in 1904, attempting to build a modern school system.[12] Since then China has shifted from a traditional to a Western knowledge system institutionally.[13] Schools in traditional China were, however, a quite different scene. They were categorized into three types: government schools, private schools, and academies (書院) which were sitting between the government and the private. Within each type, they were of different natures and levels.

Government schools were the mainstay of China's imperial education system. China's written record of schooling started from the Western Zhou period. Schools were categorized into two kinds: one (國學) located in the capital city attended by children of the royal family and ministers, the other (鄉學) in regional centers enrolling offspring from slave owners.[14] The system began to show a feature of "no distinction between ruling and education, and officials as teachers" (治教無二，官

11. Philip G. Altbach, "The Complex Roles of Universities in the Period of Globalization," in *Higher Education in the World 3: Higher Education: New Challenges and Emerging Roles for Human and Social Development*, ed. Global University Network for Innovation (GUNi) (Basingstoke: Palgrave Macmillan, 2008), 5–14.

12. Li Guojun 李國鈞 and Wang Bingzhao 王炳照, *Zhongguo jiaoyu zhidu tongshi* 中國教育制度通史 [A general history of Chinese educational system] (Jinan: Shandong Education Press, 2000).

13. It was also the time when science education had just been introduced into China. Schooling began to focus on modern subjects, especially scientific and technological disciplines. The Republican government (1912–1949) continued to establish a modern school system. The period 1912–1937 witnessed China's first peak of schooling, with a national 6-3-3-4 system of schools fully established. After half a century suffering from foreign invasion, civil wars, and political catastrophes, China's second peak of schooling was reached during 1985–2010, when China's system had become highly sophisticated and the nine-year compulsory education fulfilled nationwide. The transformation of China's knowledge system is a central and recurrent theme throughout this volume. For a start, see Rui Yang, Meng Xie, and Wen Wen, "Pilgrimage to the West: Modern Transformations of Intellectual Formulation in Social Sciences," *Higher Education* 77, no. 4 (2019): 815–829.

14. Mao Lirui 毛禮銳, *Zhongguo gudai jiaoyushi* 中國古代教育史 [History of ancient Chinese education] (Beijing: People's Publishing House, 1979).

師合一). Education aimed only at training future rulers and was not available for ordinary people. During the Spring and Autumn (771–476 BCE) and the Warring States (480–221 BCE) periods, government schooling declined. The system was only rebuilt when the Qin dynasty (221–206 BCE) unified China. The "officials-as-teachers system" was further implemented.

By the Han dynasty (206 BCE–220 CE), the Chinese empire became powerful. Government schooling was reestablished and flourished. There were two levels of schooling in the capital: one included Taixue (太學) and Hongdumen Academy (鴻都門學). Taixue was founded in 124 BCE by Emperor Wu at Dong Zhongshu's suggestion. Recruiting tribute students (貢生) from the populace, it was China's earliest higher learning institution and left a historical mark in the Chinese history of education and politics.[15] Its enrolment reached 30,000 during Emperors Shun and Zhi of the Eastern Han period (25–220 CE). Hongdumen Academy was established in 178 BCE by Emperor Ling.[16] It resulted from the emperor's personal love for arts and literature and did not last long. The other was at the basic education level. Emperor Ping of Han (9 BCE–6 CE) required all children of his family to receive schooling from specially chosen teachers. Six years after Emperor Ming ascended to throne, his mother ordered schools set up for children from the monarchy and her own family. Government schooling developed fast after that. Schooling outside the capital was started by a governor in Sichuan province, and Emperor Wu spread it nationwide. By 3 CE, it had been institutionalized.

During the Six Dynasties period (220–589 CE), an era of disunity, instability, and warfare, the Chinese empire was disrupted, and separatist regimes were set up by force of arms. The national unified school system could not last. Instead, various feudal regimes established their own school systems. During some periods, such as the Northern Wei (386–534 CE), schooling developed well with more types of schools and further specialized education. Emperor Wu of Jin (236–290 CE) established Guozixue (國子學) for the Sons of the State in 276 CE to train future rulers. Guozixue coexisted with Taixue. Since then it existed in every dynasty during feudal China.[17] During those periods, vocation-based technology education and specialized teaching emerged in China, including medical and law schools.[18]

Government schooling was rebuilt during the Sui dynasty (581–619 CE) and flourished during the Tang dynasty. The Tang period was one of progress and stability. The Chinese empire flourished, and government schooling developed further. In addition to Taixue and Guozixue, the Tang government set up many more

---

15. Yuan Zheng, "Local Government Schools in Sung China: A Reassessment," *History of Education Quarterly* 34, no. 2 (1994): 193–213.

16. Zhixi Qian, "A Study into the Incident of the Hongdumen Academy," *Frontiers of Literary Studies in China* 4, no. 4 (2010): 483–522.

17. Xiong Mingan 熊明安, *Zhongguo gaodeng jiaoyu shi* 中國高等教育史 [History of Chinese higher education] (Chongqing: Chongqing Press, 1983).

18. Mao Lirui 毛禮銳, *Zhongguo gudai jiaoyushi.*

specialized vocation-based schools covering language and literacy, mathematics, law, calligraphy, and Daoism, as well as primary schools. Taixue expanded during the period to enroll at least 8,000 students, including those from Japan and Korea. Meanwhile, government schooling also developed well at primary and secondary levels in regional centers. A comprehensive national system of regional government schools was founded with some specialized training in various subjects, including medicine and New Daoism (玄學).

The Song dynasty (960–1279 CE) inherited the Tang dynasty's government schooling system. In 1023 and 1103, schools specialized in martial and fine arts were established by Emperors Renzong (宋仁宗, 1010–1063) and Huizong (宋徽宗, 1082–1035) respectively. While the system of schools for the Sons of the State remained the same as those in the Tang dynasty, the Song government put all schools together from primary to higher learning. By the eleventh century, the primary schools in the capital housed over 1,000 pupils. Government schooling in provincial China also copied the Tang dynasty's system. In 1102, Emperor Huizong ordered all children over ten to go to local schools. The Song government issued detailed regulations on selecting students for schools at all levels up to Taixue, through examination.

Government schooling declined again during the Liao (916–1125), Jin (1115–1234), and Yuan (1271–1368) dynasties. During Liao and Jin, only Guozixue and Taixue existed in the capital, while provincial government schooling was limited mainly at the prefecture level. During the Yuan dynasty, there was only Guozixue in the capital, but government schools developed well in regional areas. Some special schools were established to teach Mongol-specific subjects, such as the Mongol language, literature, and medicine. In 1286, the Yuan government organized every fifty families as a *she* (社). Each *she* was required to found a school for their children, called *Shexue* (社學). An experienced senior person with rich knowledge and agricultural skills was nominated to teach at the school. Children learned farming skills, rites, and basic literacy.[19]

During the Ming (1368–1644) and Qing dynasties, government schools were revived. The Ming government continued to have Guozijian and Taixue in the capital, in addition to specialized schools teaching royal family history (皇宗學), martial arts, medicine, and theory of yin and yang. The Qing rulers did similarly, having more specialized schools teaching mathematics and Manchu-specific subjects, including Manchu history and language. There were also schools specifically set up for Russians studying in China. Government-run higher learning reached its peak during the late Ming dynasty, when Guozijian enrolled almost 10,000 students. The students enjoyed excellent pay and conditions, and study and living costs borne by the government. For those who were married, the government provided their wives with living stipends. The government provided financial support for

---

19. Mao Lirui 毛禮銳, *Zhongguo gudai jiaoyushi.*

the wedding of those who got married during their studies. Foreign students were treated exactly the same as the Chinese.[20]

The Ming dynasty inherited regional government schooling from the previous Yuan dynasty, schools at various levels offering medical, yin and yang, and martial arts education, and a widespread *Shexue* system in rural areas. The Qing dynasty largely continued the Ming dynasty's regional government schooling system with more specialized schools established to teach commerce, nursing, and minority studies (土司學). However, the culture at government schools, on both basic and higher education levels, during the Qing dynasty became corrupt. Neither teachers nor students were serious about learning. For students, schools were just a stepping stone to office.[21] This was in line with the wider context of the declining Manchu empire.

Somewhere between government and private schools were academies (書院). Based on the Eastern Han (25–220 CE) tradition of *jing she* (精舍) that Confucian scholars set up private schools for oral instruction on classical texts, the academies originated in 725 during the Tang dynasty. They coexisted with government schools throughout Song, Yuan, Ming, and Qing dynasties. While most of them offered higher learning, some were at the secondary education level. The translation into "academies" was accredited to the Jesuit missionary Matteo Ricci, when he visited the White Deer Grotto Academy (白鹿洞書院) in 1595. They were initially small-scale formalized versions of the Han dynasty scholars' private schools, developed later into places for scholars to train students in classical studies, interpret Confucian doctrines, and collect, collate, and publish books.[22] They took their definitive forms in the Song dynasty[23] and had a national total of 397.[24] They reached their peak during the Southern Song period (1127–1279), due to the popularization of the Neo-Confucianism movement.[25]

The Yuan rulers continued to advocate academies and exerted tighter control over them. Academy directors had to be nominated by the government and were offered official ranks and salaries. Many decisions made within academies also had to be approved by the government. By the late Yuan dynasty, there was little difference between academies and regional government schools. The early Ming rulers attached much importance to government schools and were less interested in academies. Academies were only revived by the Jiajing era (1522–1566);[26] of a total

20. Zhou Yutong 周予同, *Zhongguo xuexiao zhidu* 中國學校制度 [School system in China] (Shanghai: Commercial Press, 1931).
21. Mao Lirui 毛禮銳, *Zhongguo gudai jiaoyushi.*
22. Xinzhong Yao, *The Encyclopedia of Confucianism* (London: Routledge, 2003).
23. Hayhoe, *Chinese Universities 1895–1995.*
24. Chen Yuanhui 陳元暉, *Zhongguo gudai de shuyuan zhidu* 中國古代的書院制度 [Academies in ancient China] (Shanghai: Shanghai Education Press, 1981), 30.
25. Yao, *The Encyclopedia.*
26. Thomas H. C. Lee, *Education in Traditional China: A History* (Leiden: Brill, 2000).

of 1,239 only 184 were privately owned.[27] During this period, most academies were similar to and even the same as government schools. The Qing dynasty initially suppressed academies for political reasons. The attitude changed during the reign of Emperor Kangxi (1654–1722), to provide them with operation funds. Academy directors were nominated by provincial governors. There were over 1,900 academies nationwide, of which 128 were private.[28] Academies aimed only at preparing students for the imperial examination, hoping to win an official rank.[29] Their private nature and freethinking atmosphere had long gone.[30] In 1901, the Qing government ordered all academies to become schools.

Private schools in China began from Confucius. By the Western Zhou, schools were monopolized by the government. During the Spring and Autumn period, government schooling declined and private schools prevailed. Confucius traveled through the kingdoms and created private schools to spread his teaching. This was carried forward by his students. Mozi (470–391 BCE) was another prominent advocator of private schooling. His students continued this. By the Warring States period, private schools developed further, major advocators being Xun Kuang (313–238 BCE) and Mencius (372–289 BCE). They often had hundreds of students. Private schools, then, existed in all Chinese dynasties. Ancient Chinese rulers usually supported private schools so that the schools could serve their rule. There were some exceptions, such as the first emperor of Qin (260–210 BCE) and Emperor Taixu of Northern Wei (408–452), who banned private schools. Private schooling in China took various forms with different names during different historical periods. It included various levels of education from primary to higher learning. Teaching and learning usually focused on Confucian classics and basic literacy. Students were from families of lower classes. In China's long dynastic past, private education was largely malnourished, as the political culture allowed little room for it to develop.[31]

27. Chen Yuanhui 陳元暉, *Zhongguo gudai de shuyuan zhidu*, 67.
28. Chen Yuanhui 陳元暉, 97.
29. Zhang Yan 張雁, *Xifang daxue linian zai jingdai Zhongguo de chuanru yu yingxiang* 西方大學理念在近代中國的傳入與影響 [Western ideas of a university in China: Introduction and impact] (Hangzhou Zhejiang University Press, 2009).
30. Many historians place much hope on the academies "as a kind of counter force to the civil service examination system." See Ruth Hayhoe and Jian Liu "China's Universities, Cross-Border Education, and Dialogue among Civilizations," in *Crossing Borders in East Asian Higher Education*, ed. David W. Chapman, William K. Cummings, and Gerard A. Postiglione (Hong Kong: Springer/Comparative Education Research Center, The University of Hong Kong, 2010), 88.
31. Strictly speaking, China never had private education in the Western sense. Such a fact serves as a reminder that private education in China, past and present, cannot be observed the same way as that in the West. This is not to blame China for doing particularly poorly in this regard but simply to illustrate the need for extra care in watching China's education and society, on both ideological and practical levels. For Chinese political culture, see Rui Yang, "Political Culture and Higher Education Governance in Chinese Societies: Some Reflections," *Frontiers of Education in China* 15, no. 2 (2020): 187–221.

Dong Zhongshu's Legacy in Higher Education

Confucian ethics has had a tremendous effect on government, education, and Chinese society, and the influence has gone far beyond China. However, people do not always realize that Confucius was not always profoundly influential during his own time. Some historical figures that made Confucius influential deserve our attention. One is Dong Zhongshu (董仲舒, 179–104 BCE).[32] A scholar in the Han dynasty (206 BCE–220), Dong was one of China's most influential thinkers. He was largely responsible for establishing Confucianism as the theoretical foundation of the inchoate imperial state in 136 BCE and thus greatly shaped the Chinese culture, particularly in politics and education. He accomplished a theological justification for the emperor as the "Son of Heaven" by developing an elaborate worldview integrating Confucian ethics with naturalistic cosmology. His theory of mutual responsiveness between heaven and humanity provided the Confucian scholars with a higher law by which to judge the conduct of the ruler. It was under his suggestion that Emperor Wu of Han (c. 140–87 BCE), the seventh emperor of the Han dynasty, established Taixue, China's earliest higher learning institution.[33]

Born probably around 179 BCE in Guangchuan (in modern Hebei), Dong Zhongshu was a scholar well versed in Chinese literature. Attempting to achieve a coherent system of thought that would provide a rational explanation for the entirety of human experience, he developed the theory of the interaction between heaven and humanity, his central theme. His ultimate goal was to discover universal causative principles that would both explain the past and provide a sound foundation for the future, particularly in the sociopolitical sphere. His thought integrated yin-yang cosmology into a Confucian ethical framework. In his system the ruler has the central position as heaven's ambassador on earth. Natural catastrophes such as floods and droughts are heaven's way of warning the ruler to examine his personal conduct and correct his mistakes. The ruler therefore has the duty to preserve harmony between yang (light, positive, male) and yin (dark, negative, female) elements. He must prevent disturbances by caring for and educating his people. He may reform institutions when necessary but may never alter or destroy the basic moral principles of heaven.

According to Dong, earth, heaven, and humans have complementary roles in the universe. In an ideal state they work together in harmony. Heaven desires the welfare of humankind, people are endowed with a natural tendency to obey the dictates of heaven, and the earth provides nourishment in response to people's cultivation. Heaven is at work in worldly events, mandating certain outcomes in the course

---

32. In the literature the name was Tung Chung-shu in the Wade-Giles system of romanization. There are also debates over his birth and death dates.

33. As one of the greatest emperors in Chinese history, Emperor Wu vastly expanded China's territorial domain and organized a strong and centralized Confucian state. However, Dong Zhongshu has been little documented in the English literature and even less in the field of higher education.

of human affairs. To him, the world is not a field of self-contained natural processes but rather a field in which human life is of central importance and heaven acts. The authority of the ruler should be solidly grounded in the authority of heaven, which was codified in the classics that the Confucians had always treasured and promoted. Although his philosophy merged Confucianism with elements of Daoism, yin-yang cosmology, Mohism, Legalism, shamanism, and geomancy, he believed that Confucius had come to understand the relationship between people and heaven and was able to interpret omens and portents. Confucian scholars occupied an important role in government, interpreting the meaning of events and omens, and maintaining a check on the activities of the ruler, "rectifying rightness without scheming for profit; enlightening his Way without calculating efficaciousness."[34] Dong's philosophy provided a theological justification for regarding the emperor as the "Son of Heaven." Such political thought was undoubtedly one of the major reasons that Confucianism was accepted by Emperor Wu.

Dong's teachings deeply influenced generations of Han thinkers. His understanding of the world as an interactive cosmos eventually permeated most of Chinese society and became a fundamental element of the general Chinese worldview.[35] While he was among the most influential thinkers in Chinese history, his most important scholarly and political success was achieved during his early career. He entered the imperial service during the reign of Emperor Jing of Han and rose to high office under Emperor Wu of Han. According to his biography included in the *Book of Han* (漢書), he had become the most learned person of his time by 158 BCE. In 135 BCE, Emperor Wu was troubled by a number of questions about governance, and he solicited explanations from the best scholars nationwide. In three undatable memorials, Dong proposed to revere only Confucianism and dismiss the Hundred Schools of Thought.[36] He recommended Taixue to be the best place to restore talents, its essential task to influence (教化),[37] a place not only to train talents but also to exert influence and select political personnel. Meanwhile, Gongsun Hong (公孫弘, 200–121 BCE), then prime minister, suggested the government establish a system of scholars with disciples, so that local communities would be positively influenced while talents were rewarded.[38] Emperor Wu took his advice and ordered Taixue established in 124 BCE to host scholars and their students, with a hope that they would set a good example for the entire society.

---

34. The Chinese original is "正其誼不謀其利，明其道不計其功". See Ban Gu 班固, *Hanshu* 漢書 [Book of Han] (Beijing: Zhonghua Book Company, 1962), vol. 56, 2525.
35. Russell Kirkland, "Tung Chung-shu," in *Great Thinkers of the Eastern World*, ed. Ian P. McGreal (New York: HarperCollins, 1995), 67–70.
36. The Chinese original is "罷黜百家，獨尊儒術".
37. Meng Xianchang 孟憲承, *Zhongguo gudai jiaoyu wenxuan* 中國古代教育文選 [Selected ancient works on education] (Beijing: People's Education Press, 1996).
38. The Chinese expression of the system Gongsun Hong suggested is 博士弟子員制度.

The historical significance of Dong's proposals needs to be located in context. In 221 BCE, the state of Qin had instituted a ruthless new centralized state. It banned private schooling, allowed only study from officials, and made imperial power supreme. In 206 BCE the Qin was overthrown, but meanwhile the Chinese had seen their civilization ransacked. Rulers of the subsequent Han period struggled to understand what had happened and why. The collapse of the Qin offered a clear moral and historical lesson: there is justice in the world. But if so, why had the ruthless Qin come to power in the first place? These were the questions that Emperor Wu took to the best minds for answers. Dong thus left his extraordinary mark in the Chinese history of politics and education for: (1) authorizing and institutionalizing Confucian ethics and social mores, (2) establishing China's formal higher education institutions, and (3) starting the strong Chinese tradition of marrying state with education centered on cultivation (教化) and officials as teachers (以吏為師). Dong helped to shape the character and mode of Chinese higher education for more than 2,000 years. With a combined effect of Taixue and domination of Confucianism, all public schools in China offered regular sacrifices to Confucius, who came to be perceived as the patron saint of education. Eventually, a Confucian temple was built in every one of China's 2,000 counties. His legacy even moved beyond China. Confucian ethics and governmental organization spread later to neighboring counties, including Korea, Japan, and Vietnam.[39]

Historical Roots of Chinese Higher Education

As Ruth Hayhoe rightfully points out, the term "university" is used in Chinese literature to denote an entirely different constellation of scholarly institutions in China.[40] There was no institution in the Chinese tradition that could be called a university throughout China's history, until the late nineteenth century. This is evident in the history of Chinese higher education. China predated the development of higher learning institutions in the West by centuries. The famous Jixia Academy (稷下學宮) was established during the Warring States period, twenty years before the Platonic Academy in Greece.[41] It is regarded by some as the first university in the world, consisting of eighty professors and 3,000 students.[42] As noted, Taixue,

---

39. Sarah A. Queen, *From Chronicle to Canon: The Hermeneutics of the Spring and Autumn Annals according to Tung Chung-shu* (Cambridge: Cambridge University Press, 1996).

40. Hayhoe, "Ideas of Higher Learning," 361.

41. Richard Hartnett, *The Jixia Academy and the Birth of Higher Learning in China* (Lewiston, NY: Edwin Mellen Press, 2011).

42. Generally credited to King Xuan of Qi (齊宣王, 350–301 BCE) and given a foundation date around 318 BCE, it was a scholarly academy located in the capital of Qi (present-day Shandong). The literal translation of the name is a learning place at the gate of Ji, the harvest god." It took its name from its position outside the city's western gate and thrived until the reign of King Min of Qi (齊湣王, 323–284 BCE). The academy is important to note to the overarching theme of this book. It paved the way for the Contention of a Hundred Schools of Thought (百家爭鳴). The Jixia scholars were free to

which literally means Greatest Study or Learning, was China's earliest higher learning institution, founded at Dong Zhongshu's suggestion. It was the highest rank of educational establishment with a "Confucian" curriculum for the high-level civil service. Toward the end of the Han dynasty, as many as 30,000 students attended Taixue.[43]

Taixue taught only Confucianism.[44] Even after one year of study at Taixue and having mastery of one classic, students were eligible to be chosen by the government to become officials. By so doing, the government directly controlled their political future. This was the beginning of China's strong tradition for over two millennia, higher education aiming at preparing would-be officials for the state. Taixue thus became a subsidiary body of the bureaucratic system.[45] As part of the ruling system, Taixue was not able and indeed never attempted to go beyond the imperial framework. The first nationwide government school system in China was established in 3 CE under Emperor Ping of Han, the Taixue at the top, located in the capital, Chang'an.[46] Later, it was replaced by the Guozijian (國子監) as the top level of educational institutions and as the highest organization to oversee the national government school system. The development of Taixue and Guozijian was thus confined to the limited range allowed by Confucian ideologies.

The imperial examination system (科舉) and the academies were key elements of ancient Chinese higher learning.[47] The imperial examination was a civil service examination system in imperial China to select candidates for the state bureaucracy. This system began to take form around 400 CE, and Taixue gave rise to it during the Sui dynasty (589–618). The system reached its full institutional development in the Tang dynasty. During the Song, it crystallized into patterns that were to last right up to 1905. The system shaped China's intellectual, cultural, and political life and helped to unify the empire to an extraordinary extent. As a means of entering the government bureaucracy,[48] it allowed men of humble birth who had ability the

---

debate with one another without any of the responsibilities of high office though they were accorded its honors and emoluments. And, it started China's strong tradition of patronage between rulers and scholars. As Mark Lewis argues, "it marks a significant development. For the first time on record a state began to act as a patron of scholarship out of the apparent conviction that this was a proper function of the state or as a means of increasing its prestige." See Mark Lewis, "Warring States Political history," in *The Cambridge History of Ancient China: From the Origins of Civilization to 221 BC*, ed. Michael Loewe and Edward L. Shaughnessy (Cambridge: Cambridge University Press, 1999), 643.

43. Queen, *From Chronicle to Canon*.
44. Patricia Buckley Ebrey, *The Cambridge Illustrated History of China* (Cambridge: Cambridge University Press 1999).
45. Zhang Yan, *Xifang daxue linian zai jingdai Zhongguo de chuanru yu yingxiang*.
46. See Yuan, "Local Government Schools in Sung China."
47. Hayhoe, *Chinese Universities 1895–1995*.
48. Historians continue to debate whether or not China's imperial examination system exerted a significant influence on the examination and civil service systems in the West. See Derk Bodde, *Chinese Ideas in the West: Asiatic Studies in American Education, No. 3* (Ann Arbor, MI: UMI, 1994). Citing Ssu-yü Têng's early work, Hayhoe and Liu insist that "the transformation of the medieval universities of Europe into institutions that could help build up modern nation states, particularly in France,

possibility of rising to positions of power and influence. The ideal of achievement by merit gave legitimacy to imperial rule. The increased reliance on the exam system contributed to the Tang dynasty's shift from a military aristocracy to a gentry class of scholar-bureaucracy.

As noted, the academies emerged in the late Tang dynasty and thrived from the Song to Qing dynasties. They provided a structured learning environment that was separate from yet interacting with state institutions associated with the civil service examination system. Their private nature and freethinking atmosphere are seen by some as essential elements of traditional Chinese higher education.[49] However, such features were not maintained. The academies sit somewhere between the private and the official. Their long historical developments bore a marked brand of ideological and financial control by the government. Initially they focused on exploring Confucianism and personal intellectual cultivation rather than on training government officials, operation funds coming mainly from private sources. They became prosperous through winning recognition and financial support from government in the Song dynasty. The government extended its control via donations of books and land. Due to a gradual loss of independence from the government, the academies reached their peak during the Southern Song, became a major part of the government education system, and trained many officials. They were integrated into the government school system from the Yuan to Qing dynasties, from the appointment of lecturers to examinations, admissions, and the whereabouts of the students. By the Qing dynasty, their major aim had changed to preparing for the imperial examination students hoping to win an official rank.[50]

Chinese higher education has unique historical roots. By the eighteenth century China started to have increasing encounters with the West. As the only culture in the world with a continuous recorded history of five millennia, China had left behind countless literary classics, historical documents, cultural relics, and national records reflecting its immense scope. Education is one shining part of such remarkable achievements and contrasts sharply with those in the West. Along the Confucian scholarly tradition, Chinese higher education lacked an interest in seeking truth. It focused on knowledge of human society, with a central emphasis on connectedness and integration "between theory and practice, fact and value, individual and community, institution and political-social-natural context."[51] Such an approach

---

Austria, and Prussia, was profoundly influenced by a Chinese or East Asian model of higher learning, namely the civil service examination system. See Ssu-yü Têng, "Chinese Influence on the Western Examination System," *Harvard Journal of Asiatic Studies* 7 (1942/1943): 267–312; and Hayhoe and Liu, "China's Universities, Cross-Border Education, and Dialogue among Civilizations," 86.

49. Ruth Hayhoe, "China's Universities and Western Academic Models," *Higher Education* 18, no. 1 (1989): 49–85.

50. Zhang Yan, *Xifang daxue linian zai jingdai Zhongguo de chuanru yu yingxiang*.

51. Ruth Hayhoe, "Lessons from the Chinese Academy," in *Knowledge across Cultures: A Contribution to Dialogue among Civilisations*, ed. Ruth Hayhoe and Julia Pan (Hong Kong: Comparative Education Research Centre, The University of Hong Kong, 2001), 347.

to scholarship was centered on utility in the terms of the ruling classes. Featured by close integration within a meritocratic bureaucracy that entrusted governance to those who could demonstrate their knowledge through written examinations, higher learning institutions were loyal servants of the emperor. Higher education was to prepare would-be officials for the state. Higher education institutions were a subsidiary body of the bureaucratic system. They had no intention of going beyond the imperial framework. Private higher learning institutions also set their sights on the imperial examination in the hope of winning an official rank.

China thus started its higher learning system with a fundamentally different relationship between the state and educational institutions from that of medieval universities in Europe, leading to a strong tradition of the alliance between education and politics in Chinese history. Ancient Chinese educational institutions were far too reliant on their relations with the ruling elites. Modern universities were only established in China according to the Western experience in the late nineteenth century. Ancient Chinese higher learning institutions only had superficial resemblances with medieval universities. Ancient Chinese rulers controlled scholarship development via education, which was long treated as a path to bureaucracy. To those who governed, it was the way to select people for office, while for individuals and families the ultimate goal was always to become an official. Such officialdom-centered education was subsidiary to the government,[52] taking the form of "A good scholar would make an official" (學而優則仕). The orientation toward officialdom privileged the political function of higher education. Traditional ways of thinking have survived dramatic social and cultural changes in China's modern history, and their impact on contemporary Chinese higher education remains profound.

This is in stark comparison with European medieval universities that were a collection of individuals banded together as a *universitas*.[53] They were autonomous corporations of students and masters governed by internal rules set by the academic community itself and protected from the outset by Pope Gregory IX's papal bull. Being self-financing, depending either on their properties or on contributions from students for their income, they were independent institutions governed by

52. SoongHee Han, "Confucian States and Learning Life: Making Scholar-Officials and Social Learning a Political Contestation," *Comparative Education* 49, no. 1 (2013): 57–71.

53. The Latin word *universitas* implied a guild. The *universitas* guild is the early origin of what we characterize as a university. During the late twelfth and early thirteenth centuries, a *universitas magistrorum et scholarium* (a guild of masters and scholars) grew up around Notre Dame Cathedral. All the earliest universities, including Bologna, Paris, and Oxford, appeared from the guild, which enjoyed the right to self-determination granted by church and state. Scholastic guilds were permitted to develop their own rules and regulations and govern their own affairs without interference from external authorities. See Hastings Rashdall, *The Universities of Europe in the Middle Ages* (Oxford: Clarendon Press, 1895); Peter Classen, "Associations of Teachers and Learners: The Medieval View of the University," *Western European Education* 13, no. 3 (1981): 28–37; and Charles J. Fox and Hugh T. Miller, "Practices of the Guild: A Declaration of Independence," *Administrative Theory and Praxis* 20, no. 2 (1998): 142–158.

their own members, who elected a rector.[54] More specifically, a few features distinguished traditional Chinese higher education institutions from their counterparts in Europe: (1) their teaching staff received government salary, (2) they took major classical texts of the Confucian school as their curricular content with little disciplinary and/or practical focuses, (3) their teaching and approaches included mainly lectures and self-study. Discussion and debating were used only within a range that was limited by their relevance to Confucianism. Reciting Confucian classics was the main learning approach, and skepticism was generally lacking. The education showed clear signs of what Weber termed political pragmatism.[55]

The External Influence of China's Higher Learning Traditions

The historical influence of Chinese traditions and cultural practices has long extended outside China's territorial borders, especially in East and Southeast Asia, where China's long and sustained cultural influence runs deep. Confucianism or at least Confucian traditions are often regarded not only as the major characteristic of China but also of East Asia and some parts of Southeast Asia—especially those where Chinese migration has been considerable.[56] Imperial China was the source of considerable cultural, as well as political, influence throughout East Asia. Ever since Fairbank, East Asia has been identified by the common elements of Chinese cultural heritage.[57] Although there is some variability in the Confucianism identified by various societies in the region, common characteristics tend to include a particular stress on education. The influence of Chinese higher learning traditions are manifest widely in the development of higher education systems and institutions in East and Southeast Asian societies. These societies shared with China the

---

54. José-Ginés Mora, "Governance and Management in the New University," *Tertiary Education and Management* 7, no. 2 (2001): 95–110.

55. David L. Hall and Roger T. Ames, "A Pragmatist Understanding of Confucian Democracy," in *Confucianism for the Modern World*, ed. Daniel A. Bell and Hahm Chaibong (Cambridge: Cambridge University Press, 2003), 124–160.

56. East and Southeast Asia are China's principal regions of cultural influence. The region that has been historically influenced by Chinese culture is called the East Asian cultural sphere or Sino sphere (東亞文化圈), consisting of countries in East and Southeast Asia. Other names for the area include the Confucian world, the Sinic/Sinitic world, the Daoist world, and the Chinese culture sphere. It is fair to point out that the countries under China's long and sustained impact, including Japan, Korea, and Vietnam, have never been simply passive receptacles of Chinese culture. Instead, they have participated actively in an ongoing and creative process of cultural interaction, exchange, and reinvention. See Chun-chieh Huang, ed., *East Asian Confucianisms: Texts in Contexts* (Taipei: National Taiwan University Press and Vandenhoeck & Ruprecht, 2015); and Jeffrey L. Richey, *Confucius in East Asia: Confucianism's History in China, Korea, Japan, and Vietnam* (Ann Arbor: Association for Asian Studies, 2013). It is also necessary to note an inherent contradiction often found between narrow political nationalism and the wider appreciation of Chinese culture.

57. See Edwin O. Reischauer and John K. Fairbank, *East Asia: The Great Tradition* (London: George Allen & Unwin, 1960).

remarkably rich cultural traditions and were bound by such historical linkage to go through thick and thin together, especially after they encountered the West.[58] China is the cultural heartland in the region, and the distinct characteristics of China's traditional society strongly influenced its neighbors, especially Korea, Vietnam, and Japan. Both Korea and Vietnam derived much of their higher civilization from China, including writing systems, philosophies, and political institutions. Chinese influences were adapted to surviving local customs, and both the Korean and the Vietnamese retained separate cultural identities. Japan produced an even more distinctive version of East Asian civilization although Japan accepted many Chinese influences. China's cultural influence on Korea and Japan reached its height during the Tang dynasty.[59] A blessing or a curse aside, the shared Confucian heritage has been a fundamental part of the social and cultural base for these societies when they are confronted with the most challenging task of incorporating Western cultural values since the late nineteenth century. Indigenizing the Western idea of a university is one such mission with profound historical significance.

Korea

Featured by a Confucian curriculum and training of scholar-officials, ancient Korean higher learning was heavily influenced by China. Throughout the history of Korea, Confucianism has had a great impact on the gamut of the Korean society including politics, education, and culture. Indeed, Korea has been the society that adheres most to Confucianism outside China's territorial boundaries. Until the early twentieth century, Confucianism was its official ideology, and Confucian values remain powerful even to the present time in the society.[60] Ever since the early years of the Three Kingdoms period (57 BCE–668 CE) Confucian learning has been the most respected core of curricula in higher institutions in Korea. According to *Samguksagi* (History of the Three Kingdoms), Korea's first formal institution of higher

---

58. The bounding here is in their similar conflicts and struggles in trying to balance their own traditions and those from the West. Their situations were similar to those in China, where the idea of academic freedom and institutional autonomy never took root, since universities serving the nation state became a focus of attention and were widely accepted by the Chinese. See Chan-Fai Cheung and Guangxin Fan, "The Chinese Idea of University, 1866–1895," in *Transmitting the Ideal of Enlightenment: Chinese Universities since the Late Nineteenth Century*, ed. Ricardo King Sang Mak (Lanham, MD: University of Press of America, 2009), 24.

59. Craig A. Lockard, "The Asian Resurgence in World History Perspective," *World History Connected* 9, no. 1 (2012): 1–23.

60. However, there has been little documentation in ancient Korean historical records in relation to the introduction of Confucianism. It is widely believed that Confucianism was transmitted to Korea through continental China before the diffusion of Chinese civilization. See Charles Allen Clark, *Religions of Old Korea* (New York: Garland Publishing Inc., 1981), 91–94; James H. Grayson, *Korea: A Religious History* (Oxford: Clarendon Press, 1989), 60–61; and Sa-Soon Yun, "Confucian Thought and Korean Culture," in *Korean Cultural Heritage, Vol. II. Thought and Religion*, ed. Joung-won Kim (Seoul: Samsung Moonhwa Printing Co., 1996), 108–113.

learning, Taehak (National Confucian Academy), was founded in 372 CE during the Koguryŏ kingdom (37 BCE–668 CE). It was reestablished as Gukhak (National Confucian Academy) in 682 CE, during the Silla kingdom (57 BCE–935 CE).[61] From the fifteenth century, the Seowon (the Korean version of China's academies) was introduced and became the typical school of higher learning in the country. The Paekche kingdom (18 BCE–660 CE) also set up higher institutions to focus on Confucian classics and state-building. The Seongkyunkwan (National Confucian Academy) was founded as the highest level of learning in the capital city in 1397, during the Choson kingdom (1392–1910).

The intellectual activities during these periods were centered on learning Chinese thought and culture, which was much more highly developed than native Korean thought and culture at that time. After that period, the succeeding of the unified Silla kingdom (668–935) and the Koryo kingdom (918–1392) maintained Confucian studies as a major academic field. In the Choson period, the rulers designated Confucianism as the resource for politics, ethics, and education for over 500 years. After completing the course work, the *yusaeng* (graduates) of these institutions would be qualified to take the *Kwa-keo* (the Korean version of the Imperial Examinations), particularly *Dae-kwa* or *Mun-kwa* (Triennial Higher Examinations or Erudite Examinations) to win a post in the state bureaucracy, the Seowon holding a preparatory role. The contents of the examinations were almost exclusively Chinese classics. Similar to the situation in China, provincial and private schools either prepared their students directly for the examinations or sent them to elite higher institutions that focused on the examinations. Such a Confucian educational system depended greatly on the *Kwa-keo*, lasting until the late nineteenth century, when the Choson kingdom was invaded by Western powers and Japan.

While higher learning followed the Chinese pattern to train scholar-officials to serve the ruling class from the Three Kingdoms period to the late Choson era, Confucian traditions from China were modified, indigenized, and integrated into Korean culture and society, especially during the late Choson period. Elite Confucian institutes remained highly influential in Korea until they were systematically devalued by Japanese colonizers and Western imperialists in the late nineteenth century.[62] As a matter of fact, a movement, *Silhak* (Practical Learning) as it was called, emerged in the eighteenth century. Although not successful in their final social and political consequences, a group of reform-minded Choson scholars sought to modernize the country through acquiring Western knowledge and the sociopolitical system. Greatly forced by Western powers and Japan, the Confucian Choson rulers finally recognized the significance of Western knowledge and education and discontinued the *Kwa-keo* system by the late nineteenth century. Just like the Qing court in China, they established *Dongmunhak* (English language

61. Wan-Gee Choi, *The Traditional Education of Korea* (Seoul: Ewha Womans University Press, 2006).
62. Horace H. Underwood, *Modern Education in Korea* (New York: International Press, 1926).

institutes) in 1883, in order to import Western learning as the initial part of the modernization of the country.

Vietnam

For Vietnam, its giant northern neighbor China has been an "abiding influence."[63] In the beginning of the second century BCE, deposed members of the Chinese Qin dynasty began to move into the Tonkin and Red River Deltas after the Han dynasty gained power. They brought with them Chinese technology, language, and culture, beginning the Sinicization of Northern Vietnam. In 111 BCE, the Han began to govern the Vietnamese directly, and Vietnam was under Chinese rule until the tenth century. During this long period, Vietnamese people absorbed Chinese culture deeply and comprehensively. They were heavily influenced by Chinese art, writing, Confucian bureaucracy, and commercial practices and goods. Chinese agricultural and military organization was followed. Confucianism reached Vietnam about 2,000 years ago.[64] It has since been exercising a significant influence on the society in both social structure and learning. A Confucian bureaucracy, dominated by aristocracy, was established quite early on. Vietnamese elites attended Chinese-like schools, learned to read Chinese, studied the Confucian classics, and took the imperial examinations to enter the bureaucracy.

Quốc Tử Giám, a center for Confucian learning, established in 1076, is regarded as Vietnam's first National University, which lasted about 700 years.[65] After reaching its apogee and assuming a dominant role in society during the early Ly dynasty (1009–1225),[66] Confucianism spread its influence through every area of society, from government institutions and political activities, to economy, military affairs, literature, architecture, morality, education, and the system of civil service examinations. Confucianism touched people from different social strata, influenced their habits, and became part of their customs. Chinese-inspired civil service examinations, based on Confucian classics, were introduced to recruit officials. They were instituted as the Confucian court examination system in 1705. From 1462 to 1463 a two-tiered, triennial examination system was introduced. It functioned

---

63. This point was expressed by Anthony Welch about China's enduring influence on Vietnam. He continues to write: "Just as elements of the contemporary Vietnamese higher education system, most notably its people's universities, are examples of Chinese influence, so too are major elements in the history of Vietnamese higher learning, as any visitor to Ha Noi's ancient and beautiful *Temple of Literature* can tell." See Anthony R. Welch, "Internationalization of Vietnamese Higher Education: Retrospect and Prospect," in *Reforming Higher Education in Vietnam: Higher Education Dynamics, Vol. 29*, ed. Grant Harman, Martin Hayden, and Pham Thanh Nghi (Dordrecht: Springer, 2010), 197.

64. Korea was conquered by the Han in 109 BCE. Therefore, Confucianism reached Korea around the same time as it reached Vietnam.

65. Pham Lan Huong and Gerald W. Fry, "Education and Economic, Political, and Social Change in Vietnam," *Educational Research for Policy and Practice* 3, no. 3 (2004): 199–222.

66. Neil L. Jamieson, *Culture and Development in Vietnam* (Honolulu HI: East-West Centre, the University of Hawai'i, 1991), 6.

not only to qualify men for official posts but also as the mechanism for organizing and expanding a new social and political stratum in Vietnam, a countrywide,
Neo-Confucian indoctrinated, educated elite.[67] The examination system lasted until
1919. Permeating all aspects of the society, Confucian thought and Confucian-
inspired social institutions had wide influences on the development of education
systems in Vietnam, and legacies of these impacts remain.[68]

Japan

Japan also owes an inestimable cultural debt to the great civilization of China. By
the early nineteenth century at least, the intellectual and cultural context of the
Japanese view of Chinese civilization was servient to the Chinese self-image and
in thrall to the literary and cultural traditions of the Chinese elite. If the scholars
from China and Japan had been able to meet and talk together in the years from
1800 to 1850, or even later, they would have been in general agreement about the
history, literature, philosophy, and the society of China: they would have agreed
with the Chinese scholar on what Chinese civilization was and what it meant; they
would have also agreed on how that civilization should be studied. It is thus almost
natural for ancient Japanese higher learning to follow the Chinese tradition.[69] The
model of modern Japanese universities is derived from bureaucratic institutions,
whose ultimate origin can be traced to ancient or medieval Chinese institutions.
All teaching and administrative staff of the university were government employees
of the Ministry of Education. Its faculty-department structure was modeled after
the departmental hierarchy of bureaucratic machinery, which was developed in
China.[70]

   Formal education in Japan started in the sixth century when Chinese learning, including Confucianism, Buddhism, the Chinese writing system, and literary
tradition, was introduced into Japan. Daigaku-ryō (Imperial University of Kyoto)
was established in 671, teaching Confucian texts, mathematics, history, and law.

---

67. Nola Cooke, "Nineteenth-Century Vietnamese Confucianization in Historical Perspective: Evidence
    from the Palace Examinations (1463–1883)," *Journal of Southeast Asian Studies* 25, no. 2 (1994):
    275–312.
68. Huanyin Yang, "Confucius," *Prospects: Quarterly Review of Comparative Education* 23, no. 1–2 (1993):
    211–219.
69. As Wright wrote, "Despite signs of restiveness in the eighteenth and early nineteenth centuries, the
    dominant tradition of Japanese scholarship was Confucian; Japanese scholars of China, *Kangakusha*
    (Chinese Scholars), or *Jusha* (Confucianists), shared with Chinese literati a commitment to many of
    the ideas, the values, and the methods of study which had been evolved through the centuries in China.
    Japanese scholars tended to select the same problems for textual study, the same poetic models for
    appreciation and imitation, the same philosophic values by which they aspired to order the self and
    society." See Arthur F. Wright, "The Study of Chinese Civilization," *Journal of the History of Ideas* 21,
    no. 2 (1960): 234.
70. Shigeru Nakayama, "Independence and Choice: Western Impacts on Japanese Higher Education,"
    Higher Education 18, no. 1 (1989): 33.

The first university, Daigaku-ryō, was set up by the end of the seventh century by Emperor Tenji in the imperial capital of Kyoto. Ashikaga Gakkō, then the largest and most renowned academic institution of Japan, was founded in the ninth century[71] and restored in 1432 by Deputy Shōgun Uesugi Norizane.[72] Its students came from all over Japan to study Confucianism, *I Ching*, and Chinese medicine. By the ninth century, five institutions of higher learning in Kyoto primarily taught Confucianism and Buddhist thought and practice. Aiming to provide prospective government officials with Confucian training, the institutions were built on Chinese experience. Their graduates were placed in government positions at levels that corresponded to their success at the institutions. The Chinese examination system also acquired strong roots in Japan.[73]

Even during medieval times when education was for warriors, the curriculum consisted of Confucianism and military science. Even schools and libraries for the ruling class focused on traditional Confucian values and on military education, matching the cultural themes of the age. Toward the end of the medieval period, Japan's educational system was subjected to a new influence—Jesuit Catholic missionaries—beginning with the arrival of Francis Xavier in 1549. Only later in the Tokugawa Period (1863–1868) did Japan's schools expand their curriculum to include non-Confucian topics such as medicine, Japanese studies, and Western science. This period also saw an official school of the shogunate, called the Shoheiko, in Edo (Tokyo), where the children of the nation's leaders were educated by Confucian scholars. Confucian dominance lasted in Japanese educational institutions until the modern period in the nineteenth century with a tremendous amount of educational reform as Japan sought to catch up to the West.

Despite the great historical influence by the Chinese civilization, Japan has always endeavored to develop and maintain its own inherent cultural and intellectual identity both by itself and through borrowing from the Western civilizations. As early as the tenth century, the term *Wakon Kansai* (Japanese spirit with Chinese knowledge) was incorporated into Japanese literature, exemplifying the efforts of Japanese intellectuals to maintain an indigenous spiritual identity within the Eastern intellectual activities dominated by Chinese dynasties. During the Tokugawa period, the government established *Kokugaku* (national study) to refocus Japanese scholarship away from the then-dominant study of Confucian and Buddhist texts. The term *Wakon Yosai* (Japanese spirit with Western knowledge) was in popular use

---

71. There has been some controversy about when it was built. Some argue it was created in the twelfth century. See Louis Frédéric, *Japan Encyclopedia* (Cambridge, MA: Harvard University Press, 2002).
72. He imported many classical Chinese books, many of which are still kept in the school.
73. However, both its trajectory of development and the impact differed very much from that in Korea. The differences were mainly due to the hereditary privilege that remained the main criterion for those appointed in official posts in Japan. See Terri Kim, "Confucianism, Modernities, and Knowledge: China, South Korea and Japan," in *International Handbook of Comparative Education*, ed. Robert Cowen and Andreas M. Kazamias (New York: Springer, 2009), 857–872.

in the nineteenth and twentieth centuries, to maintain the distinction of Japanese identity from that of Western civilization.[74] Yet, unlike what many have often taken for granted, China's strong influence has also hindered Japan's modern university development to a considerable extent. As Shils and Roberts wrote, "the reception of the Western academic ethic and the academic freedom which is so integral to it was to have a hard passage in Japan's reception of the model of the European universities."[75]

74. Akiyoshi Yonezawa, Akinari Hoshino, and Sae Shimauchi, "Inter- and Intraregional Dynamics on the Idea of Universities in East Asia: Perspectives from Japan," *Studies in Higher Education* 42, no. 10 (2017): 1839–1852.

75. Edward Shils and John Roberts, "The Diffusion of European Models outside Europe," in *A History of the University in Europe. Vol III: Universities in the Nineteenth and Early Twentieth Centuries* (1800–1945), ed. Walter Rüegg (Cambridge: Cambridge University Press, 2004), 226.

Perceptions of Foreign Universities in the Nineteenth Century and the Birth of China's Modern Higher Education Institutions

In the Chinese literature, the university was first mentioned by Giulio Aleni (1582–1649) in 1623,[1] an Italian Jesuit missionary during the late Ming and early Qing dynasties. Yet, China's first modern universities did not emerge until the second half of the nineteenth century.[2] To understand their periods of history, we need to observe how the Western idea of a university was conceived and what happened later during the pregnancy. As part of China's early encounters with the West, the birth of modern universities in China must be viewed through the prism of the late Qing dynasty's profound humiliations and transformations. It was a historically

---

1. Aleni was the first to translate the word "university" into *daxue* (大學), which was drawn from Chinese classics. *Daxue* in ancient China could refer to one of two things: one is the *Great Learning*, which was one of the "Four Books" in Confucianism. The other is the entire higher learning system and its institutions. See Cai Xianjin 蔡先金, "Daxue zhiming yu Zhongguo jindai daxue qiyuan kaobian" 大學之名與中國近代大學起源考辨 [The concept of *daxue* and the origin of China's modern universities], *Journal of Higher Education* 高等教育研究 38, no. 1 (2017): 73–80. According to Hayhoe, there was no institution in Chinese tradition that could be called a university. See Hayhoe, *China's Universities 1895–1995*, 10. The translation, although beautifully expressed and richly supported intellectually, could be misleading for both Chinese and non-Chinese readers if they do not understand each other well. China's ancient situation has little resemblance to what the word means in the West. Therefore, an often-seen circumstance is both sides using the same concept, but they are indeed talking about different things, while at the same time they imagine that the other side has the same understanding. Although the consequence could be quite serious, few researchers have clearly realized this in a theoretical manner, let alone addressing the issue explicitly. For a fuller treatment of this theme, see Rui Yang, "Emulating or Integrating? Modern Transformations of Chinese Higher Education," *Journal of Asian Public Policy* 12, no. 3 (2018): 294–311.
2. A number of institutions lay claim to being the first university in China. Founded as Imperial Peking University (京師大學堂) in 1898 in Beijing as a replacement of the ancient Guozijian, Peking University claims it is the first formally established modern national university of China. Tianjin University, however, makes the same claim on the basis that its predecessor, Imperial Tientsin University (天津北洋西學學堂) and later Peiyang University (北洋大學堂), was set up in 1895. Wuhan University also claims that its processor, Ziqiang Institute (自強學堂), set up in 1893, was the first modern higher education institution. If the nationality of the founders is not taken into account, then St. Paul's College of Macau was a university founded in 1594. It claims the title of the first Western university in East Asia. On the Chinese mainland, Tengchow College (登州文會館) was set up in 1864 in Shandong, by Calvin Wilson Mateer (1836–1908), from the American Presbyterian Mission with the then most sophisticated facilities and infrastructure nationwide, and St. John's University (聖約翰大學) was established in 1879 in Shanghai by American missionaries.

extraordinary period with a series of Western military victories enshrined in "unequal treaties."[3] China's repeated defeats led to growing concern about the superiority of the West and fierce debate about how to respond. Some reform-minded scholars and officials called for the establishment of translation offices and institutions where students could study Western languages and mathematics in addition to Chinese classics. This approach came to be known as "self-strengthening."[4] Its principal goal was to maintain the strong essence of Chinese civilization while adding superior technology from abroad. During the process, the image of a weak backward China adrift in a modern world, bullied by Western powers, started to dominate China's historical memory and national identity. This victim mentality entangled with profound intellectual transformations to add to the complexity, forming the wider context in which universities began to appear.

A Century of Humiliation and Transformation

Until the early nineteenth century, China had been under the illusion that other nations were barbarian and too remote from the center of the civilized world. But China was soon shaken by much more powerful Western nations. In August 1842, China was defeated by the British Empire at the close of the First Opium War. The ensuing century scarred the Chinese psyche, whose prestige as the Celestial Empire was damaged by a series of brutal invasions by the era's great powers. Great Britain, France, Germany, Japan, Russia, and the United States of America all vied for a chunk of the Chinese empire. These events brought China to its knees, and after that, China fell quickly from an exalted position in which Chinese rulers had over the centuries placed their empire in relation to the rest of the world.[5] The Qing government signed a series of "unequal treaties," conceding Hong Kong, Macau, and other major port cities to Western control. China lost one-third of its territory, tens of millions Chinese perished, and China suffered 35 million casualties during World War II. The Chinese consider this period "a century of humiliation" (百年國恥), a period of intervention and subjugation of the Chinese Empire by Western powers and Japan between 1839 and 1949.[6]

---

3. Dong Wang, "The Discourse of Unequal Treaties in Modern China," *Pacific Affairs* 76, no. 3 (2003): 399–425.
4. Samuel C. Chu and Kwang-Ching Liu, eds., *Li Hung-chang and China's Early Modernization* (Armonk, NY: M. E. Sharpe, 1994).
5. Stephen Platt, *"New Domestic and Global Challenges: 1792–1860," in The Oxford Illustrated History of Modern China*, ed. Jeffrey N. Wasserstrom (Oxford: Oxford University Press, 2016), 37–62; and Robert Bickers, "Restoration and Reform: 1860–1900," in *The Oxford Illustrated History of Modern China*, ed. Jeffrey N. Wasserstrom (Oxford: Oxford University Press, 2016), 63–89.
6. Alison Adcock Kaufman, "The 'Century of Humiliation,' Then and Now: Chinese Perceptions of the International Order," *Pacific Focus: Inha Journal of International Studies* 25, no. 1 (2010): 1–33.

For China, to develop means to respond to the West.[7] Fairbank's "China's response to the West" and the "impact-response" framework make better sense than what was proposed by its critics.[8] China has had a strong sense of urgency to respond to the West strategically. Its responses can be highly emotional and go to extremes, making China's extraordinary stories of national collapse and revival. The long and painful period of dynastic decline, intellectual upheaval, foreign occupation, civil war, and revolution urged China to achieve national rejuvenation. A common goal that unites Chinese people is their determined pursuit of *fuqiang* (富強, wealth and power).[9] Over the last one and a half centuries, generations of Chinese have relentlessly pursued the goal of restoring China's greatness, motivated by a profound sense of shame and humiliation.[10] The historical experiences are the driving force for China to go from a ramshackle, quasi-feudal empire into one of the great powers of the twenty-first century. China has recently managed to burst forth onto the world stage with an impressive run of hyper-development and wealth creation, culminating in extraordinary dynamism. Its ascent demonstrates how the legacy of China's humiliation continues to have wide-reaching consequences as China plays a greater role in world affairs today.

The experience of subjugation and humiliation has become a central element of Chinese identity today. This sense is deeply entrenched in the Chinese psyche. The abiding quest for a restoration of national greatness in the face of a "century of humiliation" at the hands of Western powers even comes to define the modern Chinese character. The psychic trauma of historical memories of subjugation was inflicted on China's generations of ruling elite and intelligentsia. The determined quest remains the key to understanding many of China's actions today. A "strong nation" mentality still defines Chinese official worldview. The escalating tensions between China and the United States, up to the end of October 2021, can be seen as the latest phase in a continuing historical process: the remaking of China's ancient glory under the stimulus of Western contact. The West has mostly forgotten about the historical events, the Opium Wars relegated to a brief footnote in history, but

---

7. This is despite the rhetoric that modernization does not equate with Westernization. Such a theme has been well documented with classic questions including whether or not the unique Western value system needs to be transferred and how necessary are the cultural underpinnings in the form of a set of "modern" values based on individualism, as suggested by Hayek. There has been a huge body of literature and various arguments. See, for example, Deepak Lal, "Does Modernization Require Westernization?" *Independent Review* 5, no. 1 (2000): 5–24.

8. During the 1980s, Cohen presented his sympathetic critique of the dominant paradigms associated with John K. Fairbank. However, his interpretation has substantially less explanatory power. See Têng Ssu-yü and John K. Fairbank, *China's Response to the West* (Cambridge, MA: Harvard University Press, 1954); and Paul A. Cohen, *Discovering History in China: American Historical Writing on the Recent Chinese Past* (New York: Columbia University Press, 2010).

9. A more accurate translation of *fuqiang* is "prosperity and strength."

10. This is the central theme permeating Orville Schell's and John Delury's book *Wealth and Power*. See Orville Schell and John Delury, *Wealth and Power: China's Long March to the Twenty-First Century* (New York: Random House, 2013).

the Chinese have never forgotten that shame. Their sense of shame and humiliation has been underpinning the Chinese mentality until today. While China might need to walk out of the shadow of its unfortunate past and be a confident global player, for non-Chinese, especially those in the West, understanding Chinese psychology and acknowledging there might be another worldview that is as valid as theirs can help formulate policies that will avoid miscalculations and unnecessary conflicts.

With "the biggest change in more than three thousand years" as described by Li Hongzhang (李鴻章, 1823–1901),[11] the past one and a half centuries have been particularly soul-stirring to the Chinese people. Since the mid-nineteenth century, Chinese intellectuals have turned to the West for truth. China's modern education system has since been built upon Western experience, with little space for China's vast indigenous intellectual traditions. The promulgation of the "Authorized School Regulation" (欽定學堂章程) in 1902 marked an irrevocable break in the historical trajectory of the Chinese intellectual mind.[12] To some extent we can have a very broad generalization about Chinese intellectual history by dating it to two periods: pre-1902 and post-1902; that is, the traditional Chinese system up to the event and the Western system after it. The adoption of the Western system is based on a revolutionary break from China's long and rich traditions. Universities are both part of the reason for and a result of such a historical development. China's legitimized knowledge system shifted from traditional learning to Western intellectual formation. Indigenous Chinese intellectual traditions were driven out of their homeland as Western knowledge became institutionalized despite China's long and rich traditions in higher learning as the world's oldest and most durative civilization.

Facilitated by guns and ships, Western knowledge and value won the race and control the Chinese mind since the late Qing dynasty. Both institutionally and ideologically, this means a fundamental shift away from China's long and rich traditions. In an interview by *Philosophy Now* in 1999, Tu Wei-ming called this "a kind of collective amnesia, a loss of memory, in the sense of alienation from our own traditions."[13] The "loss of memory" is due to a drastic transformation from rich Chinese intellectual traditions to the Western knowledge system during the early twentieth century. The adoption was "more a matter of survival than of choice,"[14]

---

11. Li Hongzhang 李鴻章, "Chouyi zhizao lunchuan weike caiche zhe" 籌議製造輪船未可裁撤折 [Memo on not abandoning the manufacture of ships] (20 June 1872), in *Li Hongzhang quanji, vol. 5* 李鴻章全集 [Collected works of Li Hongzhang], ed. Gu Tinlong 顧廷龍 and Dai Yi 戴逸 (Hefei: Anhui Education Press, 2008), 109.

12. In 1902, Zhang Baixi (張百熙, 1847–1907), then-minister for education, drafted the "Authorized School Regulation" (欽定學堂章程), alternatively called Renyin Educational System (壬寅學制), "renyin" (壬寅) being the year 1902, which was put into effect by the Qing government. In 1904, Zhang participated in the establishment of the "Presented School Regulation" (奏定學堂章程, called "Guimao Educational System" 癸卯學制), "guimao" (癸卯), being the year 1904, which was the first modern Chinese educational system.

13. Anja Steinbauer, "Interview with Tu Wei-ming," *Philosophy Now* 23, Spring (1999): 28–31.

14. Yongling Lu and Ruth Hayhoe, "Chinese Higher Learning: The Transition Process from Classical Knowledge Patterns to Modern Disciplines 1860–1910," in *Transnational Intellectual Networks: Forms*

allowing little space for China's indigenous intellectual traditions. Western knowledge was then introduced into China gradually and systematically. This formed the intellectual and cultural context in which the Western concept of a university was initially introduced into China with a strong sense of urgency and a unique catch-up mentality that have had a profound and lingering impact ever since.[15]

Early Conception of a University

Inflected repeatedly by imperial powers in the mid-nineteenth century, Chinese intellectual and political elites became awakened to the pressing need of revitalizing the nation. For a national reconstruction, political, economic, and military modernization that drew on the historical experience of Western industrial nations appeared to be the only way for the nation to withstand Western imperial penetration. As the development theorist Eisenstadt suggests,[16] China needed a new elite who could redefine its position in the world and rebuild its connectedness with other nations and regenerate Chinese culture through integrating new ingredients into it.[17] It was against such a political backdrop that the university was introduced into China as part of the wider Self-Strengthening Movement (1861–1895),[18] which had an uneasy start together with an intense debate over China's possibility of catching up with the Western powers without altering its persistent cultural pattern.[19] The interest in and attention to modern universities in the West grew as an increasing number of more forward-looking scholar-officials, such as Wei Yuan (魏源, 1794–1857) and Zeng Guofan (曾國藩, 1811–1872), broke new ground by reinterpreting the mission of the Confucians.

For national salvation, it became imperative for China's intellectuals to enter into the community of nations. Their understanding of modern universities was developed through observing foreign practices and by reflecting on China's own

of Academic Knowledge and the Search for Cultural Identities, ed. Chrisophe Charle, Jürgen Schriewer, and Peter Wagner (Frankfurt: Campus Verlag, 2004), 269.

15. Rui Yang, "Self and the Other in the Confucian Cultural Context: Implications of China's Higher Education Development for Comparative Studies," *International Review of Education* 57, no. 3–4 (2011): 337–355.

16. According to Eisenstadt, the attitude of the elite toward changes is crucial to the result of any attempts at modernization. Those who are more adaptive to change help transform the traditional order by creating a new institutional and symbolic framework in which modernization proceeds. See Shmuel Noah Eisenstadt, *Tradition, Change, and Modernity* (New York: John Wiley and Sons, 1973), 337–338.

17. Ricardo K. S. Mak, "Introduction," in *Transmitting the Ideal of Enlightenment: Chinese Universities since the Late Nineteenth Century*, ed. Ricardo K. S. Mak (Lanham, MD: University Press of America, 2009), 5.

18. The details of the Self-strengthening Movement have been well documented by Chinese and Western scholars. In the English literature, the most thorough account remains the relevant chapters in *The Cambridge History of China*, vols. 10 and 11, ed. Denis Twitchett and John K. Fairbank (Cambridge: Cambridge University Press, 1978).

19. Kwang-ching Liu, *The Nineteenth Century: The Disintegration of the Old Order and the Impact of the West*. (Chicago, IL: The University of Chicago Press, 1968), 1–4.

longstanding legacy in higher learning, represented particularly by the academies.[20] It was thus natural for China to develop a certain understanding of universities before actually establishing such institutions. This differed greatly from the experiences in Europe and to a less extent North America, where the idea of a university developed largely in pace with the growth of the university system.[21] As a result of their frequent and bitter reflections on China's traditional higher learning, Chinese intellectual and political elites made efforts to integrate Western knowledge and methods of scientific inquiry, and educational ideals, institutions, and experiences into Chinese higher education.[22] As the society was more and more influenced by Western concepts, ideas, and values, the ideal of traditional Chinese higher learning, if not abandoned entirely, has gradually been swept aside. Even ideas such as "enlightenment" and "rationality," upon which modern Chinese universities are founded, have their roots in modern European intellectual traditions. China's early understanding of university education was from the outset greatly influenced by the experiences in Europe and the United States. Japanese practices, although much copied, were treated as a variation of the Western model.[23]

Since the 1860s, reform-minded Chinese literati began to encounter Western knowledge and modern sciences and pursued New (Western) Learning. At this time, more Chinese officials and private travelers visited Europe, the United States, and Japan and made observation of higher education systems and institutions in those societies. They started to note the universities and their operation. They fell into two categories. One included scholar-officials sent by the Chinese government as diplomats or on official tours of investigation. The other was open-minded private travelers, without any official titles and missions, who were interested in foreign societies. Many of these early international travelers were specialists in foreign

---

20. For more details of China's ancient academies, see Rui Yang, "Schooling in China," in *Routledge Handbook of Chinese Culture and Society*, ed. Kevin Latham (London: Routledge, 2020), 35.

21. Chan-Fai Cheung and Guangxin Fan notice this difference. See Chan-Fai Cheung and Guangxin Fan, "The Chinese Idea of University, 1866–1895," 13–14. However, this is a general relative comparison between China (indeed most non-Western societies) and the West. In the West, there has been disparity in time, theory following rather than proceeding practice. For instance, Cardinal John H. Newman's *The Idea of a University* aimed to defend the classical idea he held when it was challenged by the successful experiment at the University of Berlin. The Humboldtian model was much more theorized after its substantial practices. The latest discussions of the role of the research university in economic development have been based on the rich interaction between the university, industry, and government in Silicon Valley. See Henry Etzkowitz, "The Second Academic Revolution and the Rise of Entrepreneurial Science," *IEEE Technology and Society Magazine* 20, no. 2 (2001): 18–29.

22. Mak points out the great difficulties they had in achieving individual emancipation, broad-based education, and academic professionalism as in Western universities. Yet, he also explains that it is just not realistic to expect that higher education in China could be fully transformed within a few decades. Indeed, he claims that in comparing the universities in Chinese societies today with their predecessors a century ago, one might be surprised to see the progress made by China's early experiment over the years. See Mak, "Introduction," 8.

23. For a detailed account of how China attempted to learn from various Western nations and Japan, see Hayhoe, "Ideas of Higher Learning, East and West."

affairs with some knowledge of Western societies and cultures. In November 1867, China credentialed its earliest diplomatic mission to the West. Both Binchun (斌椿) (b. 1804), the head of the mission, and Zhang Deyi (張德彝, 1847–1918), a junior member of the mission, recorded their visit to Oxford University in much detail. Different from previous records on Western universities that were scattered without any in-depth investigation, their accounts aroused society's general interest in modern universities.

A number of the early travelers were intellectuals who made careful observations of universities. Typical examples included Wang Tao (王韜, 1828–1897), Li Gui (李圭, 1842–1903), and Huang Qingcheng (黃慶澄, 1863–1904). Wang Tao was the first Chinese scholar who participated in a two-way cultural exchange. Through translating Western religious books and Western sciences into Chinese and at the same time translating important ancient Chinese classics into English, he forged a bridge between China and the West. He was invited to deliver a speech at Oxford University in 1868, an event he made good use of as an opportunity to explore how universities functioned differently in various civilizations and how they related to their nation-states.[24] In his role as the representative of the Ningbo Customs, Li Gui visited the World's Fair held in Philadelphia, Pennsylvania in the United States in 1876. He then traveled to various locations in the United States, France, and Britain. Based on what he saw, he was convinced that modern education systems in Western societies were more sophisticatedly developed than the Chinese one.[25] In 1893, the governor of Anhui province sponsored Huang Qingcheng to visit Japan for two months on a political investigation. By detailing Japan's direct supervision of university operation and how Japanese universities nurtured officials for the state, Huang became the first Chinese to note the different state-university relations between Japan and Western nations.[26]

The most systematic and deliberate observation of Western universities was made by Guo Songtao (郭嵩燾, 1818–1891), China's first ambassador to the United Kingdom and France (1877–1878). When he first arrived in London, he was impressed with England's industrial might and was eager to bring back its secrets to China.[27] He carefully watched British and French universities, from academic affairs, student life, institutional management, to auxiliary university facilities, such as libraries and museums. After he returned to China, he participated in setting up

---

24. Wang Tao 王韜, *Manyou suilu* 漫遊隨錄 [Casual notes made during the wander] (Changsha: Yuelu shushe, 1985), 96–98.

25. He made observation on various aspects of Western societies including universities. See Li Gui 李圭, *Huanyou diqiu xinlu* 環遊地球新錄 [The new records of traveling around the world] (Changsha: Yuelu shushe, 1985), 237, 271, 292, 299.

26. Huang Qingcheng 黃慶澄, "Dongyou riji" 東遊日記 [The diary of this journey to the East], in *Jiawu yiqian riben youji wuzhong* 甲午以前日本遊記五種 [Five travelogues on Japan before 1894], ed. He Ruzhang 何如璋 (Changsha: Yulu shushe, 1985), 341.

27. Jenny Huangfu Day, "Searching for the Roots of Western Wealth and Power: Guo Songtao and Education in Victorian England," *Late Imperial China* 35, no. 1 (2014): 1–37.

new academies and attempted to incorporate such experiences.[28] During that time, even for an intellectual elite like Guo, it was difficult to understand the fundamental differences between Chinese and Western ways of knowledge organization and their manifestations in higher learning. For instance, he could not understand how a discipline could be divided into many courses. After realizing that the medical school of King's College London offered thirty different courses, he checked with a professor of the school whether there would be much repetition in content among the courses. He was shocked to know the answer was negative. He wondered why many subjects, such as astronomy, geography, electronic engineering, and chemistry, were studied independently and taught in the school and how each course focused on a particular field of knowledge.[29]

The scholar-officials on official trips and the private tourists facilitated both the court and the commonality in China to broaden their perspective. It is worth noting that the knowledge they acquired was not kept separate. For example, Li Hongzhang wrote a foreword for Li Gui's travel notes, and the Zongli Yamen sponsored its publication.[30] Guo Songtao also read the book and jotted down some notes in his diary before going abroad.[31] The more they compared Chinese academies with Western universities, the more ready they were to adopt sweeping changes in the Chinese education system. It appeared increasingly clear that, for national survival, a Western-style university system must be introduced into China.[32] Their observations paved the way for an early Chinese idea of the university. The experiences they observed included various patterns within the general European–North American model of university development, with unequal attention to each.

---

28. He made a great effort in establishing new and rebuilding existing academies in 1879, sixteen years before the founding of the first university in China and twenty years before Emperor Guangxu ordered the transformation of the academies to (Westernized) schools throughout the country. Unfortunately, yet not entirely surprisingly, his attempts to incorporate Western experience failed repeatedly. See Lu Baoqian 陸寶千, Guo *Songtao xiansheng nianpu buzheng ji buyi* 郭嵩燾先生年譜補正及補遺 [Guo Songtao's chronicle: Corrections and amendments] (Taipei: Zhongyang yanjiuyuan jindaishi yanjiusuo, 2005), 294, 306.

29. Guo Songtao 郭嵩燾, *Lundun Bali riji* 倫敦與巴黎日記 [Diaries on visits to London and Paris] (Changsha: Yulu shushe, 1984), Vol. 4, 210–213.

30. The Zongli Yamen (總理衙門, Office of General Management) was established by the Qing state to deal with the foreign presence in the late Qing period. It managed the dispatch of diplomats, supervised foreign trade, coastal defence, customs and customs revenues, railroads and mining, telecommunications, military labour, the Court of Colonial Affairs (*lifanyuan* 理藩院, also called *tongwensi* 同文寺), as well as the admission of students abroad. See He Shuangsheng 何雙生, "Zongli geguo shiwu yamen" 總理各國事務衙門 [Prime Minister's office of affairs concerning various nations], in *Zhongguo da baike quanshu* 中國大百科全書 Zhongguo lishi 中國歷史 [Encyclopedia of China: History of China] (Beijing: Zhongguo da baike quanshu chubanshe, 1992), Vol. 3, 1626–1627.

31. Zhong Shuhe 鍾叔河, *Cong dongfang dao xifang* 從東方到西方 [From the East to the West] (Shanghai: Shanghai remin chubanshe, 1989), 289.

32. Chan-Fai Cheung and Guangxin Fan, "The Chinese Idea of University, 1866–1895," 16.

The models did not contribute to China's early ideas of a university in equal measure; changing attitudes toward different patterns occurred over the time.[33] The British model caught most Chinese attention because the British Empire was the most powerful at the time and was the first to commit colonial outrages to force China to cede its territory, an action that led to an era of unequal treaties regarding China. The second was the French model that appeared to be attractive to Chinese observers due mainly to its centralized structure and specialized colleges to provide technical training for the social elite. In contrast, higher education in the United States and its institutions attracted later, yet increasing, attention from the Chinese for their featured decentralization. The fast development of modern Japanese universities caught the eye of many Chinese people, understandably as a mixture of the French centralized system and the American decentralized model. However, a more fundamental reason for the popularity of the Japanese experience was the perceived successful combination of Western and East Asian traditions in higher education. The Chinese particularly admired Japan for continuing the respect for imperial authority while nurturing specialized personnel for public service and nation-building.

It was no surprise that early Chinese observers focused their attention on the social role of the university, that is, on the meaning of the university as a social institution whose purpose was defined as meeting the needs of society. In line with China's political and economic discourses in the late Qing dynasty that perceived the social role of the university overwhelmingly in relation to nation-building, there was a shift from the British-American model to the Japanese model with its features of central planning and practical specialized training to serve national interests. The contribution of German universities to the fast rebuilding of the nation also won the admiration of China's early reformers, while little attention was paid seriously to university autonomy that had been practiced and emphasized much by German universities.[34] Looking retrospectively, the observations were neither systematic nor penetrating and had inconsistent and even sharp contradictions of opinions.[35] It is

---

33. Here, Altbach's work over thirty years ago on the Western influence on East Asian higher education remains highly relevant. See Altbach, "Twisted Roots." For China's struggles, Hayhoe's historical narratives at the same time continue similarly to be most informative and accurate. See Hayhoe, "Ideas of Higher Learning, East and West."
34. Chan-Fai Cheung and Guangxin Fan, "The Chinese Idea of University, 1866–1895," 24, 29.
35. Shallow understanding of the universities specifically and education more generally in the West led to some interesting and often over-simplistic comparisons. For example, Zhang Deyi (張德彝, 1847–1918) corresponded rigidly bachelor's and master's degrees and doctorate respectively to *xiucai* (秀才, a qualification earned by passing the prefectural exam), *juren* (舉人, a qualification earned by passing the provincial exam), and *jinshi* (進士, a qualification earned by passing the court exam). See Zhang Deyi, *Hanghai shuqi* 航海述奇 [My fantastic experiences during overseas voyages] (Changsha: Yuelu shushe, 1985), 521. Guo Songtao treated the three Western academic degrees similarly yet even more highly, *xiucai, juren*, and *hanlin xueshi* [翰林學士, member of the Hanlin Academy (翰林院), an institution subordinated to the central government and entrusted with the draft of official documents, with the most highly regarded literati as its members] as their correspondents in China. See Guo Songtao, *Lundun Bali riji*, 378–380.

worth noting that, as the Chinese intellectual and political elite further observed foreign universities, they also deepened their understanding of China's long and rich traditions in higher learning, not necessarily always in a negative manner.[36]

The Oldest Universities in Modern History

By 1895, when China lost to Japan in the war of 1894–1895, establishing modern higher education institutions to train much-needed specialized personnel to support modernization, particularly in the military, became even more imperative. In order to "learn from the West to defend against the West" as proposed by reform-minded intellectuals and politicians such as Wei Yuan and Zuo Zongtang (左宗棠, 1812–1885),[37] new colleges were set up to offer training in Western science and technology.[38] The first was Tongwen Guan (同文館), established in Beijing in 1862 by the Zongli Yamen. It was dedicated to training interpreters in Western languages, as a direct result of defeat in the Second Opium War.[39] In 1866, a new department of mathematics and astronomy was added to teach Western science, especially for the development of a modern military.[40] It was merged with the newly established Imperial Capital University in 1902. Others included the Fuzhou Chuanzheng Xuetang (福州船政學堂, Foochow Naval Academy) set up in 1866 under the suggestion of the governor of Fujian province, to build China's modern navy.[41] Zhang Zhidong (張之洞, 1837–1909) established Ziqiang Xuetang (自強學堂, School of Self-Strengthening) in Wuchang and Chucai Xuetang (儲才學堂, School for Gathering Talent) in Nanjing in 1893 and 1896 respectively, when he was the governor of Hubei and Hunan provinces and of Jiangsu, Jiangxi, and Anhui provinces.

---

36. For example, Liang Qichao (梁啟超, 1873–1929), Hu Shi (胡適, 1891–1962), and Mao Zedong (毛澤東, 1893–1976) all viewed the Western university model critically and called for bringing in beautiful Chinese traditions such as the liberal education in ancient academies.
37. Jane Kate Leonard, *Wei Yuan and China's Rediscovery of the Maritime World* (Cambridge, MA: Council on East Asian Studies, 1984).
38. During 1862–1898, the reformists initiated a total of forty-four modern colleges to offer, for the first time in modern China, courses on Western learning, including foreign languages, natural sciences, and practical technologies, great importance attached to military technology.
39. Knight Biggerstaff, *The Earliest Modern Government Schools in China* (Ithaca, NY: Cornell University Press, 1961).
40. The terms chosen for the name of the department were "astronomy" and "mathematics," from traditional Chinese subjects and thus appeared to be less threatening to traditionalists in the government who feared moral corruption through instruction in Western subjects. See Melissa Mouat, "The Establishment of the Tongwen Guan and the Fragile Sino-British Peace of the 1860s," *Journal of World History* 26, no. 4 (2015): 733–755.
41. Chen Yuanhui 陳元暉, Chen Xuexun 陳學恂, and Tian Zhengping 田正平, eds., *Zhongguo jindai jiaoyushi ziliao huibian: Yangwu yundong shiqi jiaoyu* 中國近代教育史資料彙編：洋務運動時期教育 [Collected documents on the modern history of Chinese education] (Shanghai: Shanghai Education Press, 2007).

One such institution that has its niche in history is the Imperial Tientsin University [天津北洋西學學堂, renamed National Beiyang University (北洋大學堂) in 1912]. In the face of Western and Japanese military incursions, the Guangxu Emperor (光緒帝, 1871–1918) issued an imperial edict to call for strategies for restoring the nation. In 1895, Sheng Xuanhuai (盛宣懷, 1844–1916), together with American missionary Charles Daniel Tenney (1857–1930), who had been the principal of the Tianjin Anglo-Chinese College (天津中西書院) since 1886 and tutor to the sons of influential politician and reformer Li Hongzhang, submitted a proposal for the Arrangement of the Constitution of the Tianjin Chinese and Western School (擬設天津中西學堂章程稟) to Wang Wenshao (王文韶, 1830–1908), then the governor-general of Zhili and Surrounding Areas and superintendent of trade for the northern ports of China. They proposed establishing the Tianjin Chinese and Western School. Although their proposed name was "Tianjin Chinese and Western School," all subjects listed in the constitution were Western. Wang then eliminated "Chinese" from the name and submitted the proposal to the emperor on September 30, 1895. It was approved two days later, on October 2.[42] The school approved by the emperor only had the word "Western" in its name.[43] On the day of the approval, the imperial decree was sent back to Tianjin. On October 18, 1895, the school was officially established.

Initially patterned after Harvard and Yale Universities and later remodeled on the Japanese Imperial University in 1903, when it reopened after the Boxer Uprising in 1900,[44] it was China's first perfectly justifiable modern university to acquire Western knowledge in a comprehensive and systematic manner.[45] It was also the first government-run university in modern China to fully adopt a Western university education model to train engineers in a way that would look familiar today. Sheng Xuanhuai, the founder, participated actively in the Self-Strengthening Movement that originated in Tianjin. China's defeat in the First Sino-Japanese War lent a real urgency to this movement, which advocated learning from the West so that China could ultimately strengthen its military and protect itself against further encroachment from Japanese and Western powers. The institution acted as a model for the founding of many of other early Western-style universities in China. At its founding, it hired a number of foreign professors to design its general education plan, curriculum development, and even textbook selection. The infrastructure, from

---

42. This is why Tianjin University celebrates its anniversary on October 2.
43. Qu Lihe 瞿立鶴, *Qingmo jiaoyu xi chao: Zhongguo jiaoyu xiandaihua zhi mengya* 清末教育西潮：中國教育現代化之萌芽 [Western tides in education: The embryonic stage of China's educational modernization] (Taipei: National Institute for Compilation and Translation, 2002), 673 and 675. See also Cai Xianjin 蔡先金, "The Concept of *daxue* and the Origin of China's Modern Universities," 78.
44. Chan-Fai Cheung and Guangxin Fan, "The Chinese Idea of University, 1866–1895," 13–33.
45. The institution was named Tianjin University by the new Communist government of the People's Republic of China in 1951. Its long tradition of engineering education remains alive. It was perfectly justifiable according to the defining characxteritics of the legacy of the European medieval university, as Hayhoe sugestes in her *China's Universities, 1895–1995*.

laboratory equipment to library resources, was up-to-date. Its constitution, which outlined in detail its scale and administration, length of study, student admission and curriculum, was China's first university constitution. The twenty-five graduates in 1899 were the first group of graduates trained by a modern-style government-run Chinese university with Western-pattern academic degrees.

The university demonstrated China's very sophisticated understanding of a university in various dimensions. It advocated a learner-centered teaching style that emphasized practical application and creative abilities. It allowed students to choose which field to specialize in and to change freely at any time within their first and second years of study. The criteria for both teacher recruitment and student admission were maintained strictly at a high level even by international standards. All advanced science and engineering courses were taught by foreign instructors who were overwhelmingly graduates from renowned universities in the United States, such as Stanford University and Massachusetts Institute of Technology. Some well-known Chinese experts and scholars, such as Mao Yisheng (茅以升, 1896–1989), were also hired.[46] By the collapse of the Qing court, while Imperial University of Peking had not yet conferred any undergraduate degrees, Imperial Tientsin University had trained nine graduates in law and thirty-five graduates in engineering. After 1895, the line of thinking of integrating Chinese and Western civilizations ended abruptly. Since China's disastrous defeat in the First Sino-Japanese War, Chinese society began to seek "wealth" and "power," focusing only on short-term successes and quick benefit.

Compared with other new-style colleges, Jinshi Daxuetang (京師大學堂, Imperial University of Peking) was much more symbolic. After many calls by reform-minded intellectuals and officials for a modern, Western-style system of schools, Sun Jianai (孫家鼐, 1827–1909) submitted his proposal for Jinshi Daxuetang to the emperor in 1896. Although the emperor backed the initiative passionately, the implementation was delayed by highly placed conservatives in the Inner Court, such as Prince Yi and Manchu Grand Councilor Gangyi. On January 29, 1898, Kang Youwei (康有為, 1858–1927) proposed the idea again in his sixth petition to the emperor during the historical Gongche Shangshu (公車上書) movement, which sought reforms and expressed opposition to the Treaty of Shimonoseki (下關條約) in 1895. On February 15, the proposal was submitted by Wang Pengyun (王鵬運, 1840–1904) to the emperor and was approved on the same day. In August

---

46. Mao was a Chinese structural engineer, who had a master's degree from Cornell University and earned the first PhD ever granted by the Carnegie Institute of Technology (now Carnegie Mellon University) in 1919. His doctoral treatise entitled *Secondary Stress on Frame Construction* is treasured at the Hunt Library of Carnegie Mellon University, and the university constructed a statue of him on campus in his honor. Credited as the founder of modern bridge engineering in China, he designed two of the most famous modern bridges in China, Qiantang River Bridge near Hangzhou and Wuhan Yangtze River Bridge in Wuhan. The former is the first dual-purpose road-and-railway bridge designed and built by a Chinese; the latter is China's first modern bridge.

some Western diplomats, especially the Italian and the German envoys, tried to stop the establishment. Their attempts were sternly rejected by Sun Jianai. In 1898, when momentum for reform gathered,[47] it was established and officially opened on December 31.[48]

Designated to be the supreme higher education institution and the highest educational administration,[49] Imperial University of Peking was founded with historical baggage to transform from an old Chinese institution of higher learning to a modern university. The emperor appointed Sun Jianai, his former tutor, to head the institution and bestowed the title Director of Educational Affairs (管學大臣) upon him. Through the work of Zhang Zhidong, a series of charters for the new colleges had been drafted and finalized by 1903. The regulations were later proclaimed by the Qing court[50] and paved the way for a new national education system that was more in line with international practice. *Zhongti xiyong* (中體西用, Chinese learning as substance, Western learning for application) was designated as the fundamental tenet of the university.[51] In practice, it was utilized as a slogan for justifying the introduction of Western learning. In this sense, Imperial University of Peking, together with Imperial Tientsin University, marked not merely the emergence of China's earliest modern universities but also the start of a gradual transition from traditional to modern Chinese higher education. As the earliest trial of a systematical transplantation of the Western educational system, they set the foundation of the university system and disciplinary education in China.

---

47. Timothy B. Weston, *The Power of Position: Beijing University, Intellectuals, and Chinese Political Culture, 1898–1929* (Berkeley, CA: University of California Press, 2004), 30.

48. Wang Xuezhen 王學珍, *Beijing daxue jishi 1898–1997* 北京大學紀事 1898–1997 [Chronicle of Peking University 1898–1997] (Beijing: Peking University Press, 2008), 5.

49. The dual instructional-administrative function of the university was prescribed in its constitution drafted by Liang Qichao. As the regulations stipulated, "now a university was set up at the capital, so all schools in provinces should be administrated by the university without any obstruction. All regulations and coursework should be put in line with the university so as to ensure a uniform and coordinated implementation." See Beijingdaxue 北京大學 and Zhongguo diyi lishi danganguan 中國第一歷史檔案館, eds., *Jingshidaxuetang dangan xuanbian* 京師大學堂檔案選編 [Selected archives of the Imperial University of Peking] (Beijing: Beijing University Press, 2001), 26.

50. They included in particular the Memorial to Set Regulations for Imperial University of Peking (奏定京師大學堂章程) and the Imperial Command on Regulations for Institutes of Higher Learning (欽定高等學堂章程). See Michael Lackner, *Coping with the Future: Theories and Practices of Divination in East Asia* (Leiden: Brill, 2018), 459.

51. *Ti-yong* (體用, essence-function) is a key theme in Chinese philosophy. The idea of *zhongti xiying* was initially proposed by Feng Guifen (1809–1874) in 1861. It was borrowed by the people around Zhang Zhidong and was further elaborated in Zhang's Exhortation to Study (勸學篇) in 1898 as Traditional (Chinese) learning as substance, New (Western) learning as application (舊學為體，新學為用). The concept then became a popular slogan among Chinese thinkers in the late nineteenth and early twentieth centuries, when they were interrogating how to approach the threat posed by encroaching Western states. On the notion of *ti-yong* in late imperial China's discourse of reform, see Joseph P. Levenson, *Confucian China and Its Modern Fate: A Trilogy* (Berkeley, CA: University of California Press, 1968), vol. 1, 57–78; and Jonathan D. Spence, *The Search for Modern China* (New York: W. W. Norton & Company, 1990), 225–226.

Missionary Colleges and Universities

In the early nineteenth century, an evangelical revival occurred at the same time as Western colonial expansion, accompanied to growing overseas missionary activity. Beginning with Robert Morrison (1782–1834) in 1807, missionary effort in China exploded during the next few decades. Supported by Protestant organizations or denominations in their home countries, thousands of missionaries lived and worked in China. The number grew from 50 in 1860 to 2,500 in 1900. Of these, 1,400 were British, 1,000 were Americans, and 100 were from continental Europe, and Scandinavia.[52] Their effort peaked in the 1920s and thereafter declined due to war and unrest in China.[53] They believed that the promotion of Western culture was an integral part of their missionary work and that the Chinese could not be converted to Christianity until they were convinced of the superiority of Western culture. Confronting China's millennia-old culture and its sophisticated intellectual traditions, the missionaries pursued their work of cultural conquest with utmost vehemence. Missionary colleges and universities were established for evangelism. They reported to overseas boards, received substantial foreign funding, and featured a liberal arts curriculum that served as a conduit for introducing core Western values and knowledge.[54]

Starting from the early twentieth century, various Christian missionary groups set up a total of fourteen higher institutions in China, at a time when China's state-run universities were being established for self-strengthening purposes. Founded in 1882, Tengchow College, which became Shantung Christian University in 1909, was the earliest Christian higher education institution in China. By 1910, there were twelve missionary higher institutions nationwide,[55] of which some were an

---

52. Larry Clinton Thompson, *William Scott Ament and the Boxer Rebellion: Heroism, Hubris, and the "Ideal Missionary"* (Jefferson, NC: McFarland Publishing Company, 2009), 14; Jane Hunter, *The Gospel of Gentility: American Women Missionaries in Turn-of-the-Century China* (New Haven, CT: Yale University Press, 1984), 6.

53. All missionaries were expelled by the new Communist government of China by 1953. It was estimated that some 50,000 foreigners served in mission work in China between 1809 and 1949, including both Protestants and Catholics. See Kathleen L. Lodwick, *How Christianity Came to China: A Brief History* (Minneapolis, MN: Fortress Press, 2016), *xv*.

54. Elizabeth J. Perry and Hang Tu, "Cultural Imperialism Redux? Reassessing the Christian Colleges of Republican China," in *China and the World—The World and China, Vol. 3, Transcultural Perspective*, ed. Barbara Mittler and Natascha Gentz (Ostasien: Verlag, 2019), 69.

55. Different people have produced different lists of such institutions mainly due to their different understandings of the nature of the identity and mission of a Christian college. See Peter Tze Ming Ng, "Reimagining Christian Higher Education in China Today," *Christian Higher Education* 17, no. 4 (2018): 185–197. This number was given by the late Chinese American historian Liu Kwang-ching (劉廣京, 1921–2006). He included Tengchow College (1882, N. Presbyterian), Peking University (1886, N. Methodist), North China College (1889, N. Methodist), St. John's University (1890, Episcopal), Canton Christian College (later Lingnan University, 1893, N. Presbyterian), Hangchow College (1897, N. Presbyterian), Soochow University (1901, S. Methodist), Boone University (1903, Episcopal, American Board, London Missionary Society), North China Union College for Women (1905, N. Presbyterian), Shanghai Baptist College (1907, N. & S. Baptist), University of Nanking (1909, N. Methodist, Disciples

outgrowth of the secondary schools. By the early 1940s, thirteen Protestant and three Roman Catholic institutions were established in China, including Yenching University and Fu Jen Catholic University in Beijing, the University of Nanking and Ginling Women's College in Nanjing, and St. John's University in Shanghai.[56] Set up by the Methodist Episcopal Church, South, in 1901, Soochow University is often seen as the first fully Western-style university in China. The institutions played a significant role in the projection of American influence at China's earliest stage of modern higher education development. St. John's University, for instance, is particularly well known for having introduced an American model of higher education into China.[57]

In 1952, the new Communist government of China decided to close all missionary institutions.[58] Looking historically, missionary colleges and universities exerted a significant influence on the early development of Chinese higher education when the nation only had three public universities. To a great extent, they set examples in educational patterns in major dimensions, from teaching and learning and scholarly inquiry, to more fundamental themes such as the purposes and ideals of a university. There is much to learn from their historical experience. For instance, both the Chinese students who studied and lived at the colleges and universities and the foreign educators who taught and administered in them reached a considerably high level of sophistication of cultural hybridization of Chinese and Western intellectual traditions. This is not to say they completely solved all the knotty issues. Yet, the height the institutions and their members reached is indeed something all Chinese societies today can only dream of. This explains the remarkable revival of a historical interest in them since the 1980s, with mainland Chinese scholars leading the way.[59]

---

of Christ, N. Presbyterian), and West China Union University (1910, N. Methodist, N. Baptist, Canadian Methodist, English Friends). See Kwang-ching Liu, "Early Christian Colleges in China," *The Journal of Asian Studies* 20, no. 1 (1960): 71–78.

56. See Jessie Gregory Lutz, *China and the Christian Colleges, 1850–1950* (Ithaca, NY: Cornell University Press, 1971), 3; Ng, "Reimagining Christian Higher Education in China Today." Here, it is also interesting to note the differences between the priorities of Protestant and Catholic churches. While both agreed that setting up educational organizations was the main means of expanding the influence and training modern personnel, Protestant churches attached great importance to higher education and achieved much in addition to their efforts in primary and secondary education.

57. Xiong Yuezhi 熊月之 and Zhou Wu 周武, eds., *Shengyuehan daxueshi* 聖約翰大學史 [History of St. John's University] (Shanghai: Shanghai renmin chubanshe, 2007).

58. See Perry and Tu, "Cultural Imperialism Redux?," 69.

59. See Peter Tze Ming Ng, "Resurgence of the Study of China's Christian Higher Education since 1980s," *Frontiers of Education in China* 14, no. 3 (2019): 364–386. There has been a recent resurgence of research interest in missionary universities in modern China in nearly all Chinese societies, especially on the Chinese mainland, where the renowned historian Zhang Kaiyuan (章開沅) has been a particularly prominent pioneer. See, for example, Zhang Kaiyuan 章開沅, *Zhongxi wenhua yu jiaohui daxue* 中西文化與教會大學 [Chinese and Western cultures and missionary universities] (Wuhan: Hubei Education Publishing House, 1991); and *Wenhua chuanbo yu jiaohui daxue* 文化傳播與教會大學 [Cultural communication and missionary universities] (Wuhan: Hubei Education Publishing House, 1996).

Most of the missionary institutions strove to soften their foreign image and adapted to their Chinese setting, as demonstrated in their academic administration and curriculum and by the outward appearance of their campuses. Many developed robust programs in Chinese studies. Some even became renowned centers of research on China, including Yenching University in Beiping, Shantung Christian University in Jinan, and St. John's University in Shanghai.[60] While such offerings were initially in response to a virulent anti-Christianity movement that swept China in the 1920s, they helped to combine a rigorous Western-style education with serious instruction in Chinese history, philosophy, and literature taught by some of the leading Sinologists of the day. Through incorporating Chinese studies into an otherwise basically Western curriculum, the institutions were able to develop a global vision of scholarship while encouraging their Chinese students to study their own highly developed Chinese civilization in the light of Western methods of research and to interpret this civilization to the West. In this sense, they were not merely "transmitters of Western religious beliefs." Their closure in the early 1950s, unfortunately, brought an abrupt end to such innovative and highly promising experiments in developing a unique educational model.[61]

Throughout the first half of the twentieth century, missionary institutions were a major force of Chinese higher education contributing significantly to China's social and educational development. Spreading in China's east, north, south, and southwest, they offered a wide range of academic programs including arts, science, education, law, engineering, and medicine. Providing girls and students from ordinary families with higher education opportunities, they trained a large number of modern personnel that were badly needed in the society. Many of them later became pillars of the nation. They began to send Chinese students to study abroad, including Yung Wing (容閎, 1828–1912), who was the first Chinese student to graduate from an American university, and Wong Fun (黃寬, 1829–1878), who received his PhD in medicine from the University of Edinburg and became China's first Western medical doctor. Within a short time, many of them achieved a reputation for academic excellence at a world-class level and were acknowledged by peer institutions and professional associations both within China and internationally. They also developed many of China's first academic disciplines and programs, including anthropology, economics, journalism, law, and sociology.[62]

For example, Yenching University was widely recognized to have accomplished much, both individually and institutionally. It was ranked as one of the two best universities in all of Asia by an international review carried out in 1928 by the University of California, rendering its graduates directly admissible to graduate

---

60. For a detailed account of such programs, see Perry and Tu, "Cultural Imperialism Redux?," 76.

61. See Perry and Tu, "Cultural Imperialism Redux?", 76.

62. Zhao Zhenzhou and Sun Yi, "Revisiting Religious Higher Education in China: Comparative Analysis of Furen University Narratives," *Asia Pacific Education Review* 21, no. 4 (2020): 630.

studies in the United States.[63] In 1937, William Hung (洪業, 1893–1980), from its Chinese studies program, was awarded the prestigious Prix Stanislas Julien from France's Académie des Inscriptions et Belles Lettres for a volume in his *Sinological Index Series*.[64] Many other institutions also had high achievements. The University of Nanking was especially known for its School of Agriculture. A research program on the cultural history of Shandong province at Shantung Christian University caught the global eye on stone monuments related to Confucianism. Fukien Christian University devoted special attention to the folklore, folk art, and music of Fujian province and had a rich curriculum in local history and literature. West China Union University founded one of China's earliest archaeological museums to study and display both tribal and Han cultures. Through such an effective gateway to global knowledge for twentieth-century Chinese, the missionary colleges and universities became a cluster of remarkable higher education institutions that had offered "world-class education" imbued with "Chinese characteristics"[65] although they are not regarded as the beginning of China's modern universities.[66]

State-Run Universities from 1898 to 1948

China's modern universities have been overwhelmingly state-led, especially at the national level. Officials and gentry alike were most active in establishing Western-style higher education institutions in response to the pressing needs of the national unity and economic progress required to withstand an increasingly aggressive imperialist threat. After the highly symbolic Imperial University was founded in 1898, the next national university was Southeast University, which was only established in Nanjing in 1921 at the suggestion of Guo Bingwen (郭秉文, 1880–1969).[67]

---

63. Chen Yuan 陳遠, *Yanjing daxue 1919–1952* 燕京大學 1919–1952 [Yenching University, 1919–1952] (Hangzhou: Zhejiang renmin chubanshe, 2013), 93.

64. Susan Chan Egan, *A Latterday Confucian: Reminiscences of William Hung (1893–1980)* (Cambridge, MA: Harvard University Press, 1987), 122, 148.

65. For more details of such achievements, especially those linked to the Harvard-Yenching Institute, see Perry and Tu, "Cultural Imperialism Redux?".

66. Researchers hold such a view for a number of reasons. Many of them tend to see missionary institutions as a violation of China's educational sovereignty by foreign powers. Reporting to their boards overseas and receiving substantial foreign funding, the institutions were founded and administered by foreign churches and priests. They were not and did not need to be approved by the Chinese government. Privileged with extraterritoriality, they offered foreign degrees without much control from Chinese authorities. See Cai Xianjin 蔡先金, "The Concept of *daxue* and the Origin of China's Modern Universities," 77. Some of the institutions, such as Yenching University, registered with the Chinese government in the mid-to-late 1920s and thus subjected their administrative structures and curriculum to a decree of state regulation.

67. Guo is often cited as one of the founding fathers of China's modern higher education. He undertook graduate studies in education with John Dewey and Paul Monroe and received his MA degree in 1912 and his PhD in 1914 from Columbia University. He was the first Chinese to earn a PhD from Teachers College. For details of his life trajectory, achievements, and legacy, see Ryan M. Allen and Ji Liu, *Kuo Ping Wen: Scholar, Reformer, Statesman* (San Francisco, CA: Long River Press, 2016).

The number of universities set up by national and provincial governments reached sixteen and ten respectively in 1927, and fifteen and eighteen in 1930. During the Second Sino-Japanese War (1937–1945), provincial universities could not survive the wartime hardships and were merged with their national counterparts. For instance, Guangxi University became national in 1939, Chongqing University in Sichuan and Henan University in 1942, and Yingshi (英士) University in Zhejiang in 1943. By 1947, China had thirty-one national universities and no provincial ones.[68]

In relation to indigenizing the Western concept of a university, these national universities were duty-bound. However, it is no surprise that, due to their state-led nature, they experienced more difficulties in their management of the relationship with the government and in winning institutional autonomy, especially in comparison with their private counterparts. However, the universities were not immune to the profound transformation in the wider society. One telling indicator was the change of university leaders from scholar-officials to professional academics. For example, of the ten presidents of Imperial University from 1898 to 1912, seven were *jinshi*, including Sun Jianai, who was indeed a *zhuangyuan*,[69] the first president, and one of the founders as well. In contrast, of the twenty-eight presidents of national universities from 1917 to 1946, twenty-seven had studied abroad. Of the twenty returnees, fourteen received doctorates, three had a master's degree, and three a bachelor's degree from renowned universities predominantly in North America, Europe, and Japan.[70] Such a difference reflects the general social changes in China during that time.

China's modern universities were created to learn from the West as part of the effort to save the nation that was burdened with misery. In this sense, China is a new country founded only a century ago.[71] As China was beset by threats of foreign incursions, civil disorder, and a bureaucracy riddled with corruption, the establishment of Western-style universities placed the central emphasis on subjects that were perceived to be useful for national salvation. Practicality became the most prominent feature of China's earliest modern universities, while the value of "useless" knowledge was greatly neglected. Such a historical fact has had both an immediate and a long-lasting impact on China's higher education development. It is no surprise that values such as academic freedom and institutional autonomy that are

---

68. Chen Jingpan 陳景磐, *Zhongguo jindai jiaoyushi* 中國近代教育史 [Modern history of Chinese education] (Taipei: Biographical literature Publishing House, 1986), 1513.

69. *Zhuangyuan* (狀元) was the title given to the top scorer in the palace examination (the highest rank of the imperial examination system) in imperial China. For details of the presidents, see Xiao Chaoran 肖超然, *Beijing daxue xiaoshi* 北京大學校史 [History of Peking University] (Shanghai, Shanghai Educational Publishing House, 1981), 321.

70. Zhou Chuan 周川 and Huang Xu 黃旭, *Bainian zhigong* 百年之功 [A hundred years of achievements] (Fuzhou: Fujian Education Press, 2005).

71. William C. Kirby, "The World of Universities in Modern China," in *Global Opportunities and Challenges for Higher Education Leaders: Briefs on Key Themes*, ed. Laura E. Rumbley, Robin Matross Helms, Patti McGill Peterson, and Philip G. Altbach (Rotterdam: Sense Publishers, 2014), 73–76.

often seen as defining characteristics of the workings of modern universities could hardly take root, let alone grow on Chinese soil. Yet, with painstaking experiments, progress was made in a number of areas and various degrees of success during different times. By the first half of the twentieth century, China had developed one of the more dynamic systems of higher education in the world, having strong, state-run universities.

Both progress and challenge were tremendous in the integration of Chinese and Western patterns on a systemic level. As Hayhoe repeatedly points out, the Western idea of the university was introduced during this period via a series of interactions and adaptations while ideals of academic freedom and autonomy were transformed into forms of intellectual freedom and social responsibility suited to the Chinese context. By the Republican era, the Chinese university had developed into a mature institution with a balance between its Chinese identity and its ability to link up to the world community of universities. Real effort was made, especially from 1911 to 1927, to establish a "university" in the sense of the defining values of autonomy and academic freedom. This was made possible because of the lack of a strong central government during the period.[72] However, as shown by the later development under both the Guomingdang and Communist governments, it has proved difficult, if not impossible, for Chinese educators to adapt a Western model of the university to the Chinese situation.[73]

From a systemic perspective, the universities successfully and comprehensively introduced Western learning into China. In so doing, they trained a wide range of professionals badly needed by the disaster-ridden society. Their graduates became the backbone of China's nation-building in all aspects. Scholarship was stressed from the outset. Research institutes affiliated with them made extraordinary achievements when the flames of battle raged in most parts of China with seemingly endless turmoil and chaos of war. Cai Yuanpei began to establish research institutes at Peking University in 1917, modeled on the German experience.[74] Research institutes grew fast nationwide and won acclaim,[75] from three in 1925 to forty-one in 1934, in a wide range of basic and applied subject areas. While usually relying on state appropriations, they also actively raised funding. With some full-time researchers, they trained quality researchers for China. Some of them admitted

---

72. For an early expression of such a view, see John K. Fairbank and Albert Feuerwerker, eds., *The Cambridge History of China*, Vol. 13: *Republican China 1912–1949*, Part 2 (Cambridge: Cambridge University Press, 1986). Hayhoe takes their opinion in her discussion of China's first modern universities and the sense of the defining values of autonomy and academic freedom of a university. See Hayhoe, *Chinese Universities 1895–1995*, 43.

73. See Hayhoe, *Chinese Universities 1895–1995*, 53, 63; Ruth Hayhoe, "Towards the Forging of a Chinese University Ethos: Zhendan and Fudan, 1903–1919," *The China Quarterly* 94 (1983): 323.

74. He only became the president of Peking University in December 1916.

75. See Zhu Ziqing 朱自清, "Lun xueshu de kongqi" 論學術的空氣 [On intellectual atmosphere], in *Zhu Ziqing quanji* 朱自清全集 [The complete works of Zhu Ziqing], ed. Zhu Qiaosen 朱喬森 (Nanjing: Jiangsu Education Press, 1993), 491.

research students and even hosted international students. A number of them ran scholarly journals. They demonstrated surprising capacity in both scholarship and education and served China's nation-building in an impressive way.[76]

Academic authors have long been taking delight in talking about institutional and individual achievements. Although the eight-year war with Japan brought great destruction and disruption to almost every field in China, Chinese state-led universities maintained tremendously high academic standards. Pioneering research was conducted in all disciplines, from science and technology, to the humanities and social studies, the findings cutting-edge. The development of China's universities during modern times was featured most prominently by their struggle with integration between Chinese and Western intellectual traditions, manifested in every aspect of university operation. This period saw a group of Chinese scholars who achieved great sophistication in interpreting China to an international audience, and vice versa. Their scholarly works were both deeply rooted in Chinese society and culture and solidly based on modern (Western) theories and methods.[77] They set an extraordinarily high bar, even compared with the bar of researchers today.

China's modern universities deserve much more documentation. As a revealing facet of modern Chinese history, the experiment has great implications for university development today. Indeed, their achievements were recognized even internationally at that time. The renowned British scholar Joseph Needham, for instance, hailed Zhejiang University as the "Cambridge of the East."[78] He was deeply impressed by the university's dedication to leading research even during the tribulations of war. Even more legendary was Southwest Associated University located in Kunming through the war years as an amalgamation of Tsinghua University, Peking University, and Nankai University. When the entire nation was experiencing great difficulties and hardships caused by the Japanese invasion, it achieved extraordinary heights in research and teaching, produced a remarkable quality of scholarship across disciplines, and educated a generation that was to take on important

76. For a comprehensive account and analysis, see Qiao Haofeng 喬浩風, *Zhongguo jindai daxue yanjiuyuansuo de fazhan jiqi zhineng yanjiu, 1902–1945* 中國近代大學研究院所的發展及其職能研究 (1902–1945) [A study of the development and functions of university research institutes in modern China (1902–1945)], PhD diss, Soochow University, 2016.

77. Fei Xiaotong would be a typical example of such scholars. See Gary Hamilton and Xiangqun Chang, "China and World Anthropology: A Conversation on the Legacy of Fei Xiaotong (1910–2005)," *Anthropology Today* 27, no. 6 (2011): 20–23.

78. See Zhejiang University, *Seeking Truth Pursuing Innovation* (Hangzhou: Zhejiang University 2020), 2; and Xiaoyan Zhu, Bing Qin, Xiaodan Zhu, Ming Liu, and Longhua Qian, "Knowledge Graph and Semantic Computing: Knowledge Computing and Language Understanding" (paper presented at the 4th China Conference, Communications in Computer and Information Science (CCKS) 2019, Hangzhou, China, August 24–27, 2019).

intellectual leadership.[79] To some extent, the arduous "period was a kind of baptism by fire for Chinese intellectuals."[80]

Private Higher Institutions

Situated between missionary and state-led higher education institutions in early twentieth-century China was another team that was established by reform-minded gentry. They are usually seen as private institutions, according to their founders and sources of funding. Overshadowed by the other two categories, they have been much less documented in the literature. China's first private higher education institution in modern times was Nanyang Gongxue, founded in 1896–1898 by order of the Qing's Office for the Development of Foreign Investments and Telegraphic Office.[81] By the turn of the century, the number of private institutions had grown, including Aurora University (震旦大學) in Shanghai in late 1902, Fudan Gongxue (復旦公學) in Shanghai in 1905, Zhongguo Gongxue (中國公學) in Shanghai in 1906, Canton Kwong Wah Medical College (私立廣東光華醫學院) in Guangzhou in 1908, and Wuchang Zhonghua University (武昌中華大學) in 1912. For some time, the Qing court did not allow non-governmental organizations or civilians to set up institutions of law and political science. In 1910, China's first private college of political science and law was finally established in Ningbo in Zhejiang province.[82] Similar colleges of law and political science were set up in the ensuing years.

More private higher institutions were founded during the following decades. In 1925, thirteen of them registered with the Ministry of Education, including Fudan University in 1917, Nankai University in 1919, and Amoy (Xiamen) University in 1920, while fourteen were approved to run as an experiment. In 1931, of the forty-one universities nationwide, nineteen were private, accounting for 46 percent of the national total. Eighteen of the thirty-four colleges nationwide were private, accounting for 53 percent of the national total. Of the thirty post-secondary institutions nationally, ten were private, accounting for 33 percent.[83] In 1947, seventy-nine of the 207 higher education institutions in China were private, accounting for 38

---

79. Luo Weier 羅威爾, *Xinan lianda de yichan* 西南聯大的遺產 [The great heritage of National Southwestern Associated University] (Beijing: CITIC Press Corporation, 2018).

80. See Hayhoe, *Chinese Universities 1895–1995*, 57–58.

81. It became Jiaotong Engineering University (交通大學) in 1921. There have been heated debates on which private higher institution was China's first. Here I take the view of Tian Zhengping and Chen Taolan. See Zhengping Tian and Taolan Chen, "A Textual Research on the First Private University in Modern China," *Frontiers of Education in China* 3, no. 4 (2008): 178–191.

82. Zhao Dachuan 趙大川, "Wanqing minuo shiqi de Zhejiang sili fazhen zhuanmen xuexiao" 晚清民國時期的浙江私立法政專門學校 [Zhejiang College of Law and Political Science during the late Qing and Republican era], *Research on Rule of Law* 法治研究 3 (2007), 2.

83. Zhou Bangdao 周邦道, *Diyici Zhongguo jiaoyu nianjian* 第一次中國教育年鑒 [The first Chinese yearbook of education] (Shanghai: Kaiming Bookstore, 1934), 1.

percent, while twenty-four of the fifty-five universities were private.[84]All private institutions were treated by the government as equally to their state-run peers, and their rights and responsibilities were laid down clearly in a number of laws and regulations, such as the University Organizational Law in 1929 and the Regulations for State and Private Universities in 1937. Suffering the most severe blow during wartime, many private institutions had to close or merge with public universities. All private institutions were nationalized when the People's Republic of China was founded.

China's modern private higher education institutions were born as a response to the nation's sharpening crisis. They cultivated many great talents such as physicist Wu Ta-You (吳大猷, 1907–2000) and mathematician Chern Shiing-Shen (陳省身, 1911–2004). From the outset, they had complex ties with governments, taking different forms and shapes and to varying degrees during different times. For both sides, it was a new learning experience at the trial stage. In general, both government support and intervention increased steadily over time. Some private universities successfully fostered their own characteristics, as demonstrated remarkably by Xiamen and Nankai Universities in their academic programs, scholarship, and service to the society. In so doing, they became well established. Collectively, the institutions made precious experimentation on university governance and accumulated valuable experience for the development of Chinese higher education. They also set good examples of fundraising. Most fundamentally, they provided the nation with a large number professionals that were much needed in modernization. They are both a result and an accelerator of China's profound social transformation in modern times.[85]

---

84. Chen Dongyuan 陳東原, *Dierci Zhongguo jiaoyu nianjian* 第二次中國教育年鑒 [The second Chinese yearbook of education] (Shanghai: Commercial Press, 1948), 147–148.

85. Song Qiurong 宋秋蓉, "Sili daxue yu jindai Zhongguo de shehui zhuanxing" 私立大學與近代中國的社會轉型 [Private universities and China's modern social transformation]," *Journal of East China Normal University* 華東師範大學學報 22, no. 1 (2004): 73–79.

3
The Chinese Idea of a University in Academic Discussions

The long-desired fundamental mission of the universities in Chinese societies is to combine Western and Chinese traditions in higher learning judiciously at various levels. The century-long transformation of their traditional higher education institutions into modern universities has aimed at conforming their education to "international practice."[1] Tremendous strides have been made over recent decades, and it is time for their higher education to honor their traditions to build the future. There are strong grounds for such a long-awaited combination. Chinese culture is both supportive of domestic social reforms and in line with global trends toward a knowledge society. It has a remarkable capacity to accommodate other cultures and absorb some of their best elements into itself. It integrates diverse streams of thought into an organic whole, as demonstrated by the introduction of Buddhism from India and its assimilation into Chinese cultural and educational development over a long period.[2] Chinese cultural traditions respond well to a range of problems and issues facing the West, with increasing persuasiveness.[3]

Chinese culture has much to contribute to the world community. While there are substantial differences and even conflicts between Chinese and Western approaches to scholarship,[4] in the minds of some of China's most renowned intellectuals these conflicts could and should be resolved.[5] China's intellectual tradition has its strengths and a great potential to contribute to the idea of the university. The passage of Chinese culture and epistemological traditions into mainstream thought, contributing broadly to global debates about the future of the human community,

1. Rui Yang, "Enter the Dragon: China's Higher Education Returns to the World Community," in *Higher Education: Handbook of Theory and Practice*, ed. John C. Smart and William G. Tierney (Dordrecht: Springer, 2009), 448, 455.
2. Ruth Hayhoe, "Peking University and the Spirit of Chinese Scholarship," *Comparative Education Review* 49, no. 4 (2005): 575–583.
3. Weiming Tu, "Beyond the Enlightenment Mentality," in *Confucianism and Ecology: The Interrelation of Heaven, Earth and Humans*, ed. Mary E. Tucker and John H. Berthwrong (Cambridge, MA: Harvard University Press, 1998), 3–21.
4. Weston, *The Power of Position*.
5. Xiaoqing Lin, *Peking University: Chinese Scholarship and Intellectuals, 1918–1937* (Albany, NY: State University of New York Press, 2005).

can facilitate a reassessment of the moral and spiritual responsibility of the university as a knowledge institution[6] and contribute to readdressing the under-theorization of the university.[7] Chinese higher education is well positioned to play a critical role in this aspect. There is a need for further examination of the historical and cultural nature of university development in China. This chapter intends to critically appraise the literature on the Chinese idea of a university in both the English and Chinese languages, aiming to tease out the scholarly and professional pursuit of this theme in a systematic way.

Here, I need to make it clear that in today's increasingly connected scholarly world, it is difficult, if not impossible, to classify the research on the Chinese idea of a university based entirely on the geographical locations where they are produced. In consideration of the nature of this theme and the existing boundaries between the literature in Chinese and English and to a much less extent between their producers, I will roughly employ a linguistic measure to divide the extant studies into three kinds: the English literature covers works from all parts of the world, including a growing number of scholars from Chinese societies. Researchers in mainland China have their fairly peculiar academic agendas and approaches. My discussion of their work focuses on their debates and publications on the Mainland, which indeed has been little known internationally. My observations of the exploration by scholars in Hong Kong and Taiwan are also centered on their discussions in Chinese, while I am aware that a great proportion of the scholars in these two societies, especially in Hong Kong, contribute frequently and regularly to the English literature. Singapore is worth noting, as little has been written there in Chinese that falls squarely on the Chinese idea of a university while much has been documented on so-called Asian values.[8]

The Chinese University in the English Literature

The idea that the European university has a special status among the institutions of knowledge production is pervasive in academic literature. Such a status also links closely to a sense of superiority based on some perceived exceptional qualities of the university. Of its characteristics, academic freedom and institutional autonomy are considered to be particularly important to distinguish the European university from other comparable organizations of higher learning and knowledge production.[9] The

6. Mark R. Schwehn, *Exiles from Eden: Religion and Academic Vocation in America* (New York: Oxford University Press, 1993); Bruce Wilshire, *The Moral Collapse of the University: Professionalism, Purity and Alienation* (Albany, NY: State University of New York Press, 1990).

7. Simon Marginson, "The Anglo-American University at Its Global High Tide," *Minerva* 44, no. 1 (2006): 65–87.

8. See, for example, Stephan Ortmann, "Singapore: The Politics of Inventing National Identity," *Journal of Current Southeast Asian Affairs* 28, no. 4 (2009): 23–46.

9. As a time-honored institution, the European university has been much documented. An example is the four-volume book series on the history and development of the European university from the medieval

privilege is openly expressed as taken for granted. For example, Walter Rüegg, who was then professor emeritus of sociology at the University of Bern in Switzerland, wrote in the Foreword of the first volume of *A History of the University in Europe*:[10]

> The university is a European institution; indeed, it is the European institution par excellence. There are various reasons for this assertion. As a community of teachers and taught, accorded certain rights, such as administrative autonomy and the determination and realization of curricula (courses of study) and of the objectives of research as well as the award of publicly recognized degrees, it is a creation of medieval Europe, which was the Europe of papal Christianity.

In a similar way, John Kenneth Hyde, a British historian known for his work on medieval cities, made the following claim:[11]

> The statement that all universities are descended either directly or by migration from these three prototypes [Oxford, Paris, and Bologna] depends, of course, on one's definition of a university. And I must define a university very strictly here. A university is something more than a center of higher education and study. One must reserve the term university for—and I'm quoting Rashdall here: "a scholastic guild, whether of masters or students, engaged in higher education and study," which was later defined, after the emergence of universities, as "studium generale."

There have been some recent changes. First, even in the West, people have begun to realize that there were ancient centers of learning with highly sophisticated intellectual traditions and higher learning institutions.[12] Second, some have pointed out that although academic freedom and institutional autonomy have been the defining feature of the European university by a wide consensus, the freedom has always been relative and the university has never been truly autonomous from its social-political context, which makes the claim to exceptionality of the European

---

origins of the institution until the present day, published by Cambridge University Press between 1992 and 2011. The volumes consist of individual contributions by international experts in the field and are considered the most comprehensive and authoritative work on the subject to date. The volumes are: Hilde de Ridder-Symoens, ed., *A History of the University in Europe*. Vol. I: *Universities in the Middle Ages* (Cambridge: Cambridge University Press, 1992); Hilde de Ridder-Symoens, ed., *A History of the University in Europe*. Vol. II: *Universities in Early Modern Europe (1500–1800)* (Cambridge: Cambridge University Press, 1996); Walter Rüegg, ed., *A History of the University in Europe*. Vol. III: *Universities in the Nineteenth and Early Twentieth Centuries (1800–1945)* (Cambridge: Cambridge University Press, 2004); and Walter Rüegg, ed., *A History of the University in Europe*. Vol. IV: *Universities since 1945* (Cambridge: Cambridge University Press, 2010).

10. Walter Rüegg, "Foreword. The University as a European Institution," in *A History of the University in Europe. Vol. 1: Universities in the Middle Ages*, ed. Hilde de Ridder-Symoens (Cambridge: Cambridge University Press, 1992), xix.

11. John Kenneth Hyde, "Universities and Cities in Medieval Italy," in *The University and the City: From Medieval Origins to the Present*, ed. Thomas Bender (Oxford: Oxford University Press, 1991), 13–14.

12. See, for example, Michael A. Peters, "Ancient Centers of Higher Learning: A Bias in the Comparative History of the University?" *Educational Philosophy and Theory* 51, no. 11 (2019): 1063–1072.

university highly questionable.[13] Third, the university is fast becoming a truly global institution for the first time in history, increasingly cut off from its roots in Europe and Europe's colonial empires and open to other, non-European and non-élite, knowledge traditions. Its relationship with modernity has been increasingly questioned. The centrality of the university in the European experience is diminishing.[14]

It is true that the university as a form of organization was peculiar to medieval Europe. Yet, there were organized forms of higher learning peculiar to India, China, and the Middle East that considerably predate the European form. The "university" is a form that originates historically in Europe, but it is only one form that ancient centers of higher learning took, and non-European monastic forms considerably predate universities in Europe. Other ancient centers of higher learning, as cultural achievements, must count for something in the one-upmanship histories we are taught. As a matter of fact, most of the characteristics that the European university had could also be found in other institutions of higher learning. The outline above explains why studies of the idea of a university in non-European traditions are so much lacking and demonstrates an increasing need for the literature to pay more attention to non-Western traditions in higher learning.

Against such a theoretical background, as Michael Peters has rightfully pointed out, "There are comparatively very little by way of texts in English about these centers of ancient learning that provide a clear and careful picture of the historical significance of these ancient centers. Many of them have only recently been part of archeological discoveries or restoration projects that also become part of new old histories of national traditions and also world history."[15] There has generally been little documentation explicitly on the Chinese idea of the university in the English literature. Some scattered studies have been conducted, especially after the turn of the century, as China's growing role became more evident in the world. In my analysis of Peking University personnel reforms in the 2000s, I devoted a section specifically to possible Chinese contributions to the idea of the university. I argue that while China's century-old transformation of traditional higher learning institutions into modern universities has always aimed at conforming Chinese education to "international practice," its central focus is to combine Chinese and Western traditions at all levels.[16]

---

13. Alexander Dmitrishin, "Deconstructing Distinctions: The European University in Comparative Historical Perspective," *Entremons: UPF Journal of World History* 5, no. 5 (2013): 1–18.
14. Peter Scott, "The End of the European University?" *European Review* 6, no. 4 (1998): 441–457.
15. See Peters, "Ancient Centers of Higher Learning," 1071. On this theme, Hayhoe's most recent work is noteworthy. Beginning with a brief vignette of Angkor Wat in Cambodia as a great center of learning, she highlights how it had been deeply influenced by the traditions of Indian monastic institutions. She also argues that the Indian traditions influenced China's ancient academies via the pattern of Buddhist monasteries. She compares the ancient Eastern legacies with the European university tradition. See Ruth Hayhoe, "The Gift of Indian Higher Learning Traditions to the Global Research University," *Asia Pacific Journal of Education* 39, no. 2 (2019): 177–189.
16. Yang, "Enter the Dragon," 455–457.

As China's influence rises in global higher education, scholars raise questions about the Chinese university. Among those who do not specialize in Chinese studies, Simon Marginson has been one of the most currently active to observe China's progress in becoming a world-class higher education system. He asks whether or not, to what extent, and in what ways the university is distinctive in China.[17] According to him, China is dynamic in higher education development. Although the modern Chinese university is still pursuing its foundational project of a force for modernization that is partly external to the nation, China's leading universities have already become highly internationalized. As the traditional role of faculty and Confucian self-cultivation in learning continue, synergies between Western and Chinese tradition are still underdeveloped. China has a strong "idea of a university" in higher education governance, featured by a focused state, autonomous disciplinary science in corporate universities, and regulation by dual university/state authority.

Much less explicit yet widely cited as a long-held major argument of higher education development in Asia is the notion of "twisted roots" by Philip Altbach, centered on the conflicts between indigenous traditions and the Western idea of a university.[18] The scenarios he described over three decades ago have largely remained unchanged. Without a linkage to the nation's rich indigenous cultural traditions, China's modern university development is doomed to reach a "glass ceiling" with "feet of clay."[19] According to him, China's impressive recent accomplishments in higher education have masked significant barriers to the ascent of Chinese universities to the top rungs of global academe. The fundamental reason is the cultural conflicts between China's enduring traditions in higher learning and the Western idea of a university. However, he has neither delved deep into what the Chinese idea of a university is nor how it plays out in the contemporary era.

Ruth Hayhoe has been observing Chinese higher education development, especially from a historical perspective. As her book title suggests, she highlights the cultural conflicts between Chinese and Western traditions in higher education.[20] Throughout her decades-long research on higher education development in China, the Chinese idea of a university has been an overarching theme although the term does not always appear explicitly in the titles and texts of her works.[21] She acclaims Chinese traditional culture and illustrates the potential of a melding of values from Western academic traditions with aspects of the Chinese traditional scholarship.[22] She is one of the few contemporary scholars in the West who systematically elaborate

17. See, for example, Simon Marginson, "Is There a Chinese 'Idea of a University'?" Invited seminar delivered at Tsinghua University Institute of Education, Beijing, June 26, 2019.
18. Altbach, "Twisted Roots."
19. Philip G. Altbach, "Chinese Higher Education: 'Glass Ceiling' and 'Feet of Clay,'" *International Higher Education* 86, Summer (2016): 11–13.
20. Hayhoe, *China's Universities, 1895–1995*.
21. See, for example, Hayhoe, "Ideas of Higher Learning East and West."
22. See, for example, Hayhoe, "Lessons from the Chinese Academy," 347.

ancient China's scholarly institutions and values in English. In *China's Universities 1895–1995: A Century of Cultural Conflicts*, she writes:[23]

> In China, a very different set of scholarly values arose over a long historical process. Given China's cultural and linguistic domination of East Asia, an understanding of some of the main values of the Chinese scholarly tradition is helpful also for interpreting the experience of other East Asian societies. It is difficult to character-ize several thousand years of Chinese scholarly institutions by reference to two or three core values. We can say with some certainty, however, that they were neither autonomy nor academic freedom, and that there was no institution in Chinese tradition that could accurately be called a university. Many years of reflection and reading have led me to believe that parallels to these European values and patterns have to be sought at two opposite poles of the Chinese experience. On the one hand there was the civil service examination system and its cognate institutions—the Hanlin Academy, the college for the sons of the emperor (*guozijian*), the institution of supreme learning (*taixue*), and the whole system of institutions at provincial, prefectural, and county levels that made possible a "ladder of success" through a series of examinations, culminating in the palace examination in the presence of the emperor himself. On the other hand, there were the *shuyuan*, scholarly soci-eties or academies, that were often financially independent through bequests of land, and usually headed by one great scholar, who attracted disciples and col-leagues through the virtuosity of his scholarship.

Interestingly, her research findings do not always support her expressed hope for an integration between Chinese and Western traditions in higher education. She has explained how Chinese and Western ideas of higher learning differ so vastly from each other that an integration of the two incompatible traditions is extremely difficult and even impossible.[24]

> The use of western terminology such as "university," "college" or "academy" to describe Chinese educational institutions, specially those of traditional China, makes one immediately aware of the vast cultural gap between these two highly developed yet very different educational traditions. Translating the Chinese schol-arly titles of *jinshi, juren* and *xiucai* by doctorate, master and bachelor degrees, as is sometimes done, demonstrates even more vividly the incompatibility of the two traditions. No wonder then it has proved difficult, if not impossible, for Chinese educators in this century to adapt a western model of the university to the Chinese situation.

Debates on Ideals of Modern Universities in Mainland China

For China, the turn of the twentieth century was a time of rapid change, described famously by Li Hongzhang as "the biggest change in more than three thousand

---

23. See Hayhoe, *China's Universities, 1895–1995*, 10.
24. Hayhoe, "Towards the Forging of a Chinese University Ethos," 323.

years."[25] In the cultural transition from traditional to modern China, the 1890s, along with the early 1900s, stand as an important watershed. As Chang Hao has put it, the period of 1895 to 1920 was "an era of transformation" in Chinese history with sharpening crisis and wide-ranging social and institutional reforms that continue to exert great influence on contemporary Chinese societies.[26] Higher education was a core part of the reforms. It was during the time that the Western concept of a university was introduced into China. Although disastrous for China as a nation, it was a golden age for higher education modernization. Unlike the Western idea of a university that developed as practical experience accumulated, the Chinese understanding of modern universities predated practice and came fast to its adulthood during the Late Qing reforms. China's earliest modern higher institutions were featured prominently by their endeavors and sophistication at the individual, institutional, and systemic levels in managing relations between China and the West in education, scholarship and university operation. They set high bars even for today's practice.

Writings about the ideals of modern universities abound in mainland China. However, it is worth noting that, in today's mainland Chinese scholarly discourse, any issues without specific clarification would be based on Western framework. To an overwhelming majority of mainland Chinese researchers, ideas of higher education would naturally mean the Western idea of higher education, which is also taken as the "modern" and the "advanced." I searched for the literature via the electronic library at the University of Hong Kong on March 28, 2021, through CNKI.[27] The key words used were "ideas of higher education" (高等教育理念). Altogether 4,635 items popped up on my computer screen. The number changed to 262 after "Chinese" (中國) was added as a key word. The result turned shockingly to six after "traditional" (傳統) was added.[28] It should also be pointed out that very few contemporary Chinese higher education researchers have the required training to understand classical Chinese literature. Except for a handful of highly specialized historians, most researchers would not look deeply into Chinese traditions in higher learning even when they discuss China's policy and practice.

---

25. Li Hongzhang, "*Chouyi zhizao lunchuan weike caiche zhe*" 籌議製造輪船未可裁撤折, 109.
26. Chang Hao 張灝, "*Zhongguo jindai sixiangshi de zhuanxing shidai*" 中國近代思想史的轉型時代 [An age of transformation in modern Chinese intellectual history]," *Twenty-First Century* 二十一世紀 52, no. 4 (1999): 29.
27. CNKI (China National Knowledge Infrastructure, 中國知網) is a key national research and information publishing institution in China. It has built a comprehensive China Integrated Knowledge Resources System, including journals, doctoral dissertations, master's theses, proceedings, newspapers, yearbooks, statistical yearbooks, ebooks, patents, standards, and so on. It is widely used by universities, research institutes, governments, think tanks, companies, hospitals, and public libraries around the world.
28. Of the six articles, three were published in reginal scholarly journals, while the other three appeared in magazines. None of them discussed in depth Chinese higher education traditions.

The scholarly literature has been burgeoning especially since the 2000s. While it is written in Chinese, the content focuses overwhelmingly on the so-called modern (Western) ideals of the university. This echoes the general scenario of China's human and social sciences where most researchers, whether by accident or design, believe that their mission is to discover universal and deterministic laws about the human world in the same way as natural science has done about the physical world. Since Western societies have developed earlier and much more highly, the Western way is often taken for granted by Chinese researchers in the humanities and social sciences. Although this evidently contradicts China's actuality, people tend to blame their practices rather than Western theories, due to the highly institutionalized ideology and deeply embedded scientism in the society.[29] Instead of focusing on indigenizing the Western idea of a university, current research is divided into a majority of discussions of the ideals of modern (Western) universities and a minority of fragmentary studies on Chinese higher learning traditions, and little on the interplay between the two.

China is a particularly significant site for the analysis of relationships between higher education and politics. In the Chinese intellectual tradition, ancient universities were entrusted with training bureaucrats who made imperial rule possible. They were organisms of empire.[30] It is thus no surprise that a central focus in the discussions of China's long and rich traditions in higher learning has been on the relationship between institutions and the state in ancient China and its implications for higher education development today. Calling ancient China's higher institutions "classical Chinese universities," Hu Ning and Liu Baocun hold that they predated their counterparts in the West and were founded ideologically on the Confucian philosophy of education, especially the *Great Learning* (*daxue*, 大學).[31] Citing Tu Youguang (塗又光, 1927–2012),[32] they stress that while the Chinese term *daxue* could mean both profound knowledge and grand schools, it means the former in the *Great Learning*. Shaped by historical figures and their contributions, China's classical universities have significant implications for today's higher education development. Two of these figures and their contributions are Dong Zhongshu and

---

29. Examples of the influence of scientism on China's humanities and social sciences are easy to find in daily practices. One example is how Chinese government and universities name their disciplines. For example, the faculties of education in East China Normal University and Nanjing Normal University are officially translated as the Faculty of Education Science and School of Education Science, respectively. For a theoretical analysis of this, see Rui Yang, "Internationalization, Indigenization and Educational Research in China," *Australian Journal of Education* 49, no. 1 (2005): 66–88.

30. Rui Yang, "Transformations of Higher Education Institutions in the Chinese Tradition," in *Handbook of the Politics of Higher Education*, ed. Brendan Cantwell, Hamish Coates, and Roger King (Cheltenham, UK: Edward Elgar, 2018), 66–78.

31. See Hu Ning 胡寧 and Liu Baocun 劉寶存, "Zhongguo gudian daxue de linian jiqi xiandai yiyi" 中國古典大學的理念及其現代意義 [The idea of China's classical universities and its modern implications], *Journal of Nanjing University of Science and Technology* 南京理工大學學報 19, no. 3 (2006): 69–72.

32. Tu Youguang 塗又光, *Zhongguo gaodeng jiaoyu shilun* 中國高等教育史論 [On the history of Chinese higher education] (Wuhan: Hubei Education Press, 1997), 36.

Taixue, and Zhu Xi (朱熹, 1130–1200) and his White Deer Grotto Academy that had free-style teaching and learning through debates.

While most Chinese higher education researchers have greatly avoided the classical Chinese idea of the university and its modern transformations, Gan Yang, as a non-expert in the field of higher education, has been particularly active in the discussions on the theme for two direct reasons. The first is the discussions on general education starting from the late 1990s. As both a strong advocate and a frontier practitioner of general education, he has been heavily involved in China's general education reforms over the past few decades. Citing Ambrose King Yeo-chi's *The Idea of a University*, he considered the approach to general education as the core of the traditional Chinese idea of a university.[33] The second is the personnel reform of Peking University in 2004. As an alumni of Beida,[34] he participated passionately in the debates and often touched on the notion of the Chinese idea of a university. He objected to the general design of the reform for aping American research universities at every step. According to him, by moving in this direction, China's universities would be doomed to become "dependent fiefdoms" of American universities:[35]

> The fundamental problem of universities operated by Chinese is that basically there can be no mention of cultural self-confidence or cultural consciousness. In other words, they have far from established a Chinese idea of the university.

In another article, he described Peking University's incentive to attract top-quality academics of Chinese origin from abroad as "picking peaches" instead of "planting peach trees."[36] Expressing strong academic nationalism in his discussions of the Chinese idea of the university, he ended his remarks with the following:[37]

> Beida! Raise your proud head and throw out your noble chest! You must not follow others so abjectly and subserviently! You should walk your path with self-respect and self-confidence for the sake of the Chinese idea of university.

Reflecting a miscalculation of global dominance, such a view fails to acknowledge that the global-local nexus is a twofold process of give and take: a dynamic interaction between global trends and local responses, and an exchange whereby global trends are reshaped to local ends.

---

33. Gan Yang 甘陽, *Huaren daxue yu tongshi jiaoyu* 華人大學與通識教育 [Chinese universities and general education] (Beijing: Sanlian Bookstore, 2002), 67.

34. Peking University is commonly called "Beida." Bei, the first character in Beijing, and da, the first character in *daxue*, together form the abbreviation.

35. Gan Yang, "The Chinese Idea of Universities and the Beida Reform," *Chinese Education and Society* 37, no. 6 (2004), 86.

36. Gan Yang, "The Beida Reform Follows the Example of 'Peach Pickers' but Should Spend More Time 'Planting Peach Trees,'" *Chinese Education and Society* 38, no. 1 (2005): 75–79.

37. Gan, "The Chinese Idea of Universities and the Beida Reform," 97.

Contributions from Hong Kong and Taiwan

Similar to the situation on the Chinese mainland,[38] the "loss of memory" is also commonly found among the people in Hong Kong and Taiwan. Serious discussions about or even related to the classical Chinese idea of higher learning have thus been much lacking in both societies as well. A few established scholars with training in both traditional and Western learning have been relatively exceptional. One of them is Professor Ambrose King Yeo-chi, whose *The Idea of a University*, published in 1983, has been widely read with admiration in the Chinese intellectual circles.[39] The book is neither deep nor systematic in the study of the Chinese idea of a university. Instead, it is a collection of Professor King's fifteen essays and speeches. His basic approach was to borrow Western concepts and practices of university operation and discuss their application in the contemporary Chinese context with reference to related concepts and practices in ancient China. The book covers a wide range of themes such as general education, modernity, and globalization. It is the fruit of his years of reflection on modern universities based on his scholarly and administrative experiences.

Professor King was born on the Chinese mainland and brought up in Taiwan. He holds a PhD from the University of Pittsburg. He became a sociologist at the Chinese University of Hong Kong in 1970 and later served as pro-vice-chancellor and vice-chancellor. Due to his direct involvement in university operation for close to forty years, he had opportunities to make close observations. In the book, he expresses his belief that both Western monastic education and traditional Chinese ancient academies attached great importance to knowledge and character-building. The ideas of the wise minds and philosophers of the past are the life-giving headwaters of today's universities. He criticizes modern universities for overemphasizing the imparting of knowledge at the expense of cultivation of the moral character. He keenly promotes the ideals of Chinese academies as a way to enhance moral education, while at the same time emphasizing the global vision and foresight that are crucial to university education. Integrating diverse streams of thought into an organic whole, he places much hope on universities to bring the contribution of Chinese civilization to human society.

The other figure in Hong Kong who has touched explicitly on the Chinese idea of a university is Professor Anthony Cheung Bing-leung (張炳良).[40] Like King Yeo-chi, he served as a university president, the president of the then-Hong Kong Institute of Education from 2008 to 2012. Citing Confucius, he reminds us that, in the Chinese tradition, the pursuit of higher learning through the transcendence of

---

38. See Anja Steinbauer, "Interview with Tu Wei-ming," 28.
39. See note 14 in Introduction.
40. Anthony B. L. Cheung, "Mission of University: Excellence with a Soul," in *The Way Towards Great Learning*, ed. The Hong Kong Institute of Education (Hong Kong: The Hong Kong Institute of Education, 2011), 12–15.

the self and of the values of living (realization of the Way or heaven [天] in the self) was always considered to be more important than the pursuit of knowledge in the texts. China's traditional academies that were run by great scholars to engage in the discovery, interpretation, and debates of the teachings of Confucius, Mencius, and other major ancient thinkers were able to maintain independent thinking and champion new and diverse perspectives, forming the humanistic pillar of traditional Chinese culture and scholarship. Throughout China's feudal and imperial history, there had always been an entrenched view among intellectuals that the Order of Dao (道統) was superior to the Order of Zheng (政統). Ancient Chinese scholars were bound by a moral way of living rather than any institutionalized form as, for example, the Church and the professions in Europe.

According to Anthony Cheung Bing-leung, while modern Chinese universities were founded on the European and American models, the importance of cultural heritage had never escaped the minds of contemporary university leaders in Chinese societies. The urge among Chinese scholars to revive and maintain the tradition of humanism in the modern university has never been lost though such cultural renaissance has become harder to come by under the current one-dimensional "world-class" university game. Despite the rising importance of Asia and all it represents, there is still insufficient emphasis given to, and work done on, the rediscovery of Asian traditions, institutions, systems, and thoughts. There is also a lack of systematic consolidation of Asian scholarship rooted in the region's historical struggles and transformations, modernization experiences, institution building, and social and economic development. A bridge needs to be built between Western and East Asian scholarship, and between Western modernity and East Asian traditions.

Therefore, international academic literature should be informed by both Western and East Asian scholarship and experience, as this region imparts a growing impact on the world trends. Due to East Asia's rise in global higher education, East Asian universities can contribute to an international and cosmopolitan understanding of East Asia's legacy and civilization by first rediscovering their regional and national scholarly traditions. East Asian-ness needs to be further understood to extend the global discourse. An ideal twenty-first-century university in Hong Kong should pursue academic excellence with a soul, well aware of its humanist mission and of its role in enriching civilization, and be able to connect both to Western modernity and to East Asia's great intellectual and scholarly traditions, linking the present and future with the past, and linking the local with the national and international. As the modern exemplifications of a long history of Chinese thought and scholarship, and the virtues of the Chinese literati, universities in a Chinese society like Hong Kong should take this rich intellectual endowment as part of their valued heritage.

In Taiwan, Professor Huang Chun-chieh (黃俊傑) has been the most prominent writer on the Chinese idea of the university.[41] He earned a PhD in history from the University of Washington in 1980 and has long been an eminent scholar especially known for his work on East Asian humanism and Confucianism. At National Taiwan University, he offers a course on The Idea of a University, in which he explores the origin, development, and contemporary issues of modern universities. Citing the ancients such as Confucius and Aristotle and distinguishing between the classical and contemporary ideas of a university, he stresses a number of shared features across Eastern and Western higher learning traditions, such as character formation, holistic personal development, and encyclopedic knowledge, as well as the difference between practical wisdom and scientific knowledge. From a comparative and international perspective, he argues that the traditional emphasis on the intrinsic value of education has been seriously challenged by contemporary uses of universities based on instrumentalism and the wider modern capitalist culture. He proposes general education as an effective approach to a nuanced balance between classical and modern ideas of a university.

---

41. Huang Chun-chieh 黃俊傑, "*Ershiyi shiji daxue linian de jidang yu tongshi jiaoyu de zhanwang*" 二十一世紀大學理念的激蕩與通識教育的展望 [The turbulent idea of a university in the twenty-first century and the prospect of general education], *Higher Education Development and Evaluation* 高教發展與評估 36, no. 5 (2020): 1–19.

4
Increasingly Alike: Formal Resemblance

Over fifteen years ago, Schofer and Meyer employed an institutional theoretical lens and pooled panel regressions to analyze the rapid worldwide expansion of higher educational enrollments over the twentieth century. In nearly all types of countries they found similar growth patterns. The expansion was sharply accelerated after 1960. They argued that a new model of society was becoming institutionalized globally.[1] In a similar theoretical vein, Zapp and Ramirez recently analyzed the formation of a global educational regime and its influence on isomorphism. This regime is supported by a rapidly growing network of international organizations that focus on conferences, initiatives, and programs supporting a global higher education agenda, by a fast increasing number of international and national accreditation agencies, by parallel increases in regional qualification frameworks, and in the implementation of national qualification frameworks. These developments combine to create integration pressures on national higher education systems.[2]

Against such a backdrop, more and more people in Chinese societies question whether or not they are on course for a global homogenization of higher education. Indeed, signs of both homogenization and differentiation are evident in higher education in Chinese societies, depending on which dimension one looks at and what lens one employs. On closer examination, one sees that higher education institutions in the societies are neither becoming strictly homogeneous and isomorphic at an institutional level nor highly differentiated and polymorphic at the sectorial and systemic level. For Chinese societies, modern universities were established based on Western experiences as a response to the West.[3] Reformers took them as a major approach to learning from Western powers.[4] They were latecomers in modern higher education, and their development means to a great extent becoming similar to Western systems and institutions, especially in infrastructure, standards,

---

1. Evan Schofer and John W. Meyer, "The Worldwide Expansion of Higher Education in the Twentieth Century," *American Sociological Review* 70, no. 6 (2005): 898–920.
2. Mike Zapp and Francisco O. Ramirez, "Beyond Internationalization and Isomorphism: The Construction of a Global Higher Education Regime," *Comparative Education* 55, no. 4 (2019): 473–493.
3. See Têng and Fairbank, *China's Response to the West*; and Cohen, *Discovering History in China*.
4. Kirby, "The World of Universities in Modern China."

measures, and organizational behaviors. It is thus positive to note that, within a relatively short period of one and a half centuries, the societies have learned from the West remarkably well to establish their highly institutionalized modern higher education systems and institutions.

Observers have different assessments of higher education development in Chinese societies, often due to the perspectives they have employed consciously and unconsciously. They tend to be lopsided and stress the hardware much more than the software. The frame of reference is also to be noted, particularly because the development appears to be different when compared with that in Western and other non-Western societies. Far too often researchers, both Chinese and non-Chinese, tend to evaluate higher education achievements in Chinese societies according only to the experience from the West, failing to see the extraordinary accomplishment that becomes much more remarkable when it is put side by side with that from other non-Western societies.[5] As a matter of fact, after a century of arduous work, Chinese societies have made substantial achievements in higher education in learning from the West. They have all established a Western-style higher education system, with strong capacity in research and innovation as well as fast growth in scientific output.

Institutional Infrastructure

As noted in previous chapters, China has a rich tradition in higher learning. Yet, modern universities are an imported concept for Chinese societies. Although China's earliest institutions of higher learning appeared in the Western Zhou dynasty, its modern higher education system was introduced from the West as a social institution during the second half of the nineteenth century. This foreign transplant has now taken root in all Chinese societies, where path and trajectory diversity in higher education development began to widen when the Chinese Communist Party (CCP) came into power on the Mainland in 1949. Since then, higher education development in mainland China has experienced twists and turns as a result of international and domestic sociopolitical turbulences, such as "Leaning to One Side,"[6]

---

5. While the achievement has been widely acknowledged, assessment of future development is not. The strikingly contrastive assessments among scholars are often due to their perspectives employed both consciously and unconsciously in their research. The current conceptualization of higher education development in Chinese societies relies almost entirely yet highly inappropriately on Western theoretical constructions. The perspectives that give weight to the impact of traditional Chinese ways of cultural thinking on contemporary development are badly needed. I have done some analyses of similar issues with assessment of higher education development in East Asia. See Rui Yang, "Foil to the West? Interrogating Perspectives for Observing East Asian Higher Education," in *Researching Higher Education: History, Development and Future*, ed. Jisun Jung, Hugo Horta, and Akiyoshi Yonezawa (Singapore: Springer, 2018), 37–50.

6. On the eve of the establishment of New China, between the spring and summer of 1949, Mao Zedong advanced the principle of "leaning to one side." It declared that China would lean to the side of the socialist camp headed by the Soviet Union on the opposite of the imperialist camp headed by the United States. See Shen Zhihua and Li Danhui, *After Leaning to One Side: China and Its Allies in the*

and the Cultural Revolution (formally the Great Proletarian Cultural revolution, 1966–1976).[7] The recent thirty-five years have witnessed particularly impressive achievements. The system has been quickly transformed into the world's largest in number of students and teachers and the second largest producer of scientific papers so far. It has been well established as contributing to the rise of the Chinese power.

Higher education institutions on the Chinese mainland are divided into two sectors: regular and adult higher education. The regular sector is the mainstream, including four-year universities and colleges and two- and three-year specialized college programs, leading to a bachelor's degree and a diploma respectively. The adult sector includes two- and four-year diploma programs of study. Students in the regular sector are overwhelmingly full-time, while students in the adult sector are usually part-time. In 2020, 41.83 million students enrolled in mainland China's 2,738 regular and 265 adult higher education institutions, a gross enrollment rate of 54.4 percent. Annual postgraduate admissions reached 1.1 million, 116,000 and 990,500 respectively at doctoral and master's levels, and a total of 3,139,600 at-school postgraduate students. Teaching and administrative staff reached 2,668,700 with 1,833,000 full-time teachers and a student-teacher ratio of 18.37:1. There were 771 private higher education institutions, enrolling 2,556 master's students and 7,913,400 undergraduate and associate degree students.[8]

Higher education development accelerated greatly after the Mainland adopted reform and opening-up policies in 1978. Since then, establishing closer links

Cold War (Stanford, CA: Stanford University Press, 2011). Higher education was patterned on the Soviet practices that were featured by pragmatism of practical training and clear specializations. See Alexander G. Korol, *Soviet Education for Science and Technology* (New York: Wiley and the Technology Press, 1957); Alex Kuraev, "Soviet Higher Education: An Alternative Construct to the Western University Paradigm," *Higher Education* 71, no. 2 (2016): 181–193. Although little documented, Soviet influence penetrated deeply into the entire sector and has since exerted a significant and lingering impact on China's reform and development in higher education. See Leo A. Orleans, "Soviet Influence on China's Higher Education," in *China's Education and the Industrialized World: Studies in Cultural Transfer*, ed. Ruth Hayhoe and Marianne Bastid (Armonk, NY: M. E. Sharpe, 1987), 184–198. The main lessons learned from the Soviet Union revolved around thought reform and structural reorganization. For a detailed account of China's learning from the Soviet Union in education, see Suzanne Pepper, *Radicalism and Education Reform in 20th-Century China: The Search for an Ideal Development Model* (New York: Cambridge University Press, 1996), 157–258.

7. The period of the Cultural Revolution was the most destabilizing decade in modern Chinese history. It forced a very different educational shutdown that devastated a generation, hobbled their opportunities for life, and has reshaped China's approach to schooling ever since. According to some, it is one of the biggest disruptions to education in the modern world. There has been a vast body of literature on the impact of the Cultural Revolution on China's education. See, for example, Julia Kwong, *Cultural Revolution in China's Schools, May 1966–April 1969* (Stanford, CA: Hoover Institution Press, 1988). Recently, there has been some new evidence on its educational disruptions. See John Giles, Albert Park, and Meiyan Wang, "The Great Proletarian Cultural Revolution, Disruptions to Education, and the Returns to Schooling in Urban China," *Economic Development and Cultural Change* 68, no. 1 (2019): 131–164.

8. Ministry of Education, "National Education Statistics Bulletin in 2020" 2020年全國教育事業發展統計公報 (Ministry of Education, 2021), http://www.moe.gov.cn/jyb_sjzl/sjzl_fztjgb/202108/t20210827_555004.html.

between higher education and the market has been a prominent reform orientation. On the phasing out of the planned economy and a much-altered role of the state, the government became increasing reluctant to continue to subsidize students. Fees started to become a reality. The rapid expansion of higher education since 1999 further accelerated this trend. The Higher Education Law (Article 13, Chapter I) stipulates decentralization in the mainland Chinese system by stating while "the State Council shall provide unified guidance and administration for higher education throughout the country," local governments "shall undertake overall coordination of higher education in their own administrative regions, administer the higher education institutions that mainly train local people, and the higher education institutions that they are authorized by the State Council to administer."[9]

Mainland public higher education institutions are increasingly corporatized, especially since the 1990s.[10] They are expected to raise a great proportion of their own revenue, enter into business enterprises, acquire and hold investment portfolios, encourage partnerships with private business firms, compete with other universities in the production and marketing of courses to students who are seen as customers, and generally engage with the market for higher education. They are run as a business producing and selling knowledge, increasingly see their students as customers or clients, and enroll as many students as possible to improve efficiency. Many public universities have a private arm (independent colleges, for example) to maximize financial gains. Corporation is also evident in other major aspects of university operation, including research. Cost-conscious corporatized universities have caused the placing of technique above ends or values, leading to the decline of the classical disciplines. The organizational principles employed under this type of regime do not engender the long-term commitment of academic staff.[11]

---

9. Ministry of Education, "Higher Education Law of the People's Republic of China" 中華人民共和國高等教育法 (Ministry of Education, 2009), http://en.moe.gov.cn/documents/laws_policies/201506/t20150626_191386.html.

10. For example, in the mid-2000s, two Korean researchers, Jong-Hak Euna and Keun Lee, worked collaboratively with Guisheng Wu from China's Tsinghua University to explore the experience of university-run enterprises in developing countries and their implications for the Chinese mainland. They found that Mainland universities since the market-oriented reform had a strong propensity to pursue economic gains and strong internal (R&D and other) resources to launch start-ups, and established their own firms. See Jong-Hak Euna and Keun Lee, "Explaining the 'University-Run Enterprises' in China: A Theoretical Framework for University-Industry Relationship in Developing Countries and Its Application to China," *Research Policy* 35, no. 9 (2006): 1329–1346.

11. Therefore, most mainland Chinese universities try to develop the relevant organizational structures and incentives. For the shape, the scope, and channels of university-industry linkages and their incentives to encourage and facilitate engagement with industry, see Weiping Wu, "Managing and Incentivizing Research Commercialization in Chinese Universities," *Journal of Technology Transfer* 35, no. 2 (2010): 203–224. The case study of two leading institutions in Shanghai, Fudan University and Shanghai Jiaotong University, shows that the product is often a combination of various factors, including historical legacy and institutional learning. In spite of being enticed to disclose inventions and pursue commercialization, university academics continue to be more interested in scholarly work.

Since the 1980s, governance reforms have been implemented to loosen the long-featured tight control by the central government over higher education institutions on the Mainland under the national principles and plans, so that institutions can build direct links to industry and other sectors, and foster initiatives and capacity to meet economic and social needs. With the central government refraining much from direct control and acting as a facilitator, institutions have gained relatively more autonomy in many domains, including student admissions, establishment of academic programs, teaching affairs, research and development, service to local community, international exchange and cooperation, internal governance restructuring, personnel, finance, and property management. Based on their teaching needs, they take the initiative in designing their own teaching plans, selecting textbooks, and organizing teaching and learning activities. Within an institution, the president, faculty, and departments enjoy much greater autonomy in mobilizing resources and making institutional decisions on matters relating to teaching, research, and personnel.[12]

As the central state diversifies educational services to encourage the non-state sector to establish and run educational institutions, more power is devolved from the central to local governments, communities, and non-state actors to take more responsibilities for education provision, financing, and regulation. The growing significance of private higher education in the mainland system has led to changes to governance in private institutions. In the early 1980s, governance of private higher institutions was featured by the natural person (founder or owner) who took sole responsibility for policy making and management. By the 1990s, there was great diversity from natural person to board of trustees, while some adopted the president responsibility under supervision/guidance of the senate. The 2000s saw specific regulations on institutional governance. Most private institutions established their board of trustees while some adopted the president responsibility under the supervision of senate or CCP committee. After the mid-2000s, the governing body was usually a board of trustees. While government control remains strong, there has been a downward movement of the center of gravity in the governance of private higher education.[13]

---

12. However, it is important to note that the central government has remained in control over key aspects. For a detailed account of the policy trajectory on the Chinese mainland, see Yannan Cao and Rui Yang, "World-Class University Construction and Higher Education Governance Reform in China: A Policy Trajectory," in *The Governance and Management of Universities in Asia*, ed. Chang Da Wan, Molly N. N. Lee, and Hoe Yeong Loke (New York: Routledge, 2019), 21–42.

13. For further discussions of the form and features of institutional governance of private higher education institutions on the Chinese mainland, see Xu Liu, "Institutional Governance in the Development of Private Universities in China," *Higher Education* 79, no. 2 (2020): 275–290. According to her, the CCP allows private entrepreneurs considerable freedom to invest in higher education while maintains control over the private institutions. See Xu Liu, "Institutional Governance of Chinese Private Universities: The Role of the Communist Party Committee," *Journal of Higher Education Policy and Management* 42, no. 1 (2020): 85–101.

Hong Kong's higher education system was established during the colonial era to produce an Anglicized ruling Chinese elite to support the colonial rule and extend British cultural influence in China and Asia. Founded in 1911, the University of Hong Kong was the first higher institution in the society. Purposely designed to use English as its medium of instruction, it had a very distinctive role to play as an instrument of British cultural imperialism in China. It was intended as a "British lighthouse in the Orient" with a broad remit to educate the new generation of Chinese youth who would lead the modernization of China.[14] The second higher education institution, the Chinese University of Hong Kong, was born in 1963, by the amalgamation of three post-secondary colleges: New Asia (1949), Chung Chi (1951), and United (1956).[15] Despite its medium of instruction of Chinese and its emphasis on Chinese knowledge and values,[16] Hong Kong higher education remained highly colonial and elitist until the 1990s. The cherished goal of East-West integration has remained a lofty aspiration only.

In 1989, the government decided to increase the gross enrolment ratio in tertiary education to 18 percent by the academic year 1994–1995. The 1990s then witnessed the birth of more higher education institutions such as the Hong Kong University of Science and Technology (1991), the Hong Kong Technical Colleges (1993), and the Hong Kong Institute of Education (1994), for a total of eight publicly funded higher education institutions. The expansion continued after the change of sovereignty in 1997. In 2000, the government announced its plan to increase the participation rate of tertiary education to 60 percent, by encouraging the non-government sector to participate in the provision of post-secondary education. A number of self-financing higher education institutes emerged to offer two-year sub-degree programs, leading to associate degrees and higher diplomas. The gross enrolment ratio consequently increased from 9.3 percent in 1980 to 68.5 percent in 2015, growing at an average annual rate of 11.96 percent. By the 2019–2020 academic year, the total enrolment was 10,148 in the eight publicly funded universities.[17]

Since 2004, the Hong Kong government has strived to develop the city into a regional education hub,[18] mainly through internationalization and diversification of

---

14. Peter Cunich, *A History of the University of Hong Kong Vol. 1, 1911–1945* (Hong Kong: Hong Kong University Press, 2012), 439.

15. A fourth college, Shaw College, was established in 1986. See Stewart R. Sutherland, *Higher Education in Hong Kong: Report of the University Grants Committee* (Hong Kong: University Grants Committee, 2002).

16. Although largely rhetorical, the university was built on a long yearned-for beautiful ideal of Chinese intellectuals: To Combine Tradition with Modernity, To Bring Together China and the West 結合傳統 與現代　融合中國與中西, http://www.cuhk.edu.hk/iso/community/content/pdf/preface.pdf.

17. University Grants Committee, "教資會資助大學主要統計數字" Key Statistics on UGC-funded Universities, https://www.ugc.edu.hk/doc/eng/ugc/publication/report/AnnualRpt1920/full.pdf

18. For example, in his 2009–2010 Policy Address, former Chief Executive Donald Tsang Yam-kuen expressed the ambition clearly: "On the development of education services, our objective is to enhance Hong Kong's status as a regional education hub, boosting Hong Kong's competitiveness and

the postsecondary education sector. Aiming to nurture talents for other industries and attract outstanding people from around the world, the government hopes to boost Hong Kong's competitiveness and facilitate its long-term development. Local higher education in Hong Kong has since been increasingly for sale to non-local buyers. After two decades of fast expansion, the sector now faces a number of issues of quality, relevance, financial resources, and equity during its current period of post-massification. Today, having some of the region's best-built universities in teaching and research, Hong Kong is home to eight publicly funded universities, of which most enjoy a good reputation internationally.[19]

A former British colony, Hong Kong was reunited with the People's Republic of China in July 1997 under the "one country, two systems" model. Following the British tradition, the University Grants Committee (UGC) plays an important role in higher education governance in Hong Kong, as a buffer between the government and universities, to avoid interference and protect institutional autonomy and academic freedom and as an honest "broker" to ensure value for public funding.[20] Through channeling government funding to public higher education institutions, the UGC's primary role is to hold them accountable for the rightful use of public resources while maintaining accountability.[21] For institutional governance of publicly funded universities, the Chief Executive of Hong Kong has only a ceremonial role, while their presidents administer the institutions under the supervision of the council. The council is the real governing body with control over institutional administration and the appointments of senior officers, while the senate oversees academic activities and conferment of awards.

As noted in previous chapters, the earliest Western-style universities founded in Chinese societies were during the late years of the Qing dynasty, concentrated in a few cities on the Chinese mainland. None of them was in Taiwan. Modern higher education development in Taiwan started during the Japanese occupation period (1895–1945). Established in 1928, Taihoku Imperial University (National Taiwan University, after 1945) was the first in the society. It was designated initially to serve

---

complementing the future development of the Mainland." See Donald Tsang Yam-kuen, *The 2009–2010 Policy Address* (Hong Kong: Government Printer, 2009), 11.

19. According to the Quacquarelli Symonds (QS) World University Rankings 2021, of the eight public universities funded by the UGC, five were ranked in the top 100 in the world. The highest ranking is the University of Hong Kong at twenty-second place, which continues to rank ahead of the Hong Kong University of Science and Technology, which is ranked joint twenty-seventh. The Chinese University of Hong Kong is not far behind at forty-third. https://www.topuniversities.com/university-rankings/asian-university-rankings/2021.

20. See Sir Howard Newby CBE, *Governance in UGC-Funded Higher Education Institutions in Hong Kong: Report of the University Grants Committee* (Hong Kong, University Grants Committee, 2015), 2.

21. Some argue that Hong Kong's academic freedom is under serious threat. For instance, Petersen and Currie expressed such a view over a decade ago. See Carole J. Petersen and Jan Currie, "Higher Education Restructuring and Academic Freedom in Hong Kong," *Policy Futures in Education* 6, no. 5 (2008): 589–600.

as an outpost of the Japanese empire in Southeast Asia.[22] Since 1960, higher education development has accelerated in Taiwan to serve socioeconomic development.
More higher education institutions were established, with increasing numbers of
professors and students. The number of higher institutions increased from 121 in
1990, to 150 in 2000, and 127 in 2017. Student enrollment was 576,623 in 1990,
1,092,102 in 2000, and 1,274,191 in 2017. The gross enrolment rate increased from
44.31 percent in 1995 to 81.51 percent in 2010. In 2019, the 152 higher education
institutions hosted 46,137 full-time academic staff members and 1,213,172 students,
for a gross enrolment of 75.48 percent.[23]

While Taiwan's higher education system has been following the US pattern in
various key aspects, including institutional organization, curriculum, degree structure, and its recent emphasis on general education, its mode of governance in higher
education has taken a quite different route. In Taiwan, higher education institutions
fall into three types: universities, colleges, and junior colleges (similar to community colleges in the United States), offering different programs and qualifications.
Institutions of different categories are supervised by different departments at the
ministry level. Yet, a strong state-led governance approach has been deep and wide
in the system, common in both general and technological tracks and in public and
private institutions. While recent years have seen more power devolved to institutions, major aspects are still tightly controlled by the central government, such as
establishing academic programs, student admission quotas, and types and levels
of tuition and fees. Higher education institutions are encouraged to take the initiative to design their institutional management, curriculum development, human
resources, and expenditure allocation.

Private higher education institutions operate according to the Private School
Law with a board of trustees. Although more accountable for fee-payers, they enjoy
relatively more autonomy, especially in institutional management and appointment
of senior managers. However, for internal governance structure, higher education
institutions of various sorts have similar structure and features. In recent decades,
higher education governance and institutional management have been greatly
influenced by neoliberal ideologies and approaches, with increasing emphasis on
efficiency, competition, and accountability. Corporate governance has been exercising significant impact on the higher education system and its institutions. For
policy makers and institutional senior managers, such a mode of governance is
increasingly desirable to enhance effectiveness and performance. Furthermore, the

---

22. See, Wen-Hsing Wu, Shun-Fen Chen and Chen-Tsou Wu, "The Development of Higher Education in
    Taiwan," *Higher Education* 18, no. 1 (1989): 136.
23. Such statistical information was retrieved from the following websites: "National Statistics, Republic of
    China (Taiwan)," https://eng.stat.gov.tw/ct.asp?xItem=41873&ctNode=6343&mp=5 and http://stats.
    moe.gov.tw/files/ebook/others/year16/16years.htm.

inconsistencies between systemic and institutional developments have created a dual governance structure both inside and outside higher education institutions.[24]

However, Taiwan's centralized administration in higher education is different from the American system of decentralization. The Ministry of Education in Taipei has the legitimate power to approve the establishment of higher learning institutions and the addition or elimination of academic programs. It is also the Ministry of Education that determines the student number, tuition rate, and required courses in all colleges and universities. Such a centralized administration was established for the purpose of quality control in the late 1920s, when Chinese higher education was in a state of chaos. Since centralization has long been a feature of Chinese political administration, governmental intervention in higher education seems tolerable to many people. The ideal of university autonomy has not been fully realized in the island's tertiary institutions. However, at the urging of many academics, the Ministry of Education is revising the Act of University. It is believed that the highly centralized system will be changed in the near future.

Sitting at the edge of peninsular Malaysia in the heart of Southeast Asia, Singapore was founded in 1965. The universities in Singapore at that time included a branch campus of the University of Malaya and Nanyang University. In 1980, they merged to form National University of Singapore. In the 1990s and the 2000s, more higher education institutions were established, including Nanyang Technological University in 1991, Singapore Management University in 2000, Singapore Institute of Technology in 2009 (funded and run privately until 2017 when it became the full-fledged publicly funded Singapore University of Social Sciences), and Singapore University of Technology and Design in 2009. The government also funds some fine arts degree programs at LASALLE College of the Arts and Nanyang Academy of Fine Arts. In addition, some private providers work jointly with overseas universities to offer programs for profit. Since 1998, some foreign higher education institutions have established independent campuses in Singapore to offer programs leading to undergraduate and postgraduate degrees.[25]

The government forms strategic partnerships between Singapore's higher education institutions and their prominent foreign counterparts. Seeing a huge demand for international education especially from Asia, Singapore tries to tap this lucrative

---

24. For further discussions of the deep impact of neoliberalism and new public management on Taiwan's higher education governance at both systemic and institutional levels, see Sheng-Ju Chan and Chia-Yu Yang, "Governance Styles in Taiwanese Universities: Features and Effects," *International Journal of Educational Development* 63, C (2018): 29–35.

25. By early 2021, the overseas institutions included the University of Adelaide (1998), INSEAD (2000), University of Chicago Graduate School of Business (2000), Queen Margaret University-Edinburgh (2002), James Cook University (2003), SP Jain School of Global Management (2004), ESSEC Business School (2005), Cardiff Metropolitan University (2005), University of Nevada Les Vegas (2006), New York University's Tisch School of the Arts (2007), Curtin University (2008), DigiPen Institute of Technology (2008), Temple University (2010), Embry-Riddle Aeronautical University (2011), and Yale University (2011).

education market.[26] The government thus promotes greater diversity and autonomy in the post-secondary education landscape. As new higher education institutions were founded, different operational models were also tried. For instance, although Singapore Management University was incorporated as a private company by an Act of the Parliament in 2000, it has been receiving substantial funding from the government, just like other publicly funded universities. Meanwhile, the government maintains centralized control through systems of accountability to, and funding from, the state. It has thus been paradoxical for the government to engineer a tertiary education market that include public, private, and even foreign players while maintaining centralized control over the achievement of its strategic agenda within its stipulated policy and time frames.

The post-secondary education system in Singapore has transformed from elite to mass form. Today young people are much more inclined to complete university education.[27] In 2016, over 52 percent of the resident population aged twenty-five and above had at least post-secondary qualifications, which was an increase from 36.7 percent in 2006. The proportion of university graduates increased by 9.5 percent between 2006 and 2016, from 19.6 percent to 29.1 percent. The percentage of residents receiving diplomas and professional qualifications increased by 3.9 percent over the same ten-year period.[28] The percentage of each age cohort enrolled in publicly funded universities increased from 5 in 1981 to 34.2 in 2016.[29] In 2020, a total of 17,500 students enrolled in the six local universities, a cohort participation rate of 42 percent.[30] Since Singapore is consistently rated by various global indexes as a global hub for innovation and research, its higher education institutions continue to be highly attractive to prospective international students.

The qualitative progress made by Singapore higher education is equally impressive, as it has globally oriented universities. Lacking natural resources, Singapore views education as a development tool. Indeed, education has always been a priority for its economic development, and this policy has even earned Singapore the nickname "Global Schoolhouse." Ever since the leadership of Lee Kuan Yew (1923–2015), education has been prioritized under the constitution. The government plays a central role in educational reform and development. It has also been adaptive,

26. The initiative is also expected to contribute to Singapore's international network. See George Yeo, Speech by Mr George Yeo, Minister for Trade and Industry, at the 'Singapore—The Global Schoolhouse' Conference, August 16, 2003.

27. Nancy W. Gleason, "Singapore's Higher Education Systems in the Era of the Fourth Industrial Revolution: Preparing Lifelong Learners," in *Higher Education in the Era of the Fourth Industrial Revolution*, ed. Nancy W. Gleason (Singapore: Palgrave Macmillan, 2018), 145–169.

28. Singapore Department of Statistics, "Population Trends 2017," https://www.singstat.gov.sg/-/media/files/publications/population/population2017.pdf.

29. Ministry of Education, "*Education Statistics Digest 2017*" (Singapore, Ministry of Education, 2017).

30. Sandra Davie, "Singapore Universities Offered 17,500 Places Last Year, 1,000 More Than Planned," *The Straits Times*, January 18, 2021, https://www.straitstimes.com/singapore/parenting-education/17500-varsity-places-given-out-last-year-1000-more-than-planned.

as reflected consistently in its approach to education. Singapore's higher education system has thus been featured by its highly prioritized economic orientation and the central state's direct intervention, reforms always being state-led and top-down. Yet, according to many observers, Singapore is at the forefront of innovation in higher education. It links economic prosperity closely to educational development. Its education system enjoys a global reputation for preparing excellent learners.[31]

In higher education development, one major policy announced in 1997 by the prime minister was to develop National University of Singapore and Nanyang Technological University into "world-class" institutions, in order to turn Singapore into the "Boston of the East." By transforming its higher education sector, Singapore is attempting to become an education hub.[32] The city-state now boasts two widely recognized world-class universities and several others that are delivering quality education. With high standards of teaching and learning, as well as scientific research, Singapore is a pioneer when it comes to higher education both in Asia and the world. Positioning itself to become an intensively knowledge-based economy, the society has great ambitions to build not only research centers but also a world-class university environment.

Social and Financial Resources

Chinese societies are strongly committed to education culturally and financially. Public spending on higher education on the Chinese mainland was high by international comparison until the late 1990s, having generous government allocation per student. While public spending per student has recently been decreasing as the market is introduced to higher education, educational costs per student have increased substantially. Public funding of higher education accounted for 29 and 19 percent of total public education expenditures respectively in 1984 and 1994.[33] Government subsidies declined as a share of total financing, while the share of financing contributed by tuition fees rose considerably. The private cost of higher education has become substantial. Since the late 1990s, a multi-source financing system has taken shape. Government funding is no longer the only source of finance, and the percentage it contributes to the total revenue has declined dramatically.

At present, higher education revenues are generated from a variety of sources, including government funding, tuition and fees, income earned through entrepreneurial activities of higher education institutions, philanthropy, and donations. For instance, the income structure for 2019 of the top ten mainland universities

31. Although some would argue that Singaporean students learn for exams.
32. For detailed discussions of such policy initiatives, see Kris Olds, "Global Assemblage: Singapore, Foreign Universities, and the Construction of a 'Global Education Hub,'" *World Development* 35, no. 6 (2007): 959–975.
33. World Bank, *Higher Education Reform: A World Bank Country Study* (Washington, DC: World Bank, 1997).

revealed that, on average, public funding made up only around one-third of their total income. As the most prestigious universities, they were much better placed to generate additional revenues in comparison with most other institutions that continue to rely heavily on government funding. In 2019, Tsinghua University had the highest planned income of all leading universities in mainland China, amounting to around 21.9 billion RMB,[34] of which 5.41 billion RMB were allocated public funds.[35] According to the release by the Ministry of Education in April 2021, Tsinghua's budget for 2021 reached 31.728 billion RMB. Compared with 2020, the total funding of most higher education institutions in the Mainland has increased, while a few have decreased. Tsinghua University increased by 557 million RMB compared to last year.[36]

Basic research spending in mainland China was historically low, about 4.8 percent during 2012–2013, compared with 10–25 percent in developed nations. In 2014, however, the appropriation for basic research increased by 12.5 percent to $6.6 billion. The expenditure on R&D increased by 23 percent a year on average in the 2000s.[37] In 2019, its years-long run of double-digit percentage increases in spending on R&D continued. Public and private science and technology (S&T) expenditures rose 12.5 percent over the previous year to 2.21 trillion yuan RMB ($322 billion). Spending on basic research accounted for 6 percent of the total; applied research, 11.3 percent; and development, 82.7 percent. The spending amounted to 2.23 percent of GDP, an increase of 0.09 percentage points from the previous year.[38] Mainland China now has the world's largest S&T workforce of more than 100 million. The government is devoting 2.1 percent of GDP to S&T in its most recent 14th Five-Year Plan (2021–2025), approaching the level of developed countries.[39]

According to the OECD, mainland China's absolute expenditures were the world's second biggest in 2018, $468 billion on R&D, while the United States' investment was $582 billion. Analysts expect mainland China to close the gap. Investment in basic research reached 6 percent of total spending for the first time after hovering

---

34. The renminbi (abbreviated RMB) is the official currency of the People's Republic of China. On April 23, 2021 1 yuan RMB equaled $US0.15.

35. See "Planned Income Structure of Leading Ten universities in China for 2019 (in billion yuan)," https://www.statista.com/statistics/1098957/china-income-structure-of-leading-universities/.

36. Chen Zhiwen, "Who Provided Tsinghua's 31.7 Billion Funding?" https://www.ww01.net/en/archives/128814.

37. Jane Qiu, "China Goes Back to Basics on Research Funding," *Nature* 507 (March 13, 2014), 148–149.

38. Dennis Normile, "China Again Boosts R&D Spending by More Than 10%," *Science* (August 28, 2020), https://www.sciencemag.org/news/2020/08/china-again-boosts-rd-spending-more-10.

39. The 2.5 percent of GDP by 2020 goal was spelled out in a fifteen-year medium- and long-term program for S&T development. For comparison, in 2018 the United States and OECD as a whole spent respectively 2.83 and 2.38 percent of GDP on R&D, while Israel and South Korea spent 4.9 and 4.5 percent of GDP respectively. See Mu-ming Poo, "Innovation and Reform: China's 14th Five-Year Plan Unfolds," *National Science Review* 8, no. 1 (2021), https://academic.oup.com/nsr/article/8/1/nwaa294/6101717.

at just over 5 percent for a decade. Combined central and local governmental expenditures on research have topped one trillion RMB. Due to sustained investment in R&D, mainland China has jumped from bit player to major contributor in global scientific activities, fast advancing to the forefront of scientific research. For instance, its annual increase rate of science papers produced each year from 2000 to 2009 was 17 percent. Considering the fact that much research published in Chinese has been largely ignored by the international scientific community, mainland China's share of and contribution to global production far exceeds the estimates by many observers.[40] It is even positioned to change the way science is practiced in the days to come.[41]

Higher education funding for publicly funded institutions in Hong Kong is predominantly by the government through the UGC. There are two main parts of government funding for public institutions. The first is recurrent grants to support regular academic work and related administrative activities of the institutions. Based on an established formula, most of these grants are disbursed to institutions on a triennial basis to tie in with the academic planning cycle in the form of a block grant to allow institutions to have a high degree of freedom in deciding on how the allocations are deployed and put to best use internally. Determination of the grants to universities is largely based on an established formula used as the key parameter to assess universities' needs. The second is capital grants that are used to finance major works projects and minor campus improvement works. Throughout the process, the UGC plays a key role as an intermediate body with responsibility for approving funding on a three-year basis under an agreement with its funded institutions. Since the early 2000s, competition has been gradually introduced into the funding system for public higher education institutions in Hong Kong, with six rounds of Matching Grant Scheme from 2003 to 2014, for example.

Meanwhile, for over a decade, the total amount of grant money for UGC-funded institutions has accounted for appropriately 25 percent of total government expenditure on education. In addition to the block grants deployed for research activities, the UGC provides earmarked research grants through its Research Grants Council on a highly competitive basis. In 2009, an HK$18 billion Research Endowment Fund was established to provide a stable flow of research funding.[42] In addition, the investment income from up to HK$4 billion of the fund will be deployed to support theme-based research, allowing the institutions to work on research proposals on themes of a longer-term nature and strategically beneficial to the development of

40. Qingnan Xie and Richard B. Freeman, "Bigger than You Thought: China's Contribution to Scientific Publications and Its Impact on the Global Economy," *China & World Economy* 27, no. 1 (2019): 1–27.

41. Patrick Boehler, "China Spending More than Europe on Science and Technology as GDP Percentage, New Figures Reveal," *South China Morning Post*, January 21, 2014.

42. The Hong Kong dollar has been pegged to the US dollar since 1983, and trades at a tight band of HK$7.75–$7.85 per US$1. When it veers too close to either end, the city's de-facto central bank—the Hong Kong Monetary Authority—intervenes by selling or buying the currency.

Hong Kong. The fund was topped up by HK$5 billion in 2013–2014. Investment income of HK$2 billion was used to replace the government recurrent subvention, and investment income of HK$3 billion was used to provide comparative research funding for local self-financing higher institutions.

Riding on its competitive edge as an international financial hub, Hong Kong intends to develop an innovation and technology strategy to ensure its sustainable development. According to the World Economic Forum 2015–2016 Global Competitiveness Report, in 2015 Hong Kong ranked a respectable number seven in overall competitiveness but fared significantly lower in the metrics of innovative capacity and availability of scientists and engineers. Hong Kong's total spending on R&D was 0.73 percent of GDP, lower than that of Singapore's 2.1 percent, Korea's 4.2 percent, mainland China's 2.1 percent (including 4 percent for Shenzhen and 6 percent for Beijing), and the OECD average of just over 2 percent.[43] In late 2017, Chief Executive Carrie Lam set out eight major areas in her Policy Address to step up efforts to increase resources for R&D, pool technology talent, provide investment funding, provide technological research infrastructure, review legislation and regulations, open up government data and better procurement arrangements, and popularize science education.

According to the statistics on Hong Kong innovation activities released on December 23, 2020, by the Census and Statistics Department, the gross domestic expenditure on research and development (GERD) of Hong Kong in 2019 amounted to HK$26,333 million, representing an increase of 8 percent when compared to the corresponding figure of 2018 (HK$24,478 million). As a ratio to the GDP in 2019, it was 0.92 percent. Analyzed by performing sector, the expenditure on R&D activities in the business, higher education, and government sectors amounted to HK$11,616 million, HK$13,432 million, and HK$1,284 million respectively in 2019.[44] Seeing innovation and technology as an important growth engine for future economic development, the government has introduced various policies and allocated over HK$100 billion to support a series of measures for its development. The Chief Executive pledged in 2017 to increase the R&D budget during her five-year term from 0.73 percent to 1.5 percent of the GDP by 2022, which equates to an annual investment of about HK$45 billion. The 2020–2021 budget has kept such a promise alive.[45]

In Taiwan, since 2000, around 4 percent of GDP is spent on education, the highest 4.59 percent in 2009 and the lowest 3.09 percent in 2013. Over 30 percent of the total education expenditure is spent on higher education. As the ideology

---

43. Lap-chee Tsui and Rita Lun, *The Ecosystem of Innovation and Technology in Hong Kong* (Hong Kong: Our Hong Kong Foundation, 2015), 5.

44. Census and Statistics Department, "Statistics on Innovation Activities for 2019," December 23, 2020, https://www.info.gov.hk/gia/general/202012/23/P2020122300233.htm.

45. Paul M. P. Chan, "The 2020–21 Budget," https://www.budget.gov.hk/2020/eng/pdf/e_budget_speech_2020-21.pdf.

of the market was introduced into Taiwan's higher education funding system in the late 2000s, there has been a decrease in educational expenditure on the higher education sector. Higher education institutions can no longer rely entirely on government funding. They have to actively seek other financial avenues. Public institutions receive more funds from the government, while the private ones depend much more on tuition and fees. In 2012, for example, 37.1 percent of the revenues of public institutions was from the government, 18.8 percent from tuition and fees, 1.5 percent from continuing education programs (designed to help individuals to explore their interests and professional development skills), 30.7 percent from joint activities between higher education institutions and public and/or private organizations, 11.9 percent from other suppliers such as university bookstores and other on-campus revenue-generating ventures, and 0.9 percent from other funding sources.[46]

In 2018, Taiwan's gross domestic expenditure on R&D was 3.36 percent of its total GDP, reaching US$20.55 billion. It was the third highest in the world, following Israel (4.9 percent) and South Korea (4.53 percent), and surpassing Japan (3.26 percent), the United States (2.83 percent), and the Chinese mainland (2.19 percent). Corporate spending is the main driving force behind Taiwan's gross domestic expenditure on R&D, making up 80.3 percent of total expenditure, which is similar to that of South Korea and above Japan (79.4 percent), the Chinese mainland (77.4 percent), and the United States (72.6 percent). Its spending on R&D is concentrated on technical development, which increased 8.2 percent from 2017, to make up 69.7 percent of total expenditure in 2018. Meanwhile, due to budget cuts in government spending and higher education, Taiwan's spending on basic research declined by 3.6 percentage points over the same period, making up only 7.3 percent of total expenditure. However, spending on applied research increased 8 percentage points from 2017 to 2018, contributing 23 percent of the total expenditure.[47]

In Singapore, the state has been generously funding its higher education institutions. Since the 2000s, however, decentralization and corporatization began to be introduced into the higher education sector. Higher tuition fees and lower public subsidy have pressured the institutions to become more efficient in resource allocation. The University Governance and Funding Review in 2000 recommended that greater autonomy be given to major universities to ensure that they remain competitive and relevant in the long run. The universities have been given greater operational autonomy with regard to staff remuneration, and the university councils have more autonomy in setting strategic directions. They have gained certain flexibility, including start-up research grants and reduced teaching load for top researchers. Yet, all senior management teams in Singaporean universities follow the government's rules and regulations, and only slow transformation is experienced.

---

46. W. James Jacob, Ka Ho Mok, Sheng Yao Cheng and Weiyan Xiong, "Changes in Chinese Higher Education: Financial Trends in China, Hong Kong and Taiwan," *International Journal of educational Development* 58, no. C (2018): 64–85.
47. Natasha Li, "Taiwan R&D Expenditure Ranked Third," *Taipei Times*, May 30, 2020, 12.

Singapore's average expenditure on tertiary education has been at 1.1 percent of its GDP. While this appears to be lower than that of OCED countries, it spends 7.1 percent of its total public expenditure compared with the average of 3.1 percent of OECD member states.[48]

The city-state has always identified higher education as a major prong for it to remain economically competitive in what is perceived as the "knowledge economy" of the twenty-first century. In recognition of the importance of R&D, the government has pledged that its R&D budget will not be reduced to guarantee that Singapore would be able to "compete in the next century as a creative nation with additional sets of skills and capabilities."[49] The recurrent government expenditure per student in a publicly funded full-time degree course increased to 53 percent from 2002/2003 to 2016/2017.[50] In the financial year 2019, it was approximately S$22,000.[51] As higher education has been heavily emphasized as a means of supporting national economic development, a good 20 percent of the national budget is spent on education.[52] Singapore is known as a regional powerhouse for technology, and the supportive government combines business-friendly policies with heavy investment in the technology sector. It has a continuous commitment to keep R&D spending at 1 percent of GDP and recently pledged to invest S$19 billion (almost US$14 billion) in scientific and technological research as part of its Research Innovation and Enterprise (RIE 2020) plan.[53]

In December 2020, Singapore announced its investment of S$25 billion (about US$18.75 billion) or 1 percent of its GDP in R&D for the next five years. The Research, Innovation and Enterprise 2025 Plan (RIE2025) is the country's third five-year plan.[54] The largest part of it, nearly 30 percent, will be used to boost the basic scientific research capability of universities and first-class research institutes. While a quarter of the funds will be used to expand the scientific research sector, 20 percent of the funds will be allocated to establish new entrepreneurial platforms. Nearly 10 percent of the funds will be used for training talent. An additional 15 percent of the budget is earmarked for future use, when new opportunities arise. The Singaporean government is determined to invest in scientific research, as seen

48. See Ministry of Education, *Report of the Committee on University Education Pathways Beyond 2015* (Singapore: Ministry of Education, 2012); OECD, *Education at a Glance* (Paris: OECD, 2013).

49. Jason Tan, "Recent Developments in Higher Education in Singapore," *International Higher Education* 14, Winter (1999): 16.

50. Ministry of Education, *Education Statistics Digest 2017*.

51. Data Quality Campaign, "State and Local Governments Can Use Federal Funding for Education Data," https://dataqualitycampaign.org/wp-content/uploads/2021/04/DQC_Fed-Funding-for-Education-Data_April-2021.pdf.

52. UNESCO Institute for Statistics, "Government Ependiture on Education, Total (% of GDP)-Singapore, Data as of September 2020," https://data.worldbank.org/indicator/SE.XPD.TOTL.GD.ZS?locations=SG.

53. National Research Foundation, *Research Innovation and Enterprise Plan* (Singapore: Research, Innovation and Enterprise Secretariat, 2016).

54. National Research Foundation, *RIE 2025 Plan* (Singapore: Government of Singapore, 2020).

from its gradual increase in the R&D budget over the years, from S$16 billion (about US$12 billion) at the launch of RIE2015 in 2011, to S$19 billion (US$14.25 billion) for RIE2020 in 2016, and S$25 billion (US$18.75 billion) in 2021.[55]

Research and Innovation

Knowledge is increasingly important for social and economic development.[56] A country with a knowledge-based economy is one where the production, diffusion, and use of technology and information are keys to economic activity and sustainable growth.[57] Knowledge and universities are changing their roles in society and have close interactions between knowledge, universities and economic growth. Seen as key drivers of innovation and major agents of economic growth, universities are the source of strength in the knowledge-based economy of the twenty-first century. They are powerful institutions for commercializing knowledge and key drivers of regional innovation systems. As Marginson wrote over a decade ago,[58] one feature of the global knowledge system is the position of the US, which has 54 of the top 100 research universities in the 2007 Shanghai Jiao Tong listing, and almost one-third of the world's scientific papers. The US is a magnet for worldwide talent, enrolling 100,000 foreign doctoral students each year. Yet, a new wave of Asian science powers is emerging in mainland China, Hong Kong, Taiwan, Singapore, and Korea. Such shifts of magnitude suggest a more pluralistic scientific and cultural environment in world higher education.

Indeed, all four Chinese societies Marginson mentions have since made even more remarkable strides in technological progress. It is especially the case with the Chinese mainland. Over the past decades, it has experienced four stages of development: "Learning-Introducing-Supplying Stage," "Introducing-Imitating-Improving Stage," "Integrating-Boosting-Creating Stage," and "Innovating-Iterating-Promoting Stage."[59] In 2019 mainland China spent about US$324 billion on R&D, nearly double the amount it spent in 2015. The heavy investment is paying off in serious technological advances, and mainland Chinese scientists stand at least as good a chance of making a global impact on science from within their own land. The Chinese mainland leads the world in patent applications at 40 percent of the

55. Winnie Tang, "Singapore Is Committed to R&D Investment—What about Hong Kong?" *Harbor Times*, January 9, 2021.
56. A knowledge-based economy focuses on production and management of knowledge. See Philip Cooke and Loet Leydesdorff, "Regional Development in the Knowledge-Based Economy: The Construction of Advantage," *The Journal of Technology Transfer* 31, no 1 (2006): 5–15.
57. OECD, *The Knowledge-Based Economy: A Set of Facts and Figures* (Paris: OECD, 1999).
58. Simon Marginson, "Higher Education in the Global Knowledge Economy," *Procedia Social and Behavioral Sciences* 2, no. 5 (2010): 6962–6980.
59. Jiasu Lei, Ying Liu, Yaoyuan Qi and Qingzhi Zhang, "40 Years of Technological Innovation in China: A Review of the Four-Stage Climbing Track," *Journal of Industrial Integration and Management* 4, no. 3 (2019): 1–22.

global total, a share more than two times larger than that of the US and four times larger than that of Japan. The number of scientific publications by its researchers in 2016 outnumbered those from the US for the first time: 426,000 versus 409,000. In some scientific fields, mainland China has started to set the pace for others to follow.[60]

Setting its goal to become a global technological leader, mainland China has built the largest science system in the world.[61] The National Natural Science Foundation of China, in its development plan for the 13th Five-Year Plan Period (2016–2020), identified 118 independent disciplines and 16 interdisciplinary areas as priorities. In July 2019, the China Association for Science and Technology released twenty frontier scientific issues and engineering problems, which will play a guiding role in China's future science and innovation development, with particular emphasis on their industrial applications. Faced by the intensified strategic race, it will be of great interest and importance to understand mainland China's new strategic thinking and actions, for instance, in its forthcoming 14th Five-Year Plan (2021–2025) and in its second Medium- and Long-Term Science and Technology Plan (2021–2035). The new thinking and new strategic moves will make it an even more important player in the global research and innovation landscape. In March 2021, mainland China for the first time unveiled an ambitious road map for plans to transform into a world-leading power by 2035, with strategy outlines of how to become a leading global innovation engine.[62]

The development of innovation and technology in Hong Kong can be traced to the 1990s. Tung Chee Hwa, the first Chief Executive of Hong Kong, called for making Hong Kong an innovation center in his 1997 Policy Address. The Innovation and Technology Committee was then established, and the Innovation and Technology Fund was set up; some projects were built afterwards to improve the infrastructure of innovation and technology. In 2000, the Innovation and Technology Commission was established to formulate policies and measures on innovation and technology. Later, five R&D centers were set up. However, developing innovation and technology in Hong Kong achieved little until 2015, when the government prioritized innovation and technology and established the Innovation and Technology Bureau and the Academy of Sciences of Hong Kong. The former is responsible for formulating comprehensive policies to guide the Innovation and

60. Philip Ball, "China's Great Leap Forward in Science," *The Guardian*, February 18, 2018, https://www.theguardian.com/science/2018/feb/18/china-great-leap-forward-science-research-innovation-investment-5g-genetics-quantum-internet.

61. According to Simon Marginson, the great flowering of scientific investigation on the Chinese mainland has exploded the belief still widely held in the Euro-American zone that Judeo-Christian civilization or Western political democracy is essential to the highest level of intellectual achievements. See Simon Marginson, "National Modernization and Global Science in China," *International Journal of Educational Development* 84, no. 12 (2021): 11.

62. Jun Mai, "Technology Key to China's Vision for the Future as a World Leading Power," *South China Morning Post*, March 6, 2021.

Technology Commission. The latter aims at bringing together the scientific research power of Hong Kong's universities, concentrating on the public education of science and technology, scientific research, science popularization, and cooperation with industrial and commercial institutions.[63]

While tiny in size, Hong Kong has a few research universities with a high international reputation. Its research is competitive in the development of the innovation and technology ecosystem. According to a report entitled "Building the Technology Bridge for Scientific Breakthroughs launched by Our Hong Kong Foundation" in late 2020,[64] 50.4 percent of Hong Kong's total expenditure in R&D in 2018 went to universities.[65] According to the Web of Science Group's Highly Cited Researchers 2019, while Hong Kong only represents 0.10 percent of the world's population, its universities account for 1.01 percent of the world's highly cited researchers.[66] The sheer excellence of Hong Kong's world-class basic research demonstrates the outsized international impact of the city's basic research. The quality of basic research has continued to rise over the years. Hong Kong's universities play a dominant and outsized role in the city's innovation ecosystem. Indeed, they are potentially a game-changer for the entire ecosystem. This is an edge for the society to capitalize on, to drive its local innovation ecosystem forward. Recently, the government has devoted significant effort to boosting the development of S&T innovation.

Taiwan's science and technology, innovation, and universities have been underestimated internationally. According to Scimago Journal & Country Rank, Taiwan came nineteenth in total output of international publications during 1996–2019 out of 240 countries and regions.[67] S&T is becoming a key driver of growth and progress for Taiwan. Its higher education and premier fundamental research institutions have expressed aspirations for globally recognized research excellence, high social responsibilities in crucial areas, and for attracting and cultivating talents. Universities have established strong links with industry. Having well-recognized strengths in science and engineering, they are determined to foster innovative research and education. Covering 2017 to 2020, the plan for S&T development issued in September 2017 is jointly implemented by seventeen ministries, departments and agencies, Academia Sinica, the Board of Science & Technology, the Department of Cyber Security, the National Development Fund, and local government. It aims to revive economic dynamics through innovation, develop smart living technologies and industries,

63. Jie Su, "Seizing Opportunities, Hong Kong's Innovation and Technology Has a Bright Future," *Economic Review* (Bank of China) 11 (2017): 1–5.
64. Our Hong Kong Foundation, *Building the Technology Bridge for Scientific Breakthroughs: Developing an Innovation Hub of the Future* (Hong Kong: Our Hong Kong Foundation, 2020).
65. This compares to just 23.6 percent in the United Kingdom, 17.8 percent in Singapore, 12.9 percent in the United States, and 7.4 percent in mainland China. See Our Hong Kong Foundation, *Building the Technology Bridge for Scientific Breakthroughs*, 2.
66. Web of Science Group, *Highly Cited Researchers 2019* (London: Clarivate Analytics, 2019).
67. Scimago Journal & Country Rank 1996–2019, httpswww.scimagojr.comcountryrank.php.

cultivate and recruit talents with diverse career paths, and enhance an innovation ecosystem for scientific research.[68]

As a catalyst for promoting the development of S&T, the Ministry of Science & Technology is Taiwan's agency for driving scientific and technological innovation. Aiming to integrate academic research with industrial development, its designated goals are to promote society-wide scientific and technological development, support academic research and developing science parks, promote partnerships between academia and industry, and encourage innovation, while also reinforcing the impetus for businesses to invest in R&D, fostering creativity, nurturing start-ups, and supporting industrial development. To promote academic research, it has implemented a number of core facility and major instrument projects to provide first-class equipment and promote resource sharing that helps researchers achieve the maximum benefit from their work. Meanwhile, the National Applied Research Laboratories aims to further scientific research by integrating and coordinating Taiwan's key laboratories in order to translate R&D results into innovative products. Through the Academia-Industry Technological Alliance, research organizations are encouraged to establish service platforms centered on core technologies.

Since the 1990s, Singapore has developed a system of higher education that is the envy of many countries and regions. The story of how it became a research nation is truly stunning. As expressed by Bertil Andersson, its highly instrumental investment in a knowledge society has been impressively strategic for the small country. Even before the year 2000, research was still not well developed in Singapore. However, today National University of Singapore and Nanyang Technological University are widely regarded as top universities in the world. Based on actual rich experience,[69] higher education in Singapore has been developing tremendously, particularly in quality, and researchers, in volume but also in quality, although some of the achievements are not explicitly reflected in the rankings. Singapore's research now enjoys a strong global reputation. With a concept of a "smart nation," Singapore has a clear awareness that its research must further enhance that smart nation. As a society of only five million people, its research is well coordinated and always well resourced.

Universities in Singapore now carry out cutting-edge research, while actively exploring commercial application at the same time. Thanks to decades of extraordinary and comprehensive social and economic development, the higher education system and institutions in Singapore have arrived at a post catch-up

---

68. Ministry of Science and Technology, Republic of China (Taiwan), *National Science and Technology Development Plan* (Taipei: Ministry of Science and Technology, 2017).

69. Bertil Andersson served as the third president of Nanyang Technological University from July 2011 to December 2017, after being chief executive of the European Science Foundation. During his time as president, he led the university to global distinction. He expressed his views in an interview with *University World News* in late 2017. See Yojana Sharma, "The Story of How Singapore Became a Research Nation," *University World News*, December 15, 2017.

stage.[70] Some unique characteristics between the higher education system and institutions and the government have been formed. The development of the scientific capacity of higher education institutions is strongly supported by the government with coordination from the industry. The past few decades have witnessed great mutual support among these stakeholders to encourage the economic contribution of academia to local economies. In the process, the government has been a critical resource provider influencing the knowledge-transfer activities of universities. Singapore is often cited as a classic example of successful building of scientific capacity, such as how it has strategically addressed the issue of "brain drain" by investing significant sums of money to create world-class scientific institutions and providing salaries and infrastructure to entice expatriates to develop their careers in Singapore.[71]

Teaching and Learning

The university is a learning and teaching community. Indeed, universities shape new people mainly in and through teaching.[72] As a prime part of the totality of modern universities, practices of teaching and learning in the four Chinese societies are required to be informed by Western concepts and principles. Although this means that they need to learn both what and how to teach and learn from the West, they have all achieved a high level of sophistication in their university teaching and learning with wide international reputation. Since all of them have experienced a shift from elite to mass higher education, there have been many corresponding changes in their teaching and learning such as student population and access. Moreover, flagship higher education institutions in these societies have similarly aimed at world-class status, an aspiration that has significant implications for teaching and learning in the universities, including content and approaches as well as orientation.

In the Chinese mainland, disciplines at undergraduate and postgraduate levels are categorized differently by different organizations. Disciplinary categorization at bachelor's and postgraduate levels is the responsibilities of the Ministry of Education and the Academic Degrees Committee, under the State Council and the Ministry of Education respectively. Disciplines in postgraduate programs are divided into thirteen categories (philosophy, economics, law, education, literature, history, science, engineering, agriculture, medicine, military science, management,

---

70. As latecomers to modernization, catch-up societies differ much in policy, practice and mindset. For an example and a brief explanation, see Jae-Yong Choung, "Editorial Paper: Transition: From Catchup to Post Catch-up," *Asian Journal of Technology Innovation* 24, no. 1 (2016): 1–7.
71. See, for example, Third World Academy of Sciences, *Building Scientific Capacity: A TWAS Perspective* (Trieste, Italy: Third World Academy of Sciences, 2004), 36.
72. Geoffrey Boulton and Colin Lucas, "What Are Universities For?" *Chinese Science Bulletin* 56, no 23 (2011): 2506–2517.

and fine arts) with 110 and 386 at first- and second-level respectively. There are twelve disciplinary categories in bachelor's programs at regular higher education institutions, which include 92 specialized fields and 506 specialties.[73] As reform deepens, closer links are built between society and university academic programs. While categorization remains in the hands of state educational authorities, setting up academic programs has been gradually transferred to institutions as they are granted increasing autonomy over their curriculum and teaching as part of the reform.[74]

All higher institutions offering bachelor's programs are required to be evaluated regularly. The Higher Education Evaluation Center was established in 2004 as the administrative body under the auspices of the Ministry of Education to organize and implement the evaluation, based on the guidelines, regulations, and evaluation criteria set by the ministry. A five-year cycle of evaluating institutions of higher education has been established in a systematic and standardized manner.[75] It maintains a database to collect the basic institutional information concerning infrastructure and other basic facilities and makes such information available to the public to strengthen public awareness of the effectiveness of higher education institutions. Program evaluation is conducted in collaboration with higher institutions and professional agencies to combine internal and external efforts to encourage institutions to set up their internal quality assurance mechanisms. Within institutions, quality assurance has been much less systematic, depending greatly on institutional situations. Yet, teaching and research evaluation is conducted vigorously by regular higher education institutions as part of their academic performance assessment.

During the pre-reform era, the university curriculum was set up by the state in a highly planned system designed to fulfill the needs of socialist construction. Higher education institutions were to follow orders from above rather than to design their own courses. Recent years have seen growing diversity, individualization, and comprehensiveness in university curriculum. Since the 1990s, seeing curriculum reform as the main human capital development strategy for coping with the challenges of the twenty-first century, the government has played a key role in the reform of curriculum-making mechanisms and in the social distribution of knowledge, skills, and dispositions through curriculum making.[76] It has implemented a few major curriculum reforms in humanities education, general education, and quality education,

---

73. Ministry of Education of the People's Republic of China, *Putong gaodengxiexiao benke zhuanye mulu* (2012) 普通高等學校本科專業目錄 (2012) [Catalogue of undergraduate majors in regular colleges and universities (2012)], September 14, 2012, http://www.moe.gov.cn/srcsite/A08/moe_1034/s3882/201209/t20120918_143152.html.

74. Mei Li and Rui Yang, *Governance Reforms in Higher Education: A Study of China* (Paris: International Institute for Educational Planning, UNESCO, 2014).

75. Kai Jiang, "Undergraduate Teaching Evaluation in China: Progress and Debate," *International Higher Education* 58, Winter (2010): 15–17.

76. Wing-Wah Law, "Understanding China's Curriculum Reform for the 21st Century," *Journal of Curriculum Studies* 46, no. 3 (2014): 332–360.

to advocate humanity, attach importance to basics, and pursue individual all-round development respectively. The reforms have been dominated by academic elitism and confined largely to most prestigious institutions. In a context of a prevailing pragmatic orientation, voices calling for a deep humanistic understanding of the idea of a university in curriculum reforms are still much lacking yet growing.

The policies on the Chinese mainland require wide use of information communication technology (ICT) at all educational institutions. Educational technology has become a well-developed research area paving the way for even further use of modern technologies in higher education institutions. The Mainland once enjoyed an international reputation in its open and distance educational programs at tertiary level. Currently, major mainland universities actively explore and utilize ICT in higher education, including Massive Open Online Courses (MOOCs).[77] The building up of necessary skills and infrastructure played a critical role in battling the COVID-19 pandemic, during which universities shut their campuses and shifted to teaching online. The use of online education in universities has since been significantly expanded, fast becoming the main mode of instruction implemented on a massive scale. Even those without much previous e-learning experience have started teaching online. The pandemic has become an impetus for mainland universities to evaluate their technical preparedness for new changes, prompting them to reflect on how they can tap into disruptive technologies such as mixed reality, data science, and artificial intelligence to better serve the needs of education and address latent disruptors.[78]

As one of the world's most competitive cities, Hong Kong is home to some of Asia Pacific's very best universities in teaching and research achievements.[79] The eight UGC-funded universities offer a wide array of high-quality programs up to doctorate degrees. In addition, there are over twenty post-secondary institutions offering a variety of locally accredited sub-degree programs. Tertiary teaching and learning in Hong Kong enjoys a global reputation, from the renowned executive business management to increasingly popular blended/experiential learning programs. The academic structure of universities in Hong Kong followed the British pattern until 2012, when undergraduate programs changed from three to four years. The new system is more aligned with many others in the world and allows more opportunities for student exchanges with most peer higher education institutions around the globe. With an additional year and in line with the times, higher education institutions in Hong Kong have revamped their curriculum with a view to nurturing global citizens with academic excellence and international outlook

77. Fengliang Li, "The Expansion of Higher Education and the Returns of Distance Education in China," *International Review of Research in Open and Distributed Learning* 19, no. 4 (2018): 242–255.
78. Rui Yang, "China's Higher Education during the COVID-19 Pandemic: Some Preliminary Observations," *Higher Education Research & Development* 39, no. 7 (2020): 1317–1321.
79. For example, this has been demonstrated consistently by the Quacquarelli Symonds (QS) World University Rankings and the Times Higher Education World University Rankings over recent years.

through interdisciplinary studies, service learning in local and global settings, exchange programs, and enriched learning experiences.

Beginning in 1995, the UGC embarked on a program of Teaching and Learning Quality Process Reviews (TLQPRs) to undertake an assessment of teaching and learning quality for publicly funded universities. Representing a type of "academic audit" first developed in the United Kingdom,[80] the TLQPRs intended to assist institutions in their efforts to improve teaching and learning quality and to enable the UGC and the institutions to discharge their obligation to maintain accountability for quality. The exercise was carried out during an eighteen-month period from September 1995 to April 1997.[81] Following the completion of the reviews, the UGC commissioned an independent evaluation of the exercise that was carried out by the Centre for Higher Education Policy Studies of the University of Twente in the Netherlands to determine the extent to which the TLQPR process had achieved its stated goals and to recommend any improvements on the process. The evaluation report published in September 1999 concluded that the TLQPRs had been successful in achieving the intended goals. A further round of TLQPR, continuing to focus on quality processes, was also recommended. The second round of TLQPRs commenced in October 2001. The third and fourth rounds of quality review were launched respectively in 2007 and 2013.

In the face of *sudden* and *unexpected* situations such as the COVID-19 pandemic, Hong Kong universities have demonstrated their infrastructural strength. Since the outbreak of the pandemic, online teaching has been widely adopted and has become the prevalent mode of teaching and learning as the universities suspended face-to-face classes. The government has recently approved an additional funding of HK$165 million to the eight public universities to promote the strategic development of virtual teaching and learning in the coming three years.[82] With this funding the universities will develop the governance framework under virtual teaching and learning, organize staff development, or explore new strategies, pedagogies, platforms, and facilities for virtual teaching and learning. The expectation is that after the pandemic they will continue to make use of virtual teaching and learning to enhance the overall effectiveness and experience of teaching and learning. The funding will facilitate more systemic collaborations among them to promote the strategic development of virtual teaching and learning and related teaching and learning strategies, quality assurance, research on teaching methods, and teaching

---

80. Philip Meade and David Woodhouse, "Evaluating the Effectiveness of the New Zealand Academic Audit Unit: Review and Outcomes," *Quality in Higher Education* 6, no. 1 (2000): 19–29.

81. William F. Massy and Nigel J. French, "Teaching and Learning Quality Process Review: What the Program Has Achieved in Hong Kong," *Quality in Higher Education* 7, no. 1 (2001): 33–45.

82. "HK Universities Get HK$165m to Develop Virtual Teaching and Learning," *The Standard*, January 21, 2021, https://www.thestandard.com.hk/breaking-news/section/4/163882/HK-universities-get-HK$165m-to-develop-virtual-teaching-and-learning.

staff development. It will help the universities to improve the quality of teaching and respond to the challenges posed by the new normal.

The past three decades or so have seen the rapid expansion of higher education in Taiwan, in which reforms in teacher training have played an important part. The system is patterned after American practices, to allow students to choose disciplines they are interested in and want to study. A large number of academic staff members in Taiwan's higher institutions are graduates from American universities. They claim to introduce the most effective training methods on a regular basis to prepare highly qualified specialists. Teacher quality has been significantly improved in recent years. Currently, doctoral degree holders account for over 80 percent of academic staff members in Taiwan's universities. The figure has increased by 15 percent in the past ten years. Full professors account for one-third of all teaching personnel. To maintain competitiveness, the Taiwanese government invests over US$8 billion in higher education regularly to encourage higher education institutions to enhance their standards for research and teaching. Teaching and learning in Taiwan's higher education institutions aim at innovation in academic research and the cultivation of intellectual ability. They offer a wide range of programs from bachelor's to doctoral levels.

In May 2005, the Ministry of Education and several universities jointly established the Higher Education Evaluation and Accreditation Council of Taiwan to regularly evaluate universities. One major task of its evaluation is program accreditation, a five-year cycle of evaluation of all departments and faculties of higher education institutions, to assess the quality of teaching and courses, as well as student learning outcomes.[83] At the institutional level, higher education institutions are required by the University Act to develop their own curriculum and conduct regular teaching evaluation at the end of each semester.[84] Most institutions establish a specific center for the enhancement of teaching and learning to assure teaching quality and resources. In 2017, the Ministry of Education launched the Program for Promoting Teaching Excellence of Universities on a competitive basis, to promote teaching excellence in Taiwan.[85] The government also strongly promotes more widespread use of ICT in tertiary teaching and learning, including MOOCs.[86]

---

83. Ruyu Hung, "Eastern Asian Higher Education at the Crossroads: A Reflection of the Accreditation/ Evaluation System of Universities in Taiwan," *National Chiayi University Journal of the Educational Research* 嘉大教育研究學刊 34, no 3 (2015): 1–24.

84. Ministry of Education, *University Act* (amended on December 11, 2019), https://law.moj.gov.tw/ENG/ LawClass/LawAll.aspx?pcode=H0030001.

85. Cheng-Cheng Yang and Yueh-Chun Huang, "Promoting Teaching Excellence of Universities in Taiwan: Policy Analysis with a Special Reference to Educational Equality," *International Education Studies* 5, no. 5 (2012): 129–140.

86. Ming-Yuan Hsieh, "Online Learning Era: Exploring the Most Decisive Determinants of MOOCs in Taiwanese Higher Education," *Eurasia Journal of Mathematics, Science & Technology Education* 12, no 5 (2016): 1163–1188.

Nearly 70 percent of Taiwan's eighteen to twenty-two cohort receive tertiary education, and the acceptance rate has been over 90 percent since 2006. Taiwan's higher education now prioritizes students' learning effectiveness, efficiency, and employability. In the White Paper on Human Resource Development released in 2014 by the Ministry of Education, Taiwan is to reorient its education toward positive social values by 2023, to enhance quality of education and learning. Government policy targets are to prepare more dedicated and efficient professional teaching personnel, integrate schooling and the job market, and strengthen students' international competiveness and future productivity. Six key competencies are identified by the education authority to enhance the capacity of the next generation: global mobility, employability, creativity, interdisciplinary ability, information competence, and citizenship. In 2003, the government began the quest for world-class universities, in order to create a higher education system of excellence. Recently the Ministry of Education has also been promoting Taiwan as an ideal study destination for overseas students, deepening international exchange, and enhancing the global competitiveness of higher education institutions.[87]

Singapore's education system is the product of a distinctive set of historical, institutional, and cultural influences. Over time, Singapore has developed an education system that is not only centralized, integrated, and coherent but also well-funded and expert-led. Its unique configuration of historical experience, instruction, institutional arrangements, and cultural beliefs has produced an exceptionally effective and successful system. Singapore is now widely seen as a premier regional hub for higher education, attracting students from the world over. Although tiny in size, Singapore's two flagship universities, National University of Singapore and Nanyang Technological University, are highly regarded globally.[88] A number of foreign universities have campuses in Singapore. These higher education institutions offer specialized courses across all disciplines. University education in Singapore aspires to prepare students not only for today's world but also for a world where there will be jobs that have yet to be invented and challenges not yet foreseen. Teaching is coherent, fit-for-purpose and pragmatic, drawing on a range of pedagogical traditions, both Eastern and Western.

In 2005, Singapore's government launched the "Teach Less, Learn More" initiative to improve the quality of teaching and enhance student learning in Singapore

---

87. Chuing Prudence Chou, "Education in Taiwan: Taiwan's Colleges and Universities," November 12, 2014, https://www.brookings.edu/opinions/education-in-taiwan-taiwans-colleges-and-universities/.
88. According to the latest report by Universitas 21, Singapore has emerged as the top fourth country worldwide and first in Asia for its provision of quality higher education. The survey, which measures fifty countries based on four indicators—resources, environment, connectivity, and output—aims to provide insights into areas for improving living standards and how quality higher education systems contribute to new ideas, bilateral trade relations and business activity. See Ross Williams and Anne Leahy, *U21 Ranking of National Higher Education Systems* (Melbourne: Applied Economic & Social Research, University of Melbourne, 2020).

through the use of innovative learning-centered pedagogies in the Singapore education system.[89] This was built on the "Thinking School, Learning Nation" vision, which was introduced in 1997 to create an education system that nurtures creativity, critical thinking, and a passion for lifelong learning.[90] The reforms urged teachers to focus on the "quality" of learning and the use of technology in classrooms, not just the "quantity" of learning and exam preparation. However, the overwhelming emphasis on research in recent years has meant that universities seeking to rise up the ranks of global rankings have tended to devote an extensive number of resources toward boosting research outcomes, leading to a concomitant lack of resources that can be directed toward adult learning. However, rebalancing research and teaching activities is highly necessary for universities to contribute to both the education and training of a credible Singaporean labor force as well as research-driven and industry-centric innovation.[91] Policy makers and academics understand this need although it is a difficult task for them to fulfill in practice.

Evidence from the Fieldwork

As shown, all four Chinese societies have achieved remarkably in higher education development over the last few decades, implementing a highly institutionalized Western-styled modern system. The account demonstrates impressive achievements in all aspects of modern higher education development by the societies, as evidenced particularly in the resources, infrastructure, and personnel housed by their systems. Their progress has been widely acknowledged by observers from the West, both in the literature[92] and in the media.[93] As their higher education institutions are shown to be continuing an impressive steady rise in recent global league tables, all systems have openly expressed gathering confidence and intensifying aspiration to catapult their premier universities to the forefront of global rankings. In order to fully assess their real potential to see whether they can truly break the Western hegemony, it is highly necessary to understand how higher education reform and development is perceived and experienced by frontiers academics, policy makers, and practitioners

---

89. Kala S. Retna and Pak Tee Ng, "Singapore Principals' Understanding and Perceptions of the Challenges of 'Teach Less, Less More' Policy," *International Journal of Educational Reform* 25, no. 4 (2016): 426–442.

90. Vanithamani Saravanan, "'Thinking Schools, Learning Nations' Implementation of Curriculum Review in Singapore," *Educational Research for Policy and Practice* 4, no. 4–5 (2005): 97–113.

91. Woo Jun Jie, "Commentary: Singapore and Singaporeans Lose When Universities Chase after World Rankings," *CNA/sl*, September 30, 2018, https://www.channelnewsasia.com/news/commentary/nus-ntu-university-rankings-times-higher-education-singapore-10766750.

92. On this theme, Simon Marginson's "Higher Education in East Asia and Singapore" is a typical example in recent years.

93. See, for example, John Morgan, "Sun Sets on Western Dominance as East Asian Confucian Model Takes Lead," *Times Higher Education*, February 24, 2011.

within the systems. The empirical data from my research fieldwork confirm both confidence and their aspiring ambitions.[94] Although these universities are latecomers in modern higher education development, the resemblance displayed by the systems to their counterparts in the West reveals systemic maturity and consequential confidence and reflections. Such similarity demonstrates the institutional sophistication of modern higher education development in the four societies, which are building a solid foundation for future development on both local and global scales. It is manifested in every aspect of university operation, including teaching, research, and administration, both in form and content.[95] This was clearly explained by some Hong Kong–based participants with rich personal experience in different higher education systems, as the following observations reveal:

> There are going to be commonalities. If you come to HKU from the UK, they're not that unfamiliar. I knew the University of Manchester very well. This institution is not that much different from Manchester. (HKU Interview 6, University Administrator)

> In general, the structure of the University here is quite similar to the universities I worked for in the UK. The terminologies used to describe some of the committees and posts are quite familiar. (HKU Interview 10, University Administrator)

> Here we have realistic goals to join the group of the world's top universities. We are bringing in people from different places of the world, introducing practices from other universities. Internally, our administration looks a lot more like the American universities whereas HKU is more like the UK universities. For a city of 8 million people, HK is doing extremely well and has many great universities (especially HKU, HKUST, and CUHK). Similarly, the county of Los Angeles has 8 million people, and they have 3 outstanding universities as well (Caltech, USC, and UCLA). In the past there's a fixation of imitating the UK's way and there was sort of an inferiority complex; I heard about this maybe 10 or 15 years ago. But I don't think that's true anymore. Hong Kong is doing extremely well. . . . The reason that NUS and top universities in Hong Kong are doing so well is because the personnel procedures, the promotion procedures, and their governments are modeling the international standards. . . . For HKUST, strengths are the commitment to the international standards in how the university is run, recruitment, etc. (HKUST Interview 1, Former Faculty Dean)

94. Portions of this section were originally published in Rui Yang, "The Cultural Mission of China's Elite Universities: Examples from Peking and Tsinghua," *Studies in Higher Education* 42, no. 10 (2017): 1825–1838. Some of the participants understandably also talked about challenges and even crisis, which will be addressed more focally in Chapter 5.
95. More broadly, this has resulted from and in line with the global expansion of Western culture. Education systems in vast non-Western societies are patterned after Western practices. See, for example, UNESCO, *World Education Report 1998* (Paris: UNESCO Publishing, 1998); and Elena L. Grigorenko, "Hitting, Missing, and in Between: A Typology of the Impact of Western Education on the Non-Western World," *Comparative Education* 43, no. 1 (2007): 165–186.

An institutional leader based at National University of Singapore elaborated such similarity elegantly, with his delicate dignity, diplomacy, and typical Chinese modesty:

Singapore is a very small system and it doesn't have the critical mass. But Singapore can always position itself as a model, to Asian countries or to Western countries. If you look at higher education, what we are developing here in Singapore? We learnt from the best experiences, from Europe, from Asia, from the US. And we don't copy. But we take the best essence and we involve our own. Take an example of our academic system. We were formerly a British colony, and we followed the UK system. In 1994, NUS switched to a US system, a modular system. If you think about it, in the past, the UK system focuses a lot on depth; the US system focuses a lot on breadth. NUS is a hybrid. We focus on depth; we are deeper than US; but we are broader than UK. That's when we implemented the US system in 1994, twenty years ago. That's an example that we evolve by looking at the best experiences. And we are quite happy that this seems to work, seems to be recognized by the ranking agencies and by academics. . . . I will not be too presumptuous to say that Singapore can overtake this or that; neither will I be too presumptuous that East Asian or the Asian system would be far superior. My sense is that there has been a lot of focus on Western organizations, universities. In the next fifty years, I think the Asian universities would share similar focus, similar attention. And Singapore, in this small way, we hope to present a model that hopefully can shed some light, maybe some things we do very well, could be an inspiration for others to study. (NUS Interview 6, University Administrator)

However, current evaluations, both global ranking systems and those expressed by the interviewees, concentrated on basic institutional infrastructure and academic achievements as the necessary first step toward world-class status, especially stressed by mainland Chinese interviewees, as shown by the following remarks:

You have seen our new buildings including the library, many of them. They were all built recently. This is a necessary part of our world-class movement. (BJ Interview 3, Faculty Dean)

Our innovation has been accelerating because we've got the money and the people (needed), plus the culture we have, we'll certainly develop further. (BJ Interview 2, Mid-Level University Administrator)

For those based at technology-oriented universities, the impact is even more evident, as their work is usually lab-based (QH Interviews 2, Professor; QH Interview 5, Mid-Level University Administrator; QH Interview 8, Faculty Dean). In contrast, there was a general lack of sufficient thought about the longstanding development of their institutions and even less about culture and modernization of their societies and related developments in politics, economy, culture, and ideologies, as shown by the following remarks:

In terms of hardware including research facilities, quality and output, the gap (between Tsinghua and the world's best universities) is becoming very thin. In terms of real matters, such as Chinese characteristics and Tsinghua style, we've got lots to think and do. (QH Interview 3, Faculty Dean)

The similarity has also been frequently reflected on and even interrogated during the fieldwork. For example, a participant with a social science background made the following remarks, citing the Research Assessment Exercise in Hong Kong as an example:

The so-called "international benchmark" is really regional, not "international" at all. There are many reasons for this, such as cultural hegemony. Different academic traditions have their own standards of excellence and don't always translate well in other systems. If someone is good in the French system, it doesn't necessarily mean they will be the same in the British system, and vice versa. There're different intellectual styles and traditions. . . . The current intellectual logic of our institution is aligning itself to the British system. We're always submitting ourselves to the judgment of the British people, according to their standards. (HKU Interview 2, Department Head)

Much more questioning was heard from the participants about the lack/loss of identity in the chase of world-class status which leads to increasing homogeneity,[96] as shown by the following comments:

This is a world-class university but almost by accident. It hasn't thought of why it wanted to be one and that is not enough. It should have a sense of identity and direction in its development and be self-fulfilling. (HKU Interview 3, University Administrator)

In Taiwan, a respondent who is a renowned scientist and a faculty dean at National Tsing Hua University in Hsinchu expressed his strong opinion about the shortage of essential values:

Our higher education system has been colonized for too long by the West. We need to find a balance (between Chinese and Western traditions). This is what we need, also what we want. It can't continue this way! (THU Interview 2)

One classic difference between universities in Chinese and Western societies is in their relations with the state. This is also the strongest criticism Chinese sicieties have received so far of their higher education development. In this aspect, another manifestation of the similarity deserves our attention. As argued throughout this

---

96. The global state of affairs places universities at the heart of national and global strategies. Due to the growing complexity, dynamism, and global nature of our current context, it is "no longer possible for an institution or organization (whether a government, university, company or any other) to act with full autonomy and resolve questions that are in themselves complex and interdependent. See, Global University Network for Innovation (GUNi), *Towards a Socially Responsible University: Balancing the Global with the Local* (Girona: GUNi, 2017), 411.

volume, modern universities are uniquely European in origin and characteristics. They are foreign transplants to Chinese societies. Despite repeated attempts to indigenize the Western idea of a university, traditional Chinese emphasis on political pragmatism[97] and the classical persistence in ontological significance of knowledge from the West have not been blended well for nearly two centuries. The strikingly different value orientations, featured respectively by "working with (or even for) government" and "speaking truth to power" according to governance mode, have led to constant conflicts in daily operation and decision-making in higher education at all levels.[98]

However, due to long-term diligent learning from the Western model, the hard work of the societies and their universities has begun to bear fruit. Fundamental values underlying the university have started to take root in all four Chinese societies, on various levels, from the individual to the systemic. For instance, one participant from the Chinese mainland's most prominent university, who is himself an academician of the Chinese Academy of Sciences and was once the president of a regional university, said explicitly that "A truly good university must first of all have academic freedom" (QH Interview 6, Former University President). The acceptance of the fundamental value by Chinese societies has indeed been highly institutionalized in their universities, especially in Hong Kong and Taiwan. Even at the highest level of policy making in higher education, the impact of such values is becoming increasingly evident, as suggested by a senior administrator at Peking University:

> It is neither possible nor desirable for us to have academic freedom in its absolute sense. Our colleagues and (university) leaders treasure the idea of academic freedom and indeed try to protect it whenever possible. There is much to do to strike a balance in reality. For example, when He Weifang (a law professor and an activist striving to reform China's judicial system) delivers talks here, people are nervous and would try hard to find ways to deal with possible situations. He was invited to join Zhejiang University. Our university reminded him not to resign until his transfer was confirmed. Yet, he did and even delivered his farewell speech. Then he was rejected by the Zhejiang provincial government. The university had to find ways to help him and thus included him into our aid program, so he could teach at another institution for a period of time before coming back. . . . We have very free class discussions here, and the university has strong traditions. As for institutional autonomy in higher education reforms, we need to do it gradually. The government has become very aware of this and more and more tolerant. After all, we have similar goals. (BJ Interview 2, Mid-Level University Administrator)

The overwhelming majority of participants acknowledged growing autonomy granted by the governments to their institutions in all the societies. The elaboration

---

97. Hall and Ames, "A Pragmatist Understanding of Confucian Democracy."
98. Rui Yang, "Indigenizing the Western Concept of the University: Chinese Experience," *Asia Pacific Education Review* 14, no. 1 (2013): 85–92.

of such encouraging developments by a participant from Peking University, who received his PhD in science from the United States and was a full professor at the time of the interview, is typical of those in all four Chinese societies:

> Culture really plays a critical role, especially so because of our autocratic tradition. Yet, I'm still optimistic because our society is changing in line with external environments toward one that is ruled by law. The society is becoming more and more mature. We shouldn't copy Oxbridge or Harvard mechanically. We'll succeed in our own context. (BJ Interview 5, Mid-Level University Administrator)

One female participant with a human science background at Tsinghua University made the following interesting remarks:

> Academic freedom is a must. Without it, we'll never get there (world-class status). Yet, I don't think it's the best part for us to start with. China's issues require Chinese solutions. (QH Interview 9)

Taking Singapore as an example, international observers have frequently expressed their concerns about academic freedom there.[99] When asked about this issue, a university leader made the following classification in a convincing manner:

> It is doable. I think we do have certain disagreements. That could be some policies that would be disagreed. But there is no problem in our faculty members criticizing the government for their policies. That's not a problem. You can see the differences between the two cultures. The West emphasizes a lot the individual; the East like China and Singapore emphasizes society more. That's why when you asked me about academic freedom, I talked about individual freedom and activity freedom. The activity is for the society. There is nothing actually preventing different countries depending on the cultural background to interpret. Who says the US ones must be the right one? (NUS Interview 6, University Administrator)

It is unsurprising that a number of participants from the societies expressed strong concerns about the corrupt role of traditional culture, especially the difficulties and obstacles it has caused in higher education development. However, it is important to note that even those who emphasized traditional cultural values as a problem and called for seeking truth and freedom (BJ Interview 8, Professor and Center Director) still agreed that much progress had been made. Such progress contributes to narrowing the conventional gap between Western and Chinese ideas of a university. It interrogates much of the mainstream literature that has predicted an impasse of higher education development in Chinese societies. This is especially the case in mainland China, due to a longstanding and misguided perception of the complete lack of academic freedom and institutional autonomy in the society.[100]

---

99. Yojana Sharma, "Minister Sets Limits to Academic Freedom in Yale-NUS Row," *University World News*, October 7, 2019.
100. See, for example, Scholars at Risk, *Obstacles to Excellence: Academic Freedom and China's Quest for World Class Universities* (New York: Scholars at Risk, 2019).

However, the government-university relationship is in a state of change in major Western societies. Universities in the Western tradition are fast becoming technological powerhouses needed by the state, finding themselves at the mercy of the government. The state promises more and more to "manage" creativity and innovation, while the academic pursuit of truth gets itself entangled with the commercial pursuit of prosperity. In Britain, for example, scholars are required to make themselves useful based on guides set up by governments through research councils. Former Prime Minister Tony Blair was reported to famously claim: "I believe it is vital that Britain's intellectual community is full and constructively engaged in the Government's agenda and priorities. Our jobs and perspectives may be different but I believe our goals are shared."[101]

Another strong factor in narrowing the gap is the growing problem of academic culture in Western academic circles. Academic culture has usually been cited as a major reason for the failure of Chinese societies to conduct cutting-edge research and deliver world-class education.[102] It has now become an issue of concern among Western academics as well.[103] Many things unprecedented have occurred over the last few decades in Western academia, in a hunger for fast, definitive answers. What has been used to accuse Chinese societies is also found in major Western higher education systems, including some of the best scholars and universities. This is not to justify some of the notorious records in academic culture in Chinese societies. It is, however, to show the conventional gap between Chinese societies and the West is narrowing in this aspect.

None of the institutional and systemic similarity or the narrowing gap in government-university relations should lead us to a conclusion that the global landscape of higher education is becoming the same. Despite the growing convergence of global governance in higher education, diversity continues to define different systems in a variety of societies and jurisdictions. Due to increasingly intensified globalization, there are some new changes that assume more and more influence on how we manage similarities and differences in higher education at various levels, as illustrated eloquently by a deep observer based at Hong Kong University of Science and Technology. While we do not necessarily agree with him on the new model, his notion of "co-production of cultural and physical product" is truly well taken.

---

101. Kenneth R. Minogue, "The Collapse of the Academic in Britain," in *Buckingham at 25: Freeing the University from State Control*, ed. James Tooley (London: The Institute of Economic Affairs, 2001), 95.
102. See, for example, Rui Yang, "Reassessing China's Higher Education Development: A Focus on Academic Culture," *Asia Pacific Education Review* 16, no. 4 (2015): 527–535; Altbach, "Chinese Higher Education: 'Glass Ceiling' and 'Feet of Clay.'"
103. Jerry Adler, "The Reformation: Can Social Scientists Save Themselves? *Pacific Standard*, April 28, 2014, https://psmag.com/the-reformation-can-social-scientists-save-themselves-8c2f834715a7.

It's very clear to me that the American century is ending in the sense that in many areas the US will no longer be the dominant power. But it's not clear what we replace it with. I worry it's going to be nobody's century and it's going to be an absence of leadership. In terms of higher education, I'm so fascinated by the idea that there may be an alternative. Because I think that basically the German model evolved into the American model in the idea of the research university. And I think I have very deep reservations about this model, of the research university, especially as it has evolved all the time. . . . I think we are really ripe for a new model that is a twenty-first century model, may be a Chinese model or an Asian model or just a global model. I think there's increasing cultural phenomenon in this area and we are getting to an age of co-production of cultural product as well as physical product. I suspect there's an Asian model, may involve China, Japan, Korea, or even Australia but it would be co-produced. . . . So my suggestion would be that the Asian model of higher education be the place where these ideas be synthesized, where the best of the world and the best traditions come together for the twenty-first century. (HKUST Interview 2, Former Faculty Dean)

5
Similar but Different: Substantive Mix

Diversity exists in almost every corner of the modern world of higher education, both within and between societies. With a rich legacy of history, higher education and its institutions in the Western tradition have continuously been entrusted new roles and functions, from classical teaching and research to the third mission as "a contribution to society,"[1] further to the current debates over the triple-helix model for innovation,[2] and "co-creation for sustainability."[3] The population they serve has expanded drastically from the elite to the middle- and increasingly working-classes. Within this process, different higher education institutions play different roles, as no institutions would be able to perform all roles equally well simultaneously. What has been greatly underestimated is the different and even conflicting nature between these different roles and functions. Such tensions appear to be much more intense and serious in vast non-Western societies that lack the underpinning cultural values needed for operating modern universities. Frequently, such tensions and differences are overlooked when people employ similar or even the same terms, concepts, and theoretical lens in their observations of higher education development and universities.

More evidently, in the Chinese tradition the term "university" is used to denote an entirely different constellation of scholarly institutions, as Ruth Hayhoe has pointed out repeatedly.[4] Although differing greatly from each other in size, the

---

1. Lorenzo Compagnucci and Francesca Spigarelli, "The Third Mission of the University: A Systematic Literature Review on Potentials and Constraints," *Technological Forecasting and Social Change* 161, C (2020): 1–30.
2. Henry Etzkowitz, *Triple Helix Innovation: Industry, University, and Government in Action* (London and New York: Routledge, 2008).
3. Gregory Trencher, Masaru Yarime, Kes McCormick, Christopher N. H. Doll, and Steven Kraines, "Beyond the Third Mission: Exploring the Emerging University Function of Co-creation for Sustainability," *Science and Public Policy* 41, no. 2 (2014): 151–179.
4. In her work published in 1994 she wrote: "A historically accurate use of the term in China would have to limit itself to the period since the late nineteenth century, when modern institutions like those of Europe and North America were established on a new basis, as traditional ones gradually disintegrated. Even though latter had more or less disappeared by the time of the revolution of 1911, the values associated with them persisted and have been manifested in conflicts over the development of higher education right up to the present time." See Hayhoe, "Ideas of Higher Learning, East and West," 361.

four societies cherish their rich historical and intellectual heritage from ancient China. Despite the shared cultural roots, their different trajectories yet parallel evolution of modern higher education development reflect their different exposure and approaches to Western influence as a result of their modern histories. At the same time, as globalization intensifies, they are pressured greatly by similar external forces. Competition that is closely connected with the global knowledge economy has become a central preoccupation in higher education. The way these societies have responded to the global environment has been a combination of both their historical and cultural legacy and their contemporary social and economic conditions. While resemblance builds the foundation for their premier universities to nip at the heels of the best in the West, the differences tell the other half of the story. Together they unfold the truth and the future of higher education development in the four societies.

In addition to the shared cultural heritage, as latecomers to modernization, the societies have all prioritized Western learning since the nineteenth century. Their universities are modeled on European and North American experiences, operating in largely Confucian sociocultural contexts and continuing tensions between Western and Chinese value orientations. Nearly all premier universities struggle with their cultural identity. In consideration of their unique historical roots, their experiences combine to become a cultural experiment that assumes gathering importance in the present context of the paradoxical movements in the world with unprecedented human connectivity on one hand and strong rejection of other values on the other. One significant yet little noticed achievement is the deep grasp of traditional and Western knowledge in specialized fields by individuals and institutions as the products of these higher education systems. The educational elites, especially in the best universities, are becoming better and better positioned to combine Chinese and Western ideas of a university in daily life and work. The experiment encourages non-Western societies to explore possibilities in a hegemonic context of Western models of university development.[5]

As a prominent feature of the experiment, such a bicultural condition contrasts sharply with the still largely mono-cultural (Western only) university operating environment in the West.[6] The experiment enables top universities in the socie-

---

5.   See Rui Yang, "The Cultural Experiment at East Asian Universities," in *Contesting Globalization and Internationalization of Higher Education: Discourse and Responses in the Asia Pacific Region*, ed. Deane E. Neubauer, Ka Ho Mok, and Sachi Edwards (Gewerbestrasse, Switzerland: Palgrave Macmillan, 2019), 33–47.

6.   Today, the main spiritual and philosophical traditions are not on an equal footing. All other traditions have to respond to the dominant West. To them, development practically means responding successfully to the West. Without Western knowledge, neither national nor individual development could be possible in any society in the present world. Therefore, theoretically and ideally, a multicultural identity is the aim generally. In the case of Chinese societies, what is practiced is to manage the traditional Chinese and the dominant Western cultural values. Similarly, the focus in other non-Western societies would be between their traditions and the Western. This does not mean one needs to stop when he

ties to bring back their cultural traditions to integrate with Western values and contribute to inter-civilizational dialogue. As the number of bicultural individuals increases, both Chinese and Western traditions are incorporated more and more into the daily operation of their elite universities. On the surface, scholars in human and social sciences in the societies work and live just like their peers in the rest of the world, but closer scrutiny reveals their distinctive bicultural identity. Although largely unnoticed, this is indeed a remarkable achievement that positions the people and their higher education nicely for even greater future success. Such a bicultural intellectual condition embraces Western learning as one of the most important elements of their modern knowledge systems.[7] In a context of globalization, it is fast becoming an advantage. It also displays a high level of cultural confidence at individual and systemic levels.

Monitoring Competing Imperatives

Higher education and knowledge are among the most globalized of all human activities.[8] Facing a dual and potentially conflicting responsibility to address local and global demands,[9] contemporary universities operate in local, national, and global dimensions that are heterogeneous in forms and purposes. Local and national higher education systems and institutions are greatly influenced by the tendency to global convergence and integration. They are globalizing, especially through international networking and global rankings, with comparable qualification frameworks, credit transfer, and quality assurance measures. As required by increasing human coexistence, teaching and research in universities need to incorporate a global dimension to educate students as global citizens and to contribute to solving global challenges through scholarly work. "The emerging global model," as a new phenomenon in the global landscape of higher education, has recently risen to prominence.[10] Built on "costly infrastructure" (HKUST Interview 1, Former Faculty Dean), such institutions are research intensive. They rely heavily on close relationships with government agencies, the private industry, and wealthy supporters. Equipped with wide connections and striving for global impact, they effectively operate beyond the control of local and national governments, often creating policy dilemmas for national governments.

---

or she reaches the bicultural stage. The ultimate aim remains to become as multicultural as possible. Indeed, the bicultural stage builds the foundation for the multicultural pursuit.

7. Timothy Reagan, *Non-Western Educational Traditions: Alternative Approaches to Educational Thought and Practice* (Mahwah, NJ: Lawrence Erlbaum Associates, 2000).
8. Simon Marginson, "Globalization of Higher Education: The Good, the Bad and the Ugly," *University World News*, May 15, 2021.
9. See Global University Network for Innovation (GUNi), *Towards a Socially Responsible University*.
10. Kathryn Mohrman, "The Research University in Transition: The Emerging Global Model," *Higher Education Policy* 21, no. 1 (2008): 5–27.

However, as Simon Marginson reminds us most recently,[11] the globalization that emerged after 1990 is not a shared space based on respect for the other and mutual learning. Instead, it is hegemonic, American-led, and grounded in European (Hellenic-Judeo-Christian) heritage. In economic terms, it is Western and primarily American; in cultural terms, it is Anglo-American. It has fostered global openness to capital and the closure of power, culture, and equality. Accordingly, the global governance of higher education has not been fully justified. Indeed, it has fallen repeatedly short of its promises and expectations. Thirty years on, Selvaratnam's description of the dominance of the Western model of university development with its accompanying Eurocentric knowledge systems has remained largely unchanged.[12] What makes today's situation particularly different is one shared characteristic among many non-Western societies that have adopted the Western models:[13] they have all shown their great admiration for elite American higher education in its best-known twentieth-century forms: the liberal arts college, the research university, and the professional school.

While there are competing forces at work on a global scale, higher education is required fundamentally to serve nation-building by delivering skills that are relevant for the social and economic development of their own societies. National qualifications continue to be very different across countries. Higher education policies and institutions need to strike a balance between integration in the global higher education order and serving domestic needs. A good example of such struggles is to manage the dynamics and consequences of seeking world-class status for their universities and higher education systems, in line with the global movement[14] and the trend in the region.[15] All the societies try hard to balance domestic and international agendas. Facing a similar global context and based on much-shared cultural roots, their approaches to managing the competing forces have been similar when compared with those of many non-Chinese societies. While there has been

11. Marginson, "Globalization of Higher Education."
12. Viswanathan Selvaratnam, "Higher Education Co-operation and Western Dominance of Knowledge Creation and Flows in Third World Countries," *Higher Education* 17, no. 1 (1988): 41–68.
13. As Ruth Hayhoe points out, the European university has become a kind of universal institution and an essential accoutrement of every modernizing society. It is integrally linked to the expansion of European civilization of which the development of China's modern universities is a part. See Hayhoe, "Ideas of Higher Learning, East and West," 361.
14. As Altbach famously said, "Everyone wants a world-class university. No country feels it can do without one. The problem is that no one knows what a world-class university is, and no one has figured out how to get one. Everyone, however, refers to the concept." See Philip G. Altbach, "The Costs and Benefits of World-Class Universities," *International Higher Education* 33, Fall (2003): 5.
15. Ka Ho Mok, "The Quest for World-Class University Status: Implications for Sustainable Development of Asian Universities," Working paper no. 8, September 2016, Centre for Global Higher Education, Oxford University.

substantial differentiation among them due to their varying goals and strategies,[16] all four societies have demonstrated remarkably impressive achievements.[17]

For higher education, globalization implies the broad social, economic, and technological forces that shape the realities of the twenty-first century. Contemporary higher education development in any society is greatly influenced by the global context, along with increasingly intensified movement of resources, technology, information, people, ideas, and cultural practices across political and cultural boundaries. While the impact on higher education policy and academic institutions is profound, our understanding of the implications is often deceivingly simple.[18] As international forces confront local traditions, stress and conflict inevitably occur. Higher education systems and institutions react to external forces based on their local footings. Highly similar policies are implemented differently to a great extent in different jurisdictions. This is evidently the case for Chinese societies where persisting cultural values continue to underlie higher education. The following report of findings from my empirical study is organized along two threads:[19] one is vertical, centered on the relations between the traditional and the modern (Western), and the other is horizontal, focusing on the nexus between the global and the local.

Many themes and case-specific issues are rich and interesting, especially in policy and practical terms. For instance, respondents from Singapore and especially Hong Kong generally care much less about any possible loss of cultural traditions. One senior professor and former pro-vice-chancellor expressed openly, "we don't care [about cultural identity], as long as we can survive" (HKU Interview 3). Similarly, a world-renowned social scientist at the National University of Singapore remarked, "Singapore has always been strategic. We don't classify things into East or West. Not even the local or the global. If they are useful, we take them and see them as Singaporean" (NSU Interview 4). Among the participants in Taiwan, generational gaps are considerable, younger people showing much less knowledge of and commitment to Chinese traditions. While generational gaps are also noticeable among those in mainland China, they take a different shape; some elites born in and after the 1970s are starting to demonstrate a growing grasp of both Chinese and Western

---

16. For instance, for mainland China, the quest to establish world-class universities has been both symbolic and practical. Symbolically, world-class universities would convey to the world Chinese value as a great civilization. Practically, higher education would be seen as essential and instrumental for social and economic development.

17. This is not to say that they do not face serious challenges. They certainly do. The focus here is on how these societies trail-blaze new approaches in a context of predominant Western models of university development and the implications of their experiences, especially for other non-Western societies.

18. Philip G. Altbach, *The International Imperative in Higher Education* (Boston, MA: Center for International Higher Education, Boston College, 2013).

19. Some of the findings of the empirical study reported here were originally published in "Turning Scars into Stars: A Reconceptualized View of University Development in Beijing, Hong Kong, Taipei and Singapore," *Frontiers of Education in China* 14, no. 1 (2019): 1–32.

traditions. Despite such lively differentiation, the following section concentrates on the commonality that emerged prominently across cases and societies.

Managing Local-Global Relations

Traditional explanations of scholarly relations between developed and developing countries are located in a historical context of colonialism.[20] Resulting from historical factors and enhanced by globalization, there exists a powerful yet unequal international knowledge network: a few countries are the center, retaining extraordinary academic power, while the rest of world is the periphery and semi-periphery. This has been the basic condition for higher education development in non-Western societies, with heightened tensions between global engagement and local service. While knowledge is international by nature, especially in an era of globalization, in the present global higher education equation real knowledge is only Western. There has been a global asymmetric structure in which certain institutional and intellectual "centers" give direction, provide models, produce research, and in general function as the pinnacles of the academic system. At the opposite end of the spectrum are universities that are peripheral in the sense that they copy developments from abroad, produce little that is original, and are generally not at the frontiers of knowledge. Universities located in Chinese countries have been heavily dependent on the institutions located in the centers.[21]

For those in the periphery, there exits an urgent need for their academic systems to lean toward the centers in order to become members of the international knowledge network so that they can access the knowledge produced by the centers, and the knowledge that they produce would have the chance to be recognized in the system. Major universities in the periphery are thus on the horns of a dilemma: while they enjoy enormous prestige domestically and play a crucial role in national and local economic and social development, they find themselves at a disadvantage in the global knowledge system. This was well expressed by a social scientist at the University of Hong Kong:

> We have colleagues who are well-known intellectuals in Hong Kong who publish in local newspapers and Chinese language books as bestsellers. This is one of the

20. Philip G. Altbach, "The American Academic Model in Comparative Perspective," in *In Defense of American Higher Education*, ed. Philip G. Altbach, Patricia J. Gumport, and D. Bruce Johnstone (Baltimore, MD: Johns Hopkins University Press, 2001), 11–37.
21. The present international knowledge network is culturally biased and politically unequal. For details of such structured asymmetric mechanisms, see Philip G. Altbach, *Comparative Higher Education: Knowledge, the University and Development* (Hong Kong: Comparative Education Research Centre, University of Hong Kong, 1998).

reasons why we have bad RAE results,[22] because these works would probably be ranked as zero since they are in Chinese. But we actually had influence in Hong Kong through those people who are engaged in the local community. It's a problem. I noticed that some of our lecturers [in the lecturing track, not professors] are very active in magazines and local societies; however, for all of us on the professorial level, we don't have time for doing that much, so we only write for the major English publishers. (HKU Interview 2, Department Head)

The problems of looking outward and inward at the same time are substantial, particularly when combined with immense pressures to contribute directly to national or local developments and to participate in the international system. This is a predicament felt especially by the top-tier universities in all Chinese societies almost daily. The situation becomes much more serious when the English language increasingly dominates science, scholarship, and instruction as never before, due to the exponential growth of the Internet.

This is a main trend in the context of rapidly developing countries that need knowledge in different areas compared to post-industrial countries. In general, universities in Greater China are now more engaged in the development needs of industries and responsive to government. But the cases differ within. (HKU Interview 4, Faculty Dean)

We have great difficulties striking a balance between global and local agendas. The quality assurance framework the Ministry of Education has for us, their criteria are somewhat different from ranking criteria which have a very strong emphasis on citation, bibliometrics, and so on. Whereas the Ministry doesn't really care how many papers you publish, they want to make sure that our graduates are employable by society and are useful to the nation. So there are some tensions. But of course being a university we know we have to satisfy both stakeholders, and we try our best to please both. (NUS Interview 1, Former Faculty Dean)

In sociology, the people who only do surveys on Singapore don't get very far. People like me get far because we didn't care about Singapore half the time, and when I do write about Singapore, I actually address political conceptual issues. Singapore is just incidental information. Colleagues do surveys on health conditions of Singaporeans and all these. First of all, it's difficult to publish internationally. And if you publish locally, you are doing government policy work. The university doesn't recognize it. So that's why I am saying "unfortunately." Everything is geared toward the so-called international standards. And these international standards are really driven by American institutions. It doesn't recognize differences in cultural conditions, differences in historical conditions, differences in the national needs, and national issues. (NUS Interview 4, Seasoned Professor)

---

22. Originally borrowed from the United Kingdom and intended to encourage world-class research and drive excellence, the Research Assessment Exercise (RAE) is part of Hong Kong's University Grants Committee's commitment to assessing the performance of the universities it funds. It assesses the research quality of Hong Kong's publically funded universities by using international benchmarks to delineate their areas of relative strength and make recommendations for further improvements.

It is necessary to pay attention to the differentiation among Chinese societies on this issue. The two case study institutions in mainland China have been identified by the central government to bid for world-class standing. For them, locally oriented issues are allowed to be less prioritized although this does not mean that they are encouraged to be out of touch with the social and economic developments in the society. However, the sheer size of the society demands solutions that are usually unprecedented in human knowledge. Global and local agendas are, therefore, reconciled for them in this sense.[23] A similar situation applies largely to the two universities in Taiwan. In contrast, the tensions between the local and the global are much more serious for Hong Kong and Singapore.

It is also important to point out the differentiation among disciplines. While many participants, especially those in the humanities and to a lesser extent in social sciences, complained about the tensions between local and global orientations, some, especially from the technological sciences, are in a very different situation. The following comments were made by a participant from engineering at the University of Hong Kong. They are in an advantageous position due to both the high level of economic development in the region and their disciplinary background.

> I am a professor and an engineer. We always try to engage with the society. In this region [Guangdong-Hong Kong-Macau Greater Bay Area], we can achieve a sound cycle of development between academic research and industrial needs. (HKU Interview 5, Department Head)

In this sense, pursuing international impact could be a double-edged sword that has to be managed with great care, a broad and long vision as well as a strong sense of responsibility. However, it appears that many premier universities in Chinese societies are likely to be able to move beyond the long-term quagmire of local-global tensions, as expressed by Professor Tan Eng Chye, the deputy president and provost of the National University of Singapore:

> I think we do have this sort of dilemma. But so far we managed to strike a very good balance. I guess our geographical position forces us to do a lot of such things. (NUS Interview 6)

Highly related to local and global competing imperatives is a dilemma between self-assessment and the evaluation by international peers. Intellectuals and universities in Chinese societies have traditionally enjoyed prominent social status. This leads to society-wide concerns about the international prestige of their best institutions and has been fueled further by global university rankings. It was one of the most frequently mentioned topics during my fieldwork. As all the case study

---

23. However, a few participants in Beijing raised the issue explicitly, such as BJ Interviews 6 and 7 and QH Interview 1.

institutions sit on the very top of their university systems, there was a common embarrassment about the gap between their domestic and international reputations.

Bringing Back Cultural Traditions

Thanks to the remarkable progress made over recent decades, university leaders in the Chinese societies are gaining confidence. While the confidence is based directly on the impressive achievements in material and institutional dimensions of higher education development, more fundamentally it displays a belief of the intellectual elites and top universities to bring back their cultural traditions to integrate with Western values. This is unprecedented since Chinese societies were forced to learn from the West in the nineteenth century. One participant from Tsinghua University in Beijing remarked, "It won't take too long for China to have Nobel Prize winners" (QH Interview 10, Center Director). The confidence was confirmed by Xu Zhihong, former president of Peking University:

> Building a world-class university takes a long time. We've got plans to become a world-class university as soon as possible. We know clearly what we're going to do. Our aim is to make our university more competitive and attract excellent academics and students. Our objectives are based on international standards.[24]

Similar confidence was consistently expressed by the interviewees across cases and societies, but particularly by those in Beijing:

> A "glass ceiling" might exist. It might be 10 meters high. We are not there yet, perhaps only 2–3 meters high. Once we are there, we might find some cracks in it, or we can see whether it's thin or thick. We might find ways to get through or avoid it. Our world-class universities will take some time to achieve, but we will get there. (BJ Interview 6, Mid-Level University Administrator)

> We need to do well by some hard indicators in order to be acknowledged internationally as world-class. . . . Our future looks bright. We have built up our hardware. We will succeed. But it's not the time yet to claim a comprehensive win. (BJ Interview 7, Mid-Level University Administrator)

Borrowing a Zen Buddhist metaphor,[25] Professor Hong Hocheng, president of National Tsing Hua University, made the following comments:

---

24. Long Xicheng, "Xu Zhihong: We Must Reform but Should Remain Steady as We Advance," *Chinese Education and Society* 37, no. 6 (2004): 52.
25. The Zen Buddhist metaphor to describe levels of life realm is: 看山是山，看水是水 (Mountains are mountains, no matter how long you eye them, water is water, no matter how hard you watch it); 看山不是山，看水不是水 (Hills are no longer hills, even if you keep looking at them, stream is no longer stream, even if you keep staring at it); 看山還是山，看水還是水 (Mountains are still mountains, when you observe them closely, water is still water, when you behold it carefully).

Looking back historically, higher education can't be separated from wider cultural change. Ever since the Opium Wars, Chinese culture has been struggling to adjust itself to rise to Western challenge. Our development is like the three-stage Buddhist practice. The initial 50 years was our [National Tsing Hua University's] first stage when we followed the West every step. . . . We are moving from seeing hills are no longer hills to seeing mountains are mountains again. We are in a transition between the second and third stages. (THU Interview 5)

Such extraordinary confidence was echoed by Professor Tan Chorh Chuan, former provost of National University of Singapore, who made the following comments in November 2010:

I believe that Asian universities are at the most exciting phase of their development and that the future for Asian universities is very bright. Asian universities nevertheless face several challenges in their development into world-class institutions. Asian universities need to make a big shift from highly specialized education models to more broad-based ones. Universities need to develop strong global education programs. Asian universities need to develop research peaks which are among the leaders in the world.[26]

During my fieldwork, participants were asked whether they were optimistic or pessimistic about their quest for world-class university status. They tended to express their optimism openly and firmly, including those who complained a great deal about their social, political, and institutional environments. Interestingly, their complaints and confidence appeared to be somewhat contradictory across cases and societies: strong optimism with clear inability to substantialize their differences from the experiences of Western universities. Stressing cultural tradition and identity was common, especially among the participants across the Taiwan Strait, as shown by a professor and a mid-level university administrator based at National Taiwan University: "We have gone far beyond initial imitation stage. We cannot blindly follow the 'global' tides, as we should maintain the uniqueness of our own culture." (THU Interview 7)

However, neither the leaders of the case study universities nor researchers in higher education have been able to come out with anything of real substance about how their university development differs from or can be different from those of their Western counterparts, conceptually and practically. For instance, despite the strong confidence expressed by Professor Tan Chorh Chuan when he was interviewed by the *Korea Times* in June 2014, he was confident enough to explore "different" paths to the success of his university but failed to deliver anything substantial that could be a solid basis for the difference he intended to achieve:

---

26. I understand that Asia here refers to East Asia, including Chinese societies together with Japan and Korea.

What we are doing is not just take what is being done in Yale but building a different model. We don't have to follow the same patterns that are happening in the West. . . . we should be doing different things and trying different models.[27]

Such a response was confirmed repeatedly by the interviewees who were major scholars and/or university leaders throughout the societies. At least two factors explain this paradox. First, since their cultural encounters with the West in the nineteenth century, Chinese societies often regard their cultural traditions as the reason for being "ignorant and backward" in a context of Western prestige.[28] Meanwhile, universities in the West are deified to the extent that it is often beyond the imagination of the universities in Chinese societies to think of any problems of their Western peers. Secondly, as Chinese societies continue to develop well and engage with the West, people gain confidence in their own traditions and become more knowledgeable about the West. Their attitude to and knowledge of cultural traditions have also changed, with a better understanding that their traditions could have a positive role to play. Confidence in their traditional culture is resuming across the societies, as illustrated by the following remarks:

It's a matter of time [to achieve world-class status] but hard to say when. We need to wait and we are all hopeful. Once we reach a certain level, we will have our own features accumulated through a long time of development. (BJ Interview 2, Mid-Level University Administrator)

Still, very few could really link strong confidence to actual higher education development in a more defined theoretical manner. The reason is that modern universities in Chinese societies have little linkage to their traditional roots. A participant who is a professor of history at Tsinghua University in Beijing made the following analysis:

We need to have our own understanding of civilization to support our work and life. Don't always focus on catching up. Catch-up mentality is utilitarian, not scientific. Our research planning shouldn't be dominated by such a mindset. With our development today, we need to rethink the future of our civilization. Otherwise, we will be bogged down in a quagmire of low-level competition. (QH Interview 9)

Without specializing in higher education, most participants understandably did not provide an intellectual foundation for their confidence. Yet, their confidence is well founded on the rich roots of Chinese culture. Such confidence was most evidently expressed by the participants in mainland China. It was also common among those in Taiwan. Comparatively, it was less voiced by those in Singapore, while those from Hong Kong expressed it the least.

---

27. Jung Min-ho, "Bright Future for Asian Universities," *Korea Times*, June 16, 2014, http://www.korea-times.co.kr/www/news/nation/2015/01/181_159335.html.
28. Vera Schwarcz, *The Chinese Enlightenment: Intellectuals and the Legacy of the May Fourth Movement of 1919* (Berkeley, CA: University of California Press, 1986).

Fostering a Bicultural Intellectual Mind

Non-Western societies have long desired to integrate their traditions with Western cultural heritages, ever since their early encounters with the West. They are confronted with a difficult choice: the dominant Western knowledge on one hand, and their strong indigenous traditions on the other, and constant tensions between the two. This has been particularly the case for Chinese societies. However, in comparison with many other non-Western societies, they have demonstrated a stronger bicultural mind to embrace the West. Western learning has become the most important part of their modern knowledge system. For example, by the 1930s, scholars studying Chinese literature within China agreed that a thorough knowledge of both Chinese and Western literature was necessary to achieve innovation in literary studies. Fu Ssu-nien (傅斯年, 1896–1950) observed in 1919, "If you are to research Chinese literature, yet never understand foreign literature, or if you are to document the history of Chinese literature yet have never read any of the history of foreign literature, you will never ever grasp the truth."[29] Similarly, Liang Shuming (梁漱溟, 1893–1988) remarked that "Chinese people will never gain a clear understanding if they only remain within the structures of Chinese society; if only they first look to others and then at themselves, then they will immediately understand."[30]

The modernization of Chinese societies involves necessarily responding to Western challenges. The desire to catch up with the West has always been fervent. Most recently, the drive for internationally competitive universities provides an impetus for their best institutions to follow the lead of European and North American universities and embrace "international" norms. Especially due to recent impressive development, top universities in Chinese societies now compare themselves with their prominent Western peers such as Oxford and Yale. Nearly all the participants mentioned major global universities in one way or another, and almost with no exception those were Western institutions. They frequently referred to major Western universities when they talked about their international networks, strategic collaboration, and the positions of their programs in global ranking systems. One participant who was then both a mid-level administrator and a deputy dean at Peking University said, "We are still in a process of catching up. At this stage, our strategic priority is to become the same as Oxford, Cambridge, Princeton, and Yale" (BJ Interview 2).

---

29. Fu Sinian 傅斯年, "Wang Guowei *zhu Song-Yuan xiqu shi*" 王國維著《宋元戲曲史》[Review of Wang Guowei's *Song-Yuan xiqu shi*]. In *Fu Sinian quanji* 傅斯年全集 [Collections of Fu Sinian], ed., Ouyang Zhesheng 歐陽哲生 (Changsha: Hunan Education Publishing House, 2003), 111.
30. Liang Shuming 梁漱溟, "Zhongguo wenhua yaoyi" 中國文化要義 [Substance of Chinese culture], In *Liang Shuming quanji vol. 3* 梁漱溟全集 [Collections of Liang Shuming vol. 3], ed., Academic Committee of Chinese Cultural Academy 中國文化書院學術委員會 (Jinan: Shandong People's Press, 2005), 9–10.

Not everyone was entirely happy with such a perspective. For instance, a participant from Taiwan expressed his strong view that "the current Taiwanese academic community has been completely Westernized. We all talk about Western components. There has been limited indigenization in Taiwanese academia. We have become a group of Western slaves." In his eyes, the best universities in Taiwan have a "split personality" and are "culturally hollow" (TU Interview 1, University Administrator). Voiced more calmly with a somewhat more balanced opinion, his colleague explained that "Taiwan initially took over the system from the US. However, we also adapted and created many aspects to suit our society. I feel Taiwan possesses Western efficiency and modernity. Yet, we have also tried to retain our own traditional values. It has been a tough process" (TU Interview 3, University Administrator). Despite their different styles and assessments, both show the bicultural intellectual condition in a top Taiwanese university.

Some, usually from the humanities and social sciences, had a broader perspective including the historical and the foreign. At Peking University, for instance, a mid-level administrator compared the history of Chinese modern universities with Oxford and Cambridge and argued that Chinese universities needed more time to establish their own identities, values, and cultures (BJ Interview 2, Mid-Level University Administrator). One dean illustrated how he introduced "Western management" into his own faculty (BJ Interview 3, Faculty Dean). A mid-level administrator who is a historian by training compared China's encounters with Western culture with Japan's experience (BJ Interview 7). A law professor pointed out some core values that originated from the West and stressed their great significance for China (BJ Interview 8, Professor and Center Director), and his comments were strongly supported by a prominent engineer at Tsinghua University in Beijing (QH Interview 6, University Administrator).

One participant who was then a mid-level administrator at Peking University and a scientist by training said, "A third-class dean stresses efficiency. A second-class dean pays attention to management. A first-class dean watches for culture" (BJ Interview 5). Here culture, management, and efficiency are all a combination of Chinese and Western values. Such remarks echo the comments by a female participant at Tsinghua University in Beijing who was associate professor with a background in business and management: "If you observe successful businessmen in China today, they all have Chinese values for conducting oneself and Western values for conducting business" (QH Interview 5, Office Director). An interviewee based at National Taiwan University who is also a renowned academic commented that "this is an implementation of Western discipline together with the inclusion of Confucian spirit. That's rather complicated, and can't be achieved in a short period of time" (TU Interview 6, Center Director).

Bicultural situations are also highly visible in the universities in Hong Kong and Singapore, as illustrated well by the following quotes from participants:

Hong Kong has historically been a melting pot of East and West, with high mobility of individuals and different values brought together. Everybody is well equipped to wear different hats and switch between different values while still feeling comfortable and create something unique in the process. Hong Kong is not just a bridge. It's a fusion of cultures with its unique creation. I hope for an effective integration of different ideas and culture and creating something truly unique, and HKU is well positioned to do so, given our history and sound knowledge in this social background. (HKU Interview 9, University Administrator)

The fact that nearly all participants included Western knowledge in their talks has to be understood in a context of contemporary Chinese society and culture that has been profoundly influenced by Western values, as a consequence of the Westernization of the world.[31] As for education, according to UNESCO,[32] the world's chief practices are Western, as initially conceptualized in ancient Greece, adapted by ancient Romans, limited by the European Middle Ages, expanded by the Renaissance, and rationalized by the Industrial and Scientific Revolutions.[33] While there are variations on the theme and differences in interpretation, it is difficult nowadays to find a widespread educational practice that is radically different from the dominant secular educational paradigm of the West.[34] Western knowledge has become part of the contemporary knowledge systems of all Chinese societies. It is impossible for them to talk about formal education without mentioning the West. This is highly visible in the speeches delivered by university presidents, in their strategic plans, and in their booklists and syllabuses. Such a combination is well illustrated by the following observation by a professor of history at Tsinghua University in Beijing:

As for [disciplinary] knowledge, I think Chinese universities should emulate the West. We need at least to have some breakthroughs in certain fields. Such breakthroughs require genuine learning from the West [spirit of seeking truth] with great respect. . . . Our problem is that our traditions have not been activated while our understanding of Western learning is shallow. We have never truly understood Western knowledge. This is why there still lacks an integration of both traditions although some progress has been made. (QH Interview 9)

Although focusing on culture, the above remarks were much echoed by scientists at a top university across the Taiwan Strait, with emphasis on science:

---

31. For reasons for and indicators of the Westernization of the world, see Serge Latouche, *The Westernization of the World: The Singnificance, Scope, and Limits of the Drive towards Global Unifiormity* (Cambridge: Polity Press, 1996).
32. See UNESCO, *World Education Report 1998*.
33. See Grigorenko, "Hitting, Missing, and in Between," 165.
34. Julian Elliott and Elena Grigorenko, eds., *Western Psychological and Educational Theory in Diverse Contexts* (London: Routledge, 2007).

The West has its merits. Western education, particularly in the pursuit of science, is very standardized. On one hand, we need to progress well in science in order to compete or synchronize with the world. On the other hand, we need to maintain our traditions and not to lose our identity. We must seek a balance between both sides. (TU Interview 2, Female, Professor, and Mid-Level University Administrator)

The essence of Western civilization is science. We have to use Western science as a foundation and analyze our own tradition and philosophy. We can then construct theory and apply it to the reality. (TU Interview 1, University Administrator)

The most distinguished element between Western and Eastern systems is the cultural dimension. For the East, we have Confucianism. These ancient factors are very deep. We should strengthen our scientific knowledge from the West and bridge the knowledge to our own culture and society. It's just not good enough to imitate everything. (TU Interview 5, Female, Professor)

In an era of globalization, being able to learn from others has become critically important for any society's sustainable development.[35] More specifically, for research on university development in Chinese societies, the combination of the traditional and the Western has some significant implications. Firstly, it interrogates seriously the conventional dichotomy of the two in the literature on higher education in these societies and treats these societies and their education and cultures as the Other. Secondly, it reminds us of the great extent to which these societies have absorbed Western knowledge in many aspects at individual, institutional, and systemic levels. And thirdly, it demonstrates that it is no longer valid to draw a clear dividing line between Chinese and Western ideas of a university.

Reactivating the Chinese Idea of a University

Modern universities worldwide are uniquely European in origin and characteristics. Today, the direction of change of universities in all Chinese societies is still heavily influenced by their elite Western counterparts. As foreign transplants, universities in Chinese societies are patterned after the Western model without integrally linking to their indigenous cultures.[36] The universities in Chinese societies therefore have a different cultural gene. For over a century, their central purpose is to combine Chinese and Western elements at all levels of their operation. However, the desired combination has never been fully achieved. In a context of global dominance by the

---

35. Chungying Cheng, "Philosophical Globalization as Reciprocal Valuation and Mutual Integration: Comments on the Papers of Tang Yijie and Roger Ames," in *Dialogue of Philosophies, Religions and Civilizations in the Era of Globalization*, ed. Zhao Dunhua (Washington DC: The Council for Research in Values and Philosophy, 2007), 70–71.
36. Philip G. Altbach, "Peripheries and Centers: Research Universities in Developing Countries," *Asia Pacific Education Review* 10, no. 1 (2009): 15–27.

Western model,[37] it has proven to be extremely difficult. All participants stressed this in one way or another. The following comments by a Taiwan-based respondent, who is an internationally renowned scholar in the humanities, serve as an example:

> We need to have our own identity and become strongly and fully based on our local society. It's not easy, but we must have our own ideas. We should examine our copying strategies. If we only follow others, although we may look good in rankings, we will lose our identity. (TU Interview 6, Center Director)

With the great difficulty, there have been various approaches, which have differentiated Chinese societies in their dealing with the two different and often incompatible value systems. The easiest way is to take the Western concept of a university only for its practicality. While this has been criticized, and no society would openly acknowledge this, it has been largely the case across the societies to one degree or another. Singapore and especially Hong Kong due to their colonial history decided to a great extent not to try to combine the two traditions but chose the Western only. In contrast, Taiwan and especially mainland China have endeavoured to reach an integration, with limited success so far. Therefore, an overwhelminmg majority of mainland respondents stressed the importance of Chinese cultural traditions. Most Taiwan-based participants agreed, as shown by the following observations:

> Our cultural roots must become visible with sufficient passion and respect. It is possible that adopting oriental approach can be more appropriate. (THU Interview 4, Professor)

> Chinese heritages in economic, political, cultural and artistic development and ancient medical development should be strengthened. (TU Interview 8, Professor)

> Shouldn't Asia define the concept of a university particularly at this time with opportunities?! (THU Interview 2, Mid-Level University Administrator)

However, not all participants were equally positive. Two respondents from the University of Hong Kong, for example, were highly critical, as shown by their remarks:

> Up till now, we are definitely influenced by the West. I can hardly see any influence of Chinese intellectual traditions on our university development. HKU has an international perspective. It won't be assessed from China's lens of scholarly achievement. (HKU Interview 5, Department Head)

> I don't think traditional Chinese culture and Confucian values influence the University. There is nothing particularly Confucian about the University of Hong Kong. . . . Also, I'm suspicious about the Confucian values in relation to the Chinese society. I've been to China but I don't see anything Confucian about this.

---

37. Scott Jaschik, "How Asian Are Asian Universities?" *Inside Higher Ed*, March 14, 2011, http://www.insidehighered.com/news/2011/03/14/asian_university_leaders_consider_identity_of_their_institutions.

What is really Confucian about Chinese society? What's Confucian about Peking University? Not in any significant way. (HKU Interview 7, Department Head)

Despite substantial differences and even conflicts between Chinese and Western approaches to scholarship,[38] in the minds of many higher education elites in Chinese societies these conflicts could and should be resolved.[39] Their rich intellectual traditions have great strengths and potential to contribute to the idea of a university:

Being conscious of our own heritage and background will help us to better understand the Western culture. We are aware that we need to make progress. That is to say, by connecting the Chinese culture to the West, we can understand where our strengths and shortcomings are from. (THU Interview 5, University Administrator)

In the current globally networked environment, university people across the societies are becoming more aware of differences and variations in their sociocultural contexts than before. This was confirmed by many participants. Indeed, the "idea of a university" is becoming more similar across societies, especially under the pressure of global rankings and competition. Yet, it should not be a fixed concept. Instead, there have been changing definitions over time.[40] Systemic and institutional responses to the present scenario of global higher education need to be critical and strategic.

Indigenizing the Western concept of a university has therefore been the most fundamental challenge for university development in non-Western societies. No Chinese societies have ever stopped making such efforts.[41] Some even achieved highly in different historical periods. In the early twentieth century, Cai Yuanpei combined the Chinese educational spirit, especially Confucian and Mohist character building, with Western systems.[42] He synthesized valuable thought and ideas from China and the West to make Peking University a center for free and open scholarly thinking. Today, the century-long hard and bitter learning from the West by Chinese societies has begun to bear fruit more evidently. The defining values of the university have begun to take root throughout these societies, most evidently at the individual level.

While Singapore and Hong Kong are turning more attention to Chinese traditions,[43] the Chinese mainland and Taiwan have been incorporating the Western idea of a university in a profound manner at various levels. As noted previously, one participant, who is an academician of the Chinese Academy of Sciences and was once the president of a regional university, said explicitly that "A truly good

38. Weston, *The Power of Position.*
39. Lin, *Peking University.*
40. Marginson, "'Ideas of a University' for the Global Era."
41. See Rui Yang, "Indigenizing the Western Concept of the University."
42. See Weston, *The Power of Position.*
43. See, for example, Anthony B. L. Cheung, *Mission of University: Excellence with a Soul.*

university must first of all have academic freedom" (QH Interview 6). Mainland China's acceptance of the fundamental value has also been much institutionalized in universities. Even at the highest level of policy making in higher education, the impact of such values has become more and more evident, as suggested by a mid-level administrator at Peking University and a Taiwan-based senior academic:

> Our university has a strong liberal tradition, well recognized in the nation's modern history. This has penetrated deep into almost every aspect of our work. Everyone here tries to defend the tradition. However, what we do and how we do it have to be appropriate in our social context. We share the purpose of seeking the truth with every other great university in the world. (BJ Interview 2, Professor, Mid-Level University Administrator)

> We are a Chinese society, still highly Confucian. Yet, we have academic freedom and institutional autonomy. Our academic governance by professors is strong. Presidents are elected and our departmental heads are autonomous. Sometimes we might have too much autonomy to hinder our reforms. (TU Interview 13, Female, Professor)

The overwhelming majority of the participants acknowledged growing autonomy granted by the governments to their institutions, as noted by BJ Interview 5 (Mid-Level University Administrator):

> Culture really plays a critical role, especially so because of our autocratic tradition. Yet, I'm still optimistic because our society is changing in line with external environments toward one ruled by law. The society is becoming more and more mature. We shouldn't copy Oxbridge or Harvard mechanically. We'll succeed in our own context.

Two participants respectively from Tsinghua University in Beijing and Hsinchu made the following interesting remarks:

> Academic freedom is certainly important. Without it, we'll never get there [world-class status]. Yet, I don't think it's the best part for us to start with. China's issues require Chinese solutions. (QH Interview 9, Female, Professor)

> Free thinking and autonomy are indeed necessary. They are very much treasured here. We don't always feel them, as they are like air. (THU Interview 7, Faculty Dean)

Participants in all four societies acknowledged growing autonomy granted to their institutions. Even those who were concerned about the negative role of traditional culture and called for "seeking truth and freedom" agreed that much progress had been made. Such progress contributes to narrowing the conventional gap between Chinese and Western ideas of a university. Singapore is often considered as lacking academic freedom. However, according to Professor Tan, such a perception is people being biased and using inappropriate criteria. To him, "working with or even for the government" can coexist with "speaking truth to power" in Singaporean universities. His following remarks, once again, remain highly relevant:

> It is doable. Even now I think we do have certain disagreements. That could be some policies that would be disagreed on. But there is no problem in our faculty members criticizing the government for their policies. That's not a problem. You can see the differences between the two cultures. The West emphasizes a lot on individuals. The East, like China and Singapore, emphasizes more on the society. That's why when you asked me about academic freedom, I talked about individual freedom and activity freedom. The activity is for the society. There is nothing actually preventing different countries depending on the cultural background to interpret; who says the US ones must be the right one? (NUS Interview 6, University Administrator)

Echoing partially the discussions on the chronic academic culture problem in Chinese societies,[44] a number of participants expressed strong reservations about traditional Chinese cultural values as a powerful barrier for them and their universities to seek truth and freedom (BJ Interview 5, Mid-Level University Administrator; BJ Interview 8, Professor and Center Director). Nevertheless, their concerns do not suffice to confirm the mainstream literature that has predicted an impasse of higher education development in Chinese societies due to a complete lack of academic freedom and institutional autonomy (QH Interview 10, Center Director).

This issue has a very different meaning for the universities in Hong Kong, where only the Western academic model is in operation with a need for incorporating more Chinese cultural elements. Singaporean universities are in a similar situation although their mode of governance has been far more Chinese than Western. Taiwanese universities have been doing many interesting experiments to combine Confucian-style tight control by the state with increasing institutional autonomy (TU Interview 2, Female, Mid-Level University Administrator). The efforts have been even more impressive in mainland China's recent higher education reforms.

There are strong grounds for combining Chinese and Western ideas of a university. Confucian culture is both supportive of university reforms and in line with the global trends toward a knowledge society. It has a remarkable capacity to accommodate other cultures and absorb some of their best elements into itself, integrating diverse streams of thought into an organic whole, as demonstrated by the introduction of Buddhism to China from India and its integration into Chinese cultural and educational development over a long period. If Chinese societies are to bring into the global community aspects of their rich educational and cultural heritage, which could open up new pathways through some of the current and potential dead ends, the case study flagship universities are the place we are likely to encounter these ideas.[45]

---

44. See Altbach, "The Past and Future of Asian Universities."
45. See Hayhoe, "Peking University and the Spirit of Chinese Scholarship."

The provisional and open perspective demonstrated by the people in Chinese societies, which is hard for those personally committed to more absolute faiths to comprehend, offers favorable conditions for the combination of both Chinese and Western traditions. It allows them to be able to appreciate opposing poles as a driving force and see opportunities in contradiction. The pragmatic approach to life further enables them to use whatever helpful means are available to settle or solve problems or issues.[46] Therefore, they do not have to choose between the seemingly contradictory Chinese and Western university models. Instead, they could have ambivalence and flexibility to achieve an integration of both, as a respondent from Taiwan's Tsing Hua University expressed:

> To say that ours are all bad is just not right. I think the two ends can be somewhat congruent, and this will eventually create a new model of education. (THU Interview 7, Faculty Dean)

Incorporating Chinese values could even bring something more than what people usually expect. An interviewee who was a dean and has a Western cultural background made the following points:

> Given my experiences of lecturing in the four societies, it can be said that [mainland] China's universities have something that Western universities lost maybe 50–60 years ago, which is the concept of respecting each other. Respect is not only a cultural issue here; it is actually intrinsically important to education. If there's no respect for people, knowledge, or ideas, how can a teacher teach, and how can educational exchange happen? There is something lost in the West over the past years. (HKU Interview 4, Faculty Dean)

---

46. Kam-Cheung Wong, "Chinese Culture and Leadership," *International Journal of Leadership in Education* 4, no. 4 (2001): 309–319.

Conclusion

In an essay on the historical trajectory of Christian higher education, Perry L. Glanzer borrowed the old iron curtain of communism only for the purposes of convenience, to divide Western and Eastern Europe, and declaimed that "universities as we know them today originated in Western Europe and not in other parts of the world."[1] He was echoing Jacques Verger, who earlier affirmed:[2]

> No one today would dispute the fact that universities, in the sense in which the term is now generally understood, were a creation of the Middle Ages, appearing for the first time between the twelfth and thirteenth centuries. It is no doubt true that other civilizations, prior to, or wholly alien to, the medieval West, such as the Roman Empire, Byzantium, Islam, or China, were familiar with forms of higher education which a number of historians, for the sake of convenience, have sometimes described as universities. Yet a closer look makes it plain that the institutional reality was altogether different and, no matter what has been said on the subject, there is no real link such as would justify us in associating them with medieval universities in the West. Until there is definite proof to the contrary, these latter must be regarded as the sole source of the model which gradually spread through the whole of Europe and then to the whole world. We are therefore concerned with what is indisputably an original institution, which can only be defined in terms of a historical analysis of its emergence and its mode of operation in concrete circumstances.

To non-Western societies, modern universities are indeed an imported concept. They originated from Europe, spreading worldwide from the mid-nineteenth century to the present time, mainly due to colonialism. Even the countries that

---

1. Perry L. Glanzer, "Will the Parent Abandon the Child? The Birth, Secularization, and Survival of Christian Higher Education in Western Europe," in *Christian Higher Education: A Global Reconnaissance*, ed. Joel A. Carpenter, Perry L. Glanzer, and Nicholas Lantinga (Grand Rapids, MI: William B. Eerdmans Publishing Company, 2014), 135.
2. Jacques Verger, "Patterns," in *A History of the University in Europe*, vol. 1, *Universities in the Middle Ages*, ed. Hilde de Ridder-Symoens (Cambridge: Cambridge University Press, 1992), 35.

escaped colonial domination adopted Western models as well, as Philip G. Altbach wrote:[3]

All university systems are a combination of national and international traditions. The basic model is European and goes back to the medieval universities of Paris and Bologna. These are the antecedents not only for the universities in North America and Europe, but also in Asia and Africa.

The inherited Western ideal of the solitary mendicant scholar, free to roam without interference and speak truth to the prelate and the prince, sits uneasily alongside the immense resources invested in contemporary universities charged with driving innovation, industry, and business in highly competitive national and international markets.[4] This is the basic reason for university inefficacy in non-Western societies.[5] In the case of Chinese societies, the strikingly different cultural roots and heritages have led to continuous conflicts between their traditional and the imposed Western values. Attempts to indigenize the Western idea of a university started, in a piecemeal way, with Matteo Ricci's arrival in China, which was the prologue to a massive play of China's embrace of Western learning. Foreign, especially American, missionary universities were set up in China and quickly became nationally and even internationally leading,[6] followed by China's earliest modern universities established by the Chinese. The lean to the former Soviet Union in the 1950s was also part of China's learning from and response to the West.[7] Recent decades have witnessed China's reentry into the international community. China looks again to the West for policy ideas and solutions to their own social problems.

Higher education systems in Chinese universities are twofold, the institutionalized one that is based on imported Western ideas and another informal (yet powerful) one that is underpinned by traditional values.[8] Although Western academic models have been shaping the universities over the twentieth century, bringing together aspects of their traditional and Western heritages has continued to be an arduous and unfinished task, ever since the nineteenth century. How the adopted

---

3. Altbach, "The American Academic Model in Comparative Perspective," 15.
4. John Fitzgerald, "Academic Freedom and the Contemporary University: Lessons from China," *Humanities Australia: The Journal of Australian Academy of the Humanities*, no. 8 (2017): 8–22, https://www.humanities.org.au/wp-content/uploads/2017/10/AAH-Hums-Aust-08-2017-Fitzgerald.pdf.
5. See Yang, "Self and the Other in the Confucian Cultural Context," 36.
6. Shen Dingping and Zhu Weifang, "Western Missionary Influence on the People's Republic of China: A Survey of Chinese Scholarly Opinion Between 1980 and 1990," *International Bulletin of Missionary Research* 22, no. 4 (1998): 154–158.
7. Perception of Russia and the Soviet Union is different in China from that in the West. In cultural and knowledge terms, Chinese people view Russia and the Soviet Union as part of the West, even if they might acknowledge it is a somewhat different from other parts of the so-called Western world. See Lo Bobo, *How the Chinese See Russia* (Paris: ifri Russia/NIS Center, 2010); and Sebastian Kaempf, "Russia: A Part of the West or Apart from the West?" *International Relations* 24, no. 3 (2010): 313–340.
8. I have discussed the two systems in my previous works. See, for example, Yang, "Reassessing China's Higher Education Development."

system functions in the societies depends much on its interactions with old traditions that remain deeply entrenched in people's mind and action. The cultural conflicts between Chinese and Western traditions have caused inefficacy of the higher education sectors in their service to the societies, both failing to grasp the essence of the Western academic model and losing the legacy of their higher learning traditions. None of the societies have figured out how to wed the standard norms of Western higher education with their traditions. The Western concept of a university has been taken only for its practicality.

Value disorder and confusion move beyond campuses. Since the institutionalization of the Western knowledge system, conflicts at the ideological level have never stopped. Although their intellectual mind should never be entirely transformed according to Western experiences, modern knowledge systems in all Chinese societies have been patterned after Western practices. The shift is part of their profound social transformation since the nineteenth century. At the same time, the complexity is that, even with their well-established modern knowledge systems that are based entirely on Western experience, all the societies continue to be greatly influenced by traditional values. Since the traditions have not been coherently incorporated into the institutionalized system, their legitimated knowledge does not match their socioeconomic realities. Therefore, despite some differentiation within the societies, they share certain ideological confusion that has been in the making ever since their early encounters with the West in the nineteenth century. The confusion is particularly evident among the educated elites, who often feel spiritually homeless and unsettled.

However, historical experience and lessons deserve our attention. For example, China successfully created a number of world-class universities over a century ago in its modern era of suffering. Such a fact is particularly significant for the theme of this book, because it demonstrates how tremendously China's early modern higher institutions achieved in integrating Chinese and Western ideas of higher learning. It proves that it is possible, albeit extremely difficult, for Chinese educators to adapt a Western model of the university to their Chinese situations. As a revealing facet of modern Chinese history, the achievement has great implications for university development today and deserves much research, especially when China intensifies the aspiration to catapult its premier universities to the forefront of global rankings. Unlike the Western idea of a university that developed as practical experience accumulated, the Chinese understanding of modern universities predated practice and came fast to its adulthood during the Late Qing reforms. Its high achievement in learning from the West was never surpassed later—not by the Communist Mainland, by Nationalist Taiwan, or by colonial Hong Kong.

Since the early twentieth century, missionary colleges have exerted a historical influence on the initial development of Chinese higher education and reached a considerably high level of sophistication of cultural hybridization of Chinese and Western intellectual traditions, even with a global vision of scholarship and a unique educational model. The institutions founded by the Chinese also achieved highly in absorbing Western learning to respond to the sharpening crisis facing the nation. China's early modern higher institutions strove hard to judiciously combine Western traditions with the ideological, intellectual, cultural, and educational specificity of the Chinese. Their developments are characterized most prominently by a combination at the individual, institutional, and systemic levels in managing relations between China and the West in education, scholarship, and university operations. It was reached soon after the Western concept of a university was introduced into China, setting high bars even for today's practice. Such a fact tells us that neither finance nor ideology is the root cause. The crux is cultural. Chinese societies have much to learn from their own history, especially from modern times, when early encounters between Chinese and Western traditions occurred.[9]

Based on both the accomplishments and limitations of higher education development in the four Chinese societies, this book attempts to bring together theory and practice, personal reflections and empirical realities. Three observations can be made here to conclude it.

First, higher education development in the four Chinese societies is part of their much wider pursuit of cultural modernity. In this sense, their higher education development can be viewed as an experiment to explore how non-Western societies should effectively respond to the globally predominant Western influence that has already become a precondition for modernization of all other societies. Globalization has now penetrated the deepest crevices of human endeavor, and many incongruous facets of human existence have been forced together into a giant tumbler,[10] bringing all peoples into direct contact at all times for the first time in human history. The moral and intellectual ground for coexistence and codetermination is fast increasing. Knowledge of and respect for others have become a necessity for the sustainability of any society.[11] The global studies in higher education, however, have largely neglected a basic fact that all the main spiritual and philosophical traditions that emerged independently in various parts of the world during the Axial Age must understand each other amid a second Axial Age.[12]

As a result of the world *history* of recent centuries, various traditions are not on an equal footing at the present time. All other traditions have to respond to the dominant Western one. To non-Western societies, development practically means

9. Rui Yang, "World-Class Universities in China's Heroic Past," *International Higher Education* 107, Summer (2021): 18–19.

10. Catherine A. Odora Hoppers, "Education, Culture and Society in a Globalizing World: Implications for Comparative and International Education," *Compare: A Journal of Comparative and International Education* 39, no. 5 (2009): 601–614.

11. Rui Yang, "Baby and Bathwater or Soup? Some Epistemological Considerations of How to Observe China and Chinese Education," *Globalization, Societies and Education* 20, no. 1 (2022): 49–55.

12. For the Axial Age, see Karl Jaspers, *The Origin and Goal of History* (London: Routledge, 2010). For the second Axial Age, see Wei-Ming Tu, "Confucian Humanism as a Spiritual Resource for Global Ethics," *Peace and Conflict Studies* 16, no. 1 (2009): 1–8.

responding successfully to the West. Without Western knowledge, neither national nor individual development could be possible in any society today. The Western mode of development with its accompanying Eurocentric knowledge systems has been adopted widely throughout the rest of the world. Non-Western societies are pressured to significantly incorporate Western knowledge and values. Due to such unequal cultural relations, they must find ways to incorporate the West without losing their own identities. Although many of them gained political independence in the twentieth century, few have accomplished greatly in managing such difficult relations. This is also the case with the four Chinese societies. Higher education has been designated such an important mission. In this sense, the growing bicultural intellectual mind manifested at various levels in their higher education systems is a significant achievement to embrace Western learning as one of the most important elements of their contemporary knowledge systems.[13]

As a significant contributor to the gathering power of Chinese societies in the present world economy and politics, their higher education assumes global importance and engages extensively.[14] For the first time since the nineteenth century, the people and institutions in the systems appear to be increasingly confident and capable of managing the longstanding difficult relations with their Western counterparts. Their experiment is intellectually liberating to encourage a broader search for possibilities that more than one tradition can contribute to a university development model. A cultural lens needs to be emphasized in the studies of the university and higher education to give weight to the impact of traditional ways of cultural thinking on contemporary development. For the four Chinese societies, their experiment is unprecedented in history in both the nature and the accomplishment of their endeavor. For the vast non-Western world, their pursuit is evidently rich in international significance.

The rich experiences of the four Chinese societies remind us that any discussion of the idea of a university today has to be preconditioned by the fact that Western academic models have become globally dominant. For non-Western societies, instead of searching for alternatives to the Western model, a realistic approach is to find creative ways to incorporate the West without losing their own cultural identities. This is why higher education development in the four societies could be seen as a cultural experiment, having significant implications for many other non-Western societies. It is fundamentally about the relations between Chinese and Western cultural values. Whether or not the societies can fulfill their long-desired integration between the two value systems is the true meaning of and biggest challenge for their higher education development. However, in the hustle and bustle of higher education reforms, although universities are by nature cultural institutions,

---

13. Reagan, *Non-Western Educational Traditions.*
14. Simon Marginson and Lili Yang, "Individual and Collective Outcomes of Higher Education: A Comparison of Anglo-American and Chinese Approaches," *Globalization, Societies and Education* 20, no. 1 (2022): 1–31.

their historical role and cultural mission are much neglected, leading to incomplete, inappropriate, and even misleading assessments of their contemporary and future development.

Second, and more specifically, according to "the idea of a university," higher education development in Chinese societies enriches, rather than overturns, the currently dominant academic models that are European in structure, organization, and concept.[15] As noted throughout previous chapters, this is caused by historical fact, especially through Western colonization in the nineteenth century. Colonizers showed little interest in intellectual pluralism. Indeed, what happed in history was just the opposite. Whether this is a curse or a blessing, it is a fact that Western influence has been deeply rooted in nearly all non-Western societies. Simple rejection on the basis of the Western character is no longer a feasible approach for non-Western societies in socioeconomic development in general and in cultural and higher education development more particularly. The truly critical part is to combine the Western with the traditional. While the dominance of Western knowledge needs to be seriously interrogated,[16] an appropriate attitude toward Western knowledge is strategically significant.

Universities have a long historical tradition and a sense of continuity over time. The nineteenth century saw the diffusion of the European model of the university throughout much of the world under conditions of imperialism and colonialism. The basic scholarly values of the European university can be summed up in the concepts of autonomy and academic freedom, in the pursuit of truth by empirical and rational methods, and the study of important texts in law, religion, literature, and philosophy.[17] The autonomy of the medieval universities was relative. The "idea of a university" has always been in a state of change. The US "land-grant" model successfully combined the Humboldtian emphasis on research and science and the key role of the state in supporting higher education based on the idea of public service and applied technology. While the American university traces its roots to the English tradition of the college, the Soviet university owes a considerable debt to both the German and French models. The change has generally been a process of evolution. The observation made by Philip G. Altbach nearly fifty years ago has remained fundamentally unaltered:[18]

---

15. Altbach, "Peripheries and Centers: Research Universities in Developing Countries."
16. There has been a wealth of literature on global knowledge asymmetries and the unequal international relations in education. For knowledge production in the social sciences in the context of globalization, see Leandro Rodriguez Medina, *Centers and Peripheries in Knowledge Production* (New York: Routledge 2013); Wiebke Keim, Ercüment Çelik, Veronika Wöhrer, and Christian Ersche, eds., *Global Knowledge Production in the Social Sciences: Made in Circulation* (Farnham: Ashgate 2014).
17. Rashdall, *The Universities of Europe in the Middle Ages*, 362. See also Gabriel Compayré, *Abelard and the Origin and Early History of Universities* (New York: AMS Press, 1969), 87–90.
18. Philip G. Altbach, *University Reform: An International Perspective* (Washington, DC: American Association for Higher Education, 1980), 5.

Virtually all the modern world's universities are based on the Western model, which can be traced to the medieval universities of Paris (the dominant model organized by the faculty) and Bologna (developed by the students). Oxford and Cambridge, later developments of the medieval models, were the prototypes for North American institutions, and the nineteenth-century German university served as the basis for graduate education in the United States, Japan, and the rest of Europe. Even the universities of the Third World are almost exclusively Western in origin either imposed by colonialism or freely adopted in the struggle for modernization.

Indeed, higher education in all four societies has been discussed to a great extent as a Western term with Chinese caveats. None of the societies has been seeking a distinctive pattern by design. While their strategies have often appeared to be top-down and carefully planned, their practice has been largely experimental and even improvisational in the university development model despite many contrasting approaches and strategies among them.[19] However, this does not mean that they blindly follow the Western model. Consciously and unconsciously their experiment has been based on their sociocultural actualities, while their consequences have not been always as originally expected. Their successes and failures have repeatedly confirmed plurality as the only possibility, because it allows the space for both traditions to interact with each other, instead of mutual exclusivity. From a historical and cultural perspective, higher education development in the societies is a continuity and part of their much wider social transformations to foster their modernity as a response to the West, based on their own roots.

From the lens of higher education, all the societies respond to the dominant Western models of academic development. They only search for effective approaches and strategies, rather than looking for an alternative to the Western model. Such an attitude does not negate the need for innovative thinking, especially because the relations between their traditional and Western ideas of higher learning are often conflicting. According to the predominant Western model of university development, by both intention and reality, their experiment has been more an evolution, or at most reform, rather than a revolution. Their extensive higher education development over the previous decades compares especially remarkably with those of most other non-Western societies. While some scholars point out the fact that the notion of "world-class" status in the societies has been largely imitative rather than

---

19. Such an experimental sense and almost improvisational approach toward governance in higher education is a hallmark of the reforms in the societies, mainland China as the best example. This is important to note with strong theoretical and practical implications. Looking retrospectively and holistically, their reforms did not stop because there was never an absolute blueprint about what a world-class Chinese higher education system and/or university would look like at the end of the reform process. This can be seen as a continuity of Deng Xiaoping's pragmatist legacy, as shown by his theories of "Black Cat White Cat" and "Crossing the River by Feeling the Stones." For Deng's pragmatist legacy, see Lucian W. Pye, "On Chinese Pragmatism in the 1980s," *The China Quarterly* 106, June (1986): 207–234.

creative as a criticism,[20] I would argue that this is perhaps precisely the reason for the systems to be able to achieve so much, given Western supremacy as the basic condition in global higher education.

All four Chinese societies aspire to create truly world-class universities, which calls for an integration between their traditional and Western ideas of a university. A university rooted in Chinese educational heritage does not have to reject Western knowledge while providing services to their communities. The efforts and achievements by Chinese societies show real possibility of carrying forward and even further developing the presently dominant Western model by exploring how they have, and have not, achieved in establishing world-class universities on their soil, and how their experience could contribute to the betterment of the "idea of a university." All the societies have demonstrated both an embracing attitude toward and rich knowledge of the West. For their higher education and academic elites, it is impossible to discuss education without mentioning the West. After a century of painstaking learning from the West, there is a real possibility of striking a balance between Chinese and Western ideas of a university that have been conventionally perceived as mutually exclusive.

Chinese societies will never be fully Westernized, nor should they be. Many fundamental differences between Chinese and Western cultural values make it impossible to fully assimilate each other. Higher education systems in Chinese societies have been resilient and active in shaping their own agendas. The fact that there was no real parallel in the Chinese tradition to the notion of academic freedom that emerged in Europe has long been cited as the fundamental reason for tensions.[21] However, their remarkable progress over the past decades proves that they can learn effectively from the West to enable themselves to turn Western academic models to serve their own needs. A move from passivity to proactivity is in the making in all the four societies. Thanks to stellar achievements, successful reconciliation between significant aspects of Chinese and Western philosophical heritages appears to be increasingly likely. As their flagship universities become internationally leading, rich Chinese intellectual traditions have the strengths to contribute greatly to the idea of a university.

Third, higher education development in the four Chinese societies reiterates that an impassable chasm between Chinese and Western ideas of a university does not exist.[22] The lingering dominance of the Western model of university

---

20. Kathryn Mohrman, "Sino-American Educational Exchange and the Drive to Create World-class Universities," in *Bridging Minds across the Pacific: U.S.-China Educational Exchanges, 1978–2003*, ed. Cheng Li (Lanham, MD: Lexington Books, 2005), 219–235.
21. See Hayhoe, "Ideas of Higher Learning, East and West," 372.
22. See Peters, "Ancient Centers of Higher Learning," 1063.

development needs to be questioned.[23] Indeed, having a Gramscian hegemony,[24] the Western university has been seen as natural, normal, and generally beneficial almost everywhere throughout the world, including places without a colonial past.[25] Recently, however, the notion of the global university as one thing is being seriously challenged. While there can be little doubt that the age of the global university is upon us, there is little consensus on how it exactly looks. Universities exist in specific places and are inevitably shaped by local traditions, political conflicts, resource limitations, and competitive pressures. Gathering evidence points to an emerging fact that the global university can take many forms as it responds to an array of social, economic, and political forces that stem from particular historical contexts.

The studies of recent higher education development in the Chinese societies further confirm that some conventional understanding of the European university is insufficiently well based. The university has been seen as "the European institution par excellence."[26] It is said to be peculiar to medieval Europe as a form of social organization.[27] Such claims are increasingly questioned, especially recently. If the "university" was a European institution, it is no longer exclusively the child of medieval Europe.[28] Rather, it is now truly a global institution with national and regional characteristics, often grafted onto institutions and traditions of higher learning that predate the birth of the medieval university. While the university was peculiar to medieval Europe as a form of organization, it is only one form that ancient centers of higher learning took. There were organizational forms of higher learning peculiar to India, China, and the Middle East that considerably predate the European form.

The experience of Chinese societies contributes to challenging the idea that there is a single path for higher education in an age of global social and economic development. To a large extent this perspective flows from a historical interpretive vantage point. As we know, in their course of development, universities in non-Western societies clearly face a different set of issues from those of their counterparts in North America and Europe. This book has investigated both the historical and contemporary circumstances of modern university development in a major cultural sphere in the world. By so doing, it offers a useful corrective to much of the extant literature on the global university, which has failed to capture the richness

---

23. See, for example, Sharon Stein, "The Persistent Challenges of Addressing Epistemic Dominance in Higher Education: Considering the Case of Curriculum Internationalization," *Comparative Education Review* 61 (S1, 2017): s25–s50.

24. Benedetto Fontana, *Hegemony and Power: On the Relation between Gramsci and Machiavelli* (Minneapolis, MN: University of Minnesota Press, 1993), 57.

25. See, for example, John N. Hawkins, "East-West? Tradition and the Development of Hybrid Higher Education in Asia," in *The Dynamics of Higher Education Development in East Asia*, ed. Deane Neubauer, Jung Cheol Shin, and John N. Hawkins (New York: Palgrave Macmillan, 2013), 51–67.

26. Rüegg, "Foreword. The University as a European Institution," xix.

27. George Makdisi, "Madrasa and University in the Middle Ages," *Studia Islamica* 32, no. 1 (1970): 255–264.

28. See Peters, "Ancient Centers of Higher Learning," 1063.

of the diversity. While this volume does not attempt to reach any final conclusion, it aims to facilitate vigorous debates in both policy and scholarly circles on this increasingly important theme. As globalization reframes traditional conceptions of the university, calls are growing fast for further work on this subject. Taking a broad historical perspective, it places the challenges facing today's universities in historical context and reveals that the global university is not one thing but many.

The European university has not been accurately understood even by its definitive characteristics: academic freedom and institutional autonomy. Its freedom and autonomy were neither absolute nor unswerving in history. Most of its specific characteristics could also be found in other institutions of higher learning and knowledge production in non-Western societies. While academic autonomy is possibly the only distinguishing characteristic attributed to the European university by a wide consensus, the university has never been truly autonomous from its sociopolitical context, which makes the claim to exceptionality of the European university highly questionable.[29] The uniqueness of the European university is diluted as the rest of the world establishes universities underpinned by Western values of academic freedom and institutional autonomy. Ironically, while such values are increasingly cherished in many parts of the world, they face growing threat in their own heartland. Universities in the Western tradition find themselves at the mercy of their governments.[30]

For a long time, becoming international has meant treading in Western steps in the face of overweening power from the West. Every move made during the past one and a half centuries was to respond to the dominant Western model although the moves were supposed to be based solidly on the local footing. Central to the development of higher education, however, has been the promise of a successful synthesis of knowledge drawn from the best of Chinese and Western traditions, something that remains more tantalizing (even elusive) than real in the eyes of some people. Higher education development in Chinese societies has always been a dual process of cultural homogenization and Westernization. The growing bicultural mind is intellectually liberating to equip their universities, especially the elite ones, to accomplish the cultural mission to embrace Western values and cleave to Chinese traditions, challenging the seemingly contradictory Chinese and Western ideas of a university. Moving beyond an either-or dilemma, it provides much food for thought for most other non-Western societies as well.

29. Dmitrishin, "Deconstructing Distinctions."
30. Minogue, "The Collapse of the Academic in Britain."

Bibliography

Adler, Jerry. "The Reformation: Can Social Scientists Save Themselves?" *Pacific Standard*, April 28, 2014. https://psmag.com/the-reformation-can-social-scientists-save-themselves-8c2f834715a7.

Akomolafe, Adebayo, and Ijeoma Dike. "Decolonizing Education: Enunciating the Emancipatory Promise of Non-Western Aternatives to Higher Education." Paper presentated at the XII International Seminar on Globalization of Higher Education: Challenges & Opportunities, New Delhi, India, January 4–5, 2011.

Allen, Ryan M., and Ji Liu. *Kuo Ping Wen: Scholar, Reformer, Statesman*. San Francisco, CA: Long River Press, 2016.

Altbach, Philip G. *University Reform: An International Perspective*. Washington, DC: American Association for Higher Education, 1980.

Altbach, Philip G. "Twisted Roots: The Western Impact on Asian Higher Education." *Higher Education* 18, no. 1 (1989): 9–29.

Altbach, Philip G. *Comparative Higher Education: Knowledge, the University and Development*. Hong Kong: Comparative Education Research Centre, University of Hong Kong, 1998.

Altbach, Philip G. "The American Academic Model in Comparative Perspective." In *In Defense of American Higher Education*, edited by Philip G. Altbach, Patricia J. Gumport, and D. Bruce Johnstone, 11–37. Baltimore, MD: Johns Hopkins University Press, 2001.

Altbach, Philip G. "The Costs and Benefits of World-Class Universities." *International Higher Education* 33, Fall (2003): 5–8.

Altbach, Philip G. "The Complex Roles of Universities in the Period of Globalization." In *Higher Education in the World 3: Higher Education: New Challenges and Emerging Roles for Human and Social Development*, edited by Global University Network for Innovation (GUNi), 5–14. Basingstoke: Palgrave Macmillan, 2008.

Altbach, Philip G. "Peripheries and Centers: Research Universities in Developing Countries." *Asia Pacific Education Review* 10, no. 1 (2009): 15–27.

Altbach, Philip G. "The Asian Higher Education Century?" *International Higher Education* 59, Spring (2010): 3–5.

Altbach, Philip G. *The International Imperative in Higher Education*. Boston, MA: Center for International Higher Education, Boston College, 2013.

Altbach, Philip G. "Chinese Higher Education: 'Glass Ceiling' and 'Feet of Clay.'" *International Higher Education* 86, Summer (2016): 11–13.

Ball, Philip. "China's Great Leap Forward in Science." *The Guardian*, February 18, 2018. https://www.theguardian.com/science/2018/feb/18/china-great-leap-forward-science-research-innovation-investment-5g-genetics-quantum-internet.

Ban Gu 班固. *Hanshu* 漢書 [Book of Han]. Beijing: Zhonghua Book Company, 1962.

Beijingdaxue 北京大學, and Zhongguo diyi lishi danganguan 中國第一歷史檔案館, eds. *Jingshidaxuetang dangan xuanbian* 京師大學堂檔案選編 [Selected archives of the Imperial University of Peking]. Beijing: Peking University Press, 2001.

Bickers, Robert. "Restoration and Reform: 1860–1900." In *The Oxford Illustrated History of Modern China*, edited by Jeffrey N. Wasserstrom, 63–89. Oxford: Oxford University Press, 2016.

Biggerstaff, Knight. *The Earliest Modern Government Schools in China*. Ithaca, NY: Cornell University Press, 1961.

Bodde, Derk. *Chinese Ideas in the West: Asiatic Studies in American Education, No. 3*. Ann Arbor, MI: UMI, 1994.

Boehler, Patrick. "China Spending More than Europe on Science and Technology as GDP Percentage, New Figures Reveal." *South China Morning Post*, January 21, 2014.

Boulton, Geoffrey, and Colin Lucas, "What Are Universities For?" *Chinese Science Bulletin* 56, no. 23 (2011): 2506–2517.

Bové, Paul A. *Edward Said and the Work of the Critic: Speaking Truth to Power*. Durham, NC: Duke University Press, 2000.

Brook, Timothy. "Rethinking Syncretism: The Unity of the Three Teachings and their Joint Worship in Late-Imperial China." *Journal of Chinese Religions* 21, no. 1 (1993): 13–44.

Cai Xianjin 蔡先金. "Daxue zhiming yu Zhongguo jindai daxue qiyuan kaobian" 大學之名與中國近代大學起源考辨 [The concept of *daxue* and the origin of China's modern universities]. *Journal of Higher Education* 高等教育研究 38, no. 1 (2017): 73–80.

Cao, Yannan and Rui Yang. "World-Class University Construction and Higher Education Governance Reform in China: A Policy Trajectory." In *The Governance and Management of Universities in Asia*, edited by Chang Da Wan, Molly N. N. Lee, and Hoe Yeong Loke (New York: Routledge, 2019), 21–42.

Chan Egan, Susan. *A Latterday Confucian: Reminiscences of William Hung (1893–1980)*. Cambridge, MA: Harvard University Press, 1987.

Chan, Sheng-Ju, and Chia-Yu Yang. "Governance Styles in Taiwanese Universities: Features and Effects." *International Journal of Educational Development* 63, C (2018): 29–35.

Chang Hao 張灝. "Zhongguo jindai sixiangshi de zhuanxing shidai" 中國近代思想史的轉型時代 [An age of transformation in modern Chinese intellectual history]. *Twenty-First Century* 二十一世紀 52, no. 4 (1999): 29–39.

Chen Dongyuan 陳東原. *Dierci Zhongguo jiaoyu nianjian* 第二次中國教育年鑒 [The second Chinese yearbook of education]. Shanghai: Commercial Press, 1948.

Chen Jingpan 陳景磐. *Zhongguo jindai jiaoyushi* 中國近代教育史 [Modern history of Chinese education]. Taipei: Biographical Literature Publishing House, 1986.

Chen, Jingpan. *Confucius as a Teacher: Philosophy of Confucius with Special Reference to Its Educational Implications*. Beijing: China Foreign Languages Press, 1990.

Chen Yinke 陳寅恪. "Feng Youlan Zhongguo zhexueshi xiace shencha baogao" 馮友蘭《中國哲學史》下冊審查報告 [Report on my inspection of vol. 2 of Feng Youlan's history of Chinese philosophy]. In *Chen Yinke Ji* 陳寅恪集 [The works of Chen Yinke], vol. 2, 282–286. Beijing: Sanlian shudian, 2001.

Chen Yuan 陳遠. *Yanjing daxue 1919-1952* 燕京大學 1919–1952 [Yenching University, 1919–1952]. Hangzhou: Zhejiang renmin chubanshe, 2013.

Chen Yuanhui 陳元暉. *Zhongguo gudai de shuyuan zhidu* 中國古代的書院制度 [Academies in ancient China]. Shanghai: Shanghai Education Press, 1981.

Chen Yuanhui 陳元暉, Chen Xuexun 陳學恂, and Tian Zhengping 田正平, eds. *Zhongguo jindai jiaoyushi ziliao huibian: Yangwu yundong shiqi jiaoyu* 中國近代教育史資料彙編：洋務運動時期教育 [Collected documents on the modern history of Chinese education]. Shanghai: Shanghai Education Press, 2007.

Cheng, Chungying. "Philosophical Globalization as Reciprocal Valuation and Mutual Integration: Comments on the Papers of Tang Yijie and Roger Ames." In *Dialogue of Philosophies, Religions and Civilizations in the Era of Globalization*, edited by Zhao Dunhua, 65–76. Washington DC: The Council for Research in Values and Philosophy, 2007.

Cheung, Anthony B. L. "Mission of University: Excellence with a Soul." In *The Way Towards Great Learning*, edited by the Hong Kong Institute of Education, 12–15. Hong Kong: The Hong Kong Institute of Education, 2011.

Cheung, Chan-Fai, and Guangxin Fan. "The Chinese Idea of University, 1866–1895." In *Transmitting the Ideal of Enlightenment: Chinese Universities since the Late Nineteenth Century*, edited by Ricardo King Sang Mak, 13–33. Lanham, MD: University of Press of America, 2009.

Choi, Wan-Gee. *The Traditional Education of Korea*. Seoul: Ewha Womans University Press, 2006.

Choung, Jae-Yong. "Editorial Paper: Transition: From Catchup to Post Catch-up." *Asian Journal of Technology Innovation* 24, no. 1 (2016): 1–7.

Chu, Samuel C., and Kwang-Ching Liu, eds. *Li Hung-chang and China's Early Modernization*. Armonk, NY: M. E. Sharpe, 1994.

Clark, Charles Allen. *Religions of Old Korea*. New York: Garland Publishing Inc., 1981.

Clark, Kerr. "The Internal and External Threats to the University of the Twenty-First Century (with Comments)." *Minerva* 30, no. 2 (1992): 130–162.

Classen, Peter. "Associations of Teachers and Learners: The Medieval View of the University." *Western European Education* 13, no. 3 (1981): 28–37.

Cleverley, John. *Schooling of China: Tradition and Modernity in Chinese Education*. Sydney: Allen & Unwin, 1985.

Cohen, Paul A. *Discovering History in China: American Historical Writing on the Recent Chinese Past*. New York: Columbia University Press, 2010.

Compagnucci, Lorenzo, and Francesca Spigarelli. "The Third Mission of the University: A Systematic Literature Review on Potentials and Constraints." *Technological Forecasting and Social Change* 161, C (2020): 1–30.

Compayré, Gabriel. *Abelard and the Origin and Early History of Universities*. New York: AMS Press, 1969.

Cooke, Nola. "Nineteenth-Century Vietnamese Confucianization in Historical Perspective: Evidence from the Palace Examinations (1463–1883)." *Journal of Southeast Asian Studies* 25, no. 2 (1994): 275–312.

Cooke, Philip, and Loet Leydesdorff. "Regional Development in the Knowledge-Based Economy: The Construction of Advantage." *The Journal of Technology Transfer* 31, no. 1 (2006): 5–15.

Cunich, Peter. *A History of the University of Hong Kong Vol. 1, 1911–1945*. Hong Kong: Hong Kong University Press, 2012.

Davie, Sandra. "Singapore Universities Offered 17,500 Places Last Year, 1,000 More Than Planned." *The Straits Times*, January 18, 2021, https://www.straitstimes.com/singapore/parenting-education/17500-varsity-places-given-out-last-year-1000-more-than-planned.

Day, Huangfu Jenny. "Searching for the Roots of Western Wealth and Power: Guo Songtao and Education in Victorian England." *Late Imperial China* 35, no. 1 (2014): 1–37.

de Ridder-Symoens, Hilde, ed. *A History of the University in Europe*. Vol. I: *Universities in the Middle Ages*. Cambridge: Cambridge University Press, 1992.

de Ridder-Symoens, Hilde, ed. *A History of the University in Europe*. Vol. II: *Universities in Early Modern Europe (1500–1800)*. Cambridge: Cambridge University Press, 1996.

Dmitrishin, Alexander. "Deconstructing Distinctions: The European University in Comparative Historical Perspective." *Entremons: UPF Journal of World History* 5, no. 5 (2013): 1–18.

Ebrey, Patricia Buckley. *The Cambridge Illustrated History of China*. Cambridge: Cambridge University Press, 1999.

Eisenstadt, Shmuel Noah. *Tradition, Change, and Modernity*. New York: John Wiley and Sons, 1973.

Elliott, Julian, and Elena Grigorenko, eds. *Western Psychological and Educational Theory in Diverse Contexts*. London: Routledge, 2007.

Etzkowitz, Henry. "The Second Academic Revolution and the Rise of Entrepreneurial Science." *IEEE Technology and Society Magazine* 20, no. 2 (2001): 18–29.

Etzkowitz, Henry. *Triple Helix Innovation: Industry, University, and Government in Action*. New York: Routledge, 2008.

Euna, Jong-Hak, and Keun Lee. "Explaining the 'University-Run Enterprises' in China: A Theoretical Framework for University-Industry Relationship in Developing Countries and Its Application to China." *Research Policy* 35, no. 9 (2006): 1329–1346.

Fairbank, John K., and Albert Feuerwerker, eds. *The Cambridge History of China, Vol. 13: Republican China 1912–1949*, Part 2. Cambridge: Cambridge University Press, 1986.

Fitzgerald, John. "Academic Freedom and the Contemporary University: Lessons from China." *Humanities Australia: The Journal of Australian Academy of the Humanities*, no. 8 (2017): 8–22. https://www.humanities.org.au/wp-content/uploads/2017/10/AAH-Hums-Aust-08-2017-Fitzgerald.pdf.

Foltz, Richard. *Religions of the Silk Road: Premodern Patterns of Globalization*. New York: Palgrave Macmillan, 2010.

Fontana, Benedetto. *Hegemony and Power: On the Relation between Gramsci and Machiavelli*. Minneapolis, MN: University of Minnesota Press, 1993.

Fox, Charles J., and Hugh T. Miller. "Practices of the Guild: A Declaration of Independence." *Administrative Theory and Praxis* 20, no. 2 (1998): 142–158.

Frédéric, Louis. *Japan Encyclopedia*. Cambridge, MA: Harvard University Press, 2002.

Fu Sinian 傅斯年. "Wang Guowei zhu Song-Yuan xiqu shi" 王國維著《宋元戲曲史》 [Review of Wang Guowei's Song-Yuan *xiqu shi*]. In *Fu Sinian quanji* 傅斯年全集 [Collections of Fu Sinian], edited by Ouyang Zhesheng 歐陽哲生, 111–113. Changsha: Hunan Education Publishing House, 2003.

Fung, Yu-lan. *A Short History of Chinese Philosophy*. New York: Macmillan, 1948.

Gan Yang 甘陽. *Huaren daxue yu tongshi jiaoyu* 華人大學與通識教育 [Chinese universities and general education]. Beijing: Sanlian Bookstore, 2002.

Gan, Yang. "The Chinese Idea of Universities and the Beida Reform." *Chinese Education and Society* 37, no. 6 (2004): 85–97.

Gan, Yang. "The Beida Reform Follows the Example of 'Peach Pickers' but Should Spend More Time 'Planting Peach Trees.'" *Chinese Education and Society* 38, no. 1 (2005): 75–79.

Giles, John, Albert Park, and Meiyan Wang. "The Great Proletarian Cultural Revolution, Disruptions to Education, and the Returns to Schooling in Urban China." *Economic Development and Cultural Change* 68, no. 1 (2019): 131–164.

Glanzer, Perry L. "Will the Parent Abandon the Child? The Birth, Secularization, and Survival of Christian Higher Education in Western Europe." In *Christian Higher Education: A Global Reconnaissance*, edited by Joel A. Carpenter, Perry L. Glanzer, and Nicholas Lantinga, 134–162. Grand Rapids, MI: William B. Eerdmans Publishing Company, 2014.

Gleason, Nancy W. "Singapore's Higher Education Systems in the Era of the Fourth Industrial Revolution: Preparing Lifelong Learners." In *Higher Education in the Era of the Fourth Industrial Revolution*, edited by Nancy W. Gleason, 145–169. Singapore: Palgrave Macmillan, 2018.

Global University Network for Innovation (GUNi). *Towards a Socially Responsible University: Balancing the Global with the Local*. Girona: GUNi, 2017.

Grayson, James H. *Korea: A Religious History*. Oxford: Clarendon Press, 1989.

Grigorenko, Elena L. "Hitting, Missing, and in Between: A Typology of the Impact of Western Education on the Non-Western World." *Comparative Education* 43, no. 1 (2007): 165–186.

Guo Qijia 郭齊家. *Zhongguo gudai xuexiao* 中國古代學校 [Schools in ancient China]. Beijing: Commercial Press, 1998.

Guo Songtao 郭嵩燾. *Lundun Bali riji* 倫敦與巴黎日記 [Diaries on visits to London and Paris]. Changsha: Yulu shushe, 1984.

Hall, David L., and Roger T. Ames. "A Pragmatist Understanding of Confucian Democracy." In *Confucianism for the Modern World*, edited by Daniel A. Bell and Hahm Chaibong, 124–160. Cambridge: Cambridge University Press, 2003.

Hamilton, Gary, and Xiangqun Chang. "China and World Anthropology: A Conversation on the Legacy of Fei Xiaotong (1910–2005)." *Anthropology Today* 27, no. 6 (2011): 20–23.

Han, SoongHee. "Confucian States and Learning Life: Making Scholar-Officials and Social Learning a Political Contestation." *Comparative Education* 49, no. 1 (2013): 57–71.

Hansen, Valerie. "Path of Buddhism into China: The View from Turfan." *Asia Major* 11, no. 2 (1998): 37–66.

Hartnett, Richard. *The Jixia Academy and the Birth of Higher Learning in China*. Lewiston, NY: Edwin Mellen Press, 2011.

Hawkins, John N. "East-West? Tradition and the Development of Hybrid Higher Education in Asia." In *The Dynamics of Higher Education Development in East Asia*, edited by Deane Neubauer, Jung Cheol Shin, and John N. Hawkins, 51–67. New York: Palgrave Macmillan, 2013.

Hayhoe, Ruth. "Towards the Forging of a Chinese University Ethos: Zhendan and Fudan, 1903–1919." *The China Quarterly* 94 (1983): 323–341.

Hayhoe, Ruth. "China's Universities and Western Academic Models." *Higher Education* 18, no. 1 (1989): 49–85.

Hayhoe, Ruth. "Ideas of Higher Learning East and West: Conflicting Values in the Development of the Chinese University." *Minerva* 32, no. 4 (1994): 361–382.

Hayhoe, Ruth. *China's Universities 1895–1995: A Century of Cultural Conflict*. New York: Garland, 1996.

Hayhoe, Ruth. "Lessons from the Chinese Academy." In *Knowledge across Cultures: A Contribution to Dialogue among Civilisations*, edited by Ruth Hayhoe and Julia Pan, 334–370. Hong Kong: Comparative Education Research Centre, the University of Hong Kong, 2001.

Hayhoe, Ruth. "Peking University and the Spirit of Chinese Scholarship." *Comparative Education Review* 49, no. 4 (2005): 575–583.

Hayhoe, Ruth. "The Gift of Indian Higher Learning Traditions to the Global Research University." *Asia Pacific Journal of Education* 39, no. 2 (2019): 177–189.

Hayhoe, Ruth, and Jian Liu. "China's Universities, Cross-Border Education, and Dialogue among Civilizations." In *Crossing Borders in East Asian Higher Education*, edited by David W. Chapman, William K. Cummings, and Gerard A. Postiglione, 77–100. Hong Kong: Springer/Comparative Education Research Center, The University of Hong Kong, 2010.

He Shuangsheng 何雙生. "Zongli geguo shiwu yamen" 總理各國事務衙門 [Prime Minister's office of affairs concerning various nations]. In *Zhongguo da baike quanshu* 中國大百科全書 *Zhongguo lishi* 中國歷史 [Encyclopedia of China: History of China], Vol. 3, 1626–1627. Beijing: Zhongguo da baike quanshu chubanshe, 1992.

Hsieh, Ming-Yuan. "Online Learning Era: Exploring the Most Decisive Determinants of MOOCs in Taiwanese Higher Education." *Eurasia Journal of Mathematics, Science & Technology Education* 12, no. 5 (2016): 1163–1188.

Hu Ning 胡寧, and Liu Baocun 劉寶存. "Zhongguo gudian daxue de linian jiqi xiandai yiyi" 中國古典大學的理念及其現代意義 [The idea of China's classical universities and its modern implications]. *Journal of Nanjing University of Science and Technology* 南京理工大學學報 19, no. 3 (2006): 69–72.

Huang, Chun-chieh, ed. *East Asian Confucianisms: Texts in Contexts*. Taipei: National Taiwan University Press and Vandenhoeck & Ruprecht, 2015.

Huang Chun-chieh 黃俊傑. "Ershiyi shiji daxue linian de jidang yu tongshi jiaoyu de zhanwang" 二十一世紀大學理念的激蕩與通識教育的展望 [The turbulent idea of a university in the twenty-first century and the prospect of general education]. *Higher Education Development and Evaluation* 高教發展與評估 36, no. 5 (2020): 1–19.

Huang Ji 黃濟. "Zhongguo gudai jiaoyu zhexue sixiang de fazhan lichen ji zhuyao tedian" 中國古代教育哲學思想的發展歷程及主要特點 [Educational philosophy in ancient

China: Developmental stages and characteristics]. *Journal of Beijing Normal University* 北京師範大學學報 6 (1994): 28–34.

Huang Qingcheng 黃慶澄. "Dongyou riji" 東遊日記 [The diary of this journey to the East]. In *Jiawu yiqian riben youji wuzhong* 甲午以前日本遊記五種 [Five travelogues on Japan before 1894], edited by He Ruzhang 何如, 319–380. Changsha: Yulu shushe, 1985.

Hung, Ruyu. "Eastern Asian Higher Education at the Crossroads: A Reflection of the Accreditation/Evaluation System of Universities in Taiwan." *National Chiayi University Journal of the Educational Research* 嘉大教育研究學刊 34, no. 3 (2015): 1–24.

Hunter, Jane. *The Gospel of Gentility: American Women Missionaries in Turn-of-the-Century China*. New Haven, CT: Yale University Press, 1984.

Huong, Pham Lan, and Gerald W. Fry. "Education and Economic, Political, and Social Change in Vietnam." *Educational Research for Policy and Practice* 3, no. 3 (2004): 199–222.

Husén, Torsten. "The Idea of the University: Changing Roles, Current Crisis and Future Challenges." *Prospects* 21, no. 1 (1991): 171–188.

Hyde, John Kenneth. "Universities and Cities in Medieval Italy." In *The University and the City: From Medieval Origins to the Present*, edited by Thomas Bender, 13–21. Oxford: Oxford University Press, 1991.

Jacob, W. James, Ka Ho Mok, Sheng Yao Cheng, and Weiyan Xiong, "Changes in Chinese Higher Education: Financial Trends in China, Hong Kong and Taiwan." *International Journal of Educational Development* 58, C (2018): 64–85.

Jamieson, Neil L. *Culture and Development in Vietnam*. Honolulu, HI: East-West Centre, The University of Hawai'i, 1991.

Jaschik, Scott. "How Asian Are Asian Universities?" *Inside Higher Ed*, March 14, 2011. http://www.insidehighered.com/news/2011/03/14/asian_university_leaders_consider_identity_of_their_institutions.

Jaspers, Karl. *The Origin and Goal of History*. London: Routledge, 2010.

Jiang, Kai. "Undergraduate Teaching Evaluation in China: Progress and Debate." *International Higher Education* 58, Winter (2010): 15–17.

Jung, Min-ho. "Bright Future for Asian Universities." *Korea Times*, June 16, 2014. http://www.koreatimes.co.kr/www/news/nation/2015/01/181_159335.html.

Kaempf, Sebastian. "Russia: A Part of the West or Apart from the West?" *International Relations* 24, no. 3 (2010): 313–340.

Kaufman, Alison Adcock. "The 'Century of Humiliation,' Then and Now: Chinese Perceptions of the International Order." *Pacific Focus: Inha Journal of Inernational Studies* 25, no. 1 (2010): 1–33.

Keim, Wiebke, Ercüment Çelik, Veronika Wöhrer, and Christian Ersche, eds. *Global Knowledge Production in the Social Sciences: Made in Circulation*. Farnham: Ashgate 2014.

Kerr, Clark. "The Internal and External Threats to the University of the Twenty-First Century (Comments)." *Minerva* 30, no. 2 (1992): 130–152.

Kim, Terri. "Confucianism, Modernities, and Knowledge: China, South Korea and Japan." In *International Handbook of Comparative Education*, edited by Robert Cowen and Andreas M. Kazamias, 857–872. New York: Springer, 2009.

King Yeo-chi Ambrose 金耀基. *Daxue zhi Linian* 大學之理念 [The idea of a University]. Beijing: Joint Publishing, 2001.

Kirby, William C. "The World of Universities in Modern China." In *Global Opportunities and Challenges for Higher Education Leaders: Briefs on Key Themes*, edited by Laura E. Rumbley, Robin Matross Helms, Patti McGill Peterson, and Philip G. Altbach, 73–76. Rotterdam: Sense Publishers, 2014.

Kirkland, Russell. "Tung Chung-shu." In *Great Thinkers of the Eastern World*, edited by Ian P. McGreal, 67–70. New York: HarperCollins, 1995.

Korol, Alexander G. *Soviet Education for Science and Technology*. New York: Wiley and the Technology Press, 1957.

Kwong, Julia. *Cultural Revolution in China's Schools, May 1966–April 1969*. Stanford, CA: Hoover Institution Press, 1988.

Kuraev, Alex. "Soviet Higher Education: An Alternative Construct to the Western University Paradigm." *Higher Education* 71, no. 2 (2016): 181–193.

Lackner, Michael. *Coping with the Future: Theories and Practices of Divination in East Asia*. Leiden: Brill, 2018.

Lal, Deepak. "Does Modernization Require Westernization?" *Independent Review* 5, no. 1 (2000): 5–24.

Latouche, Serge. *The Westernization of the World: The Significance, Scope, and Limits of the Drive towards Global Unifiormity*. Cambridge: Polity Press, 1996.

Law, Wing-Wah. "Understanding China's Curriculum Reform for the 21st Century." *Journal of Curriculum Studies* 46, no. 3 (2014): 332–360.

Lee, Ming-huei. *Confucianism: Its Roots and Global Significance*. Honolulu, HI: University of Hawai'i Press, 2017.

Lee, Thomas H. C. *Education in Traditional China: A History*. Leiden: Brill, 2000.

Lei, Jiasu, Ying Liu, Yaoyuan Qi, and Qingzhi Zhang. "40 Years of Technological Innovation in China: A Review of the Four-Stage Climbing Track." *Journal of Industrial Integration and Management* 4, no. 3 (2019): 1–22.

Leonard, Jane Kate. *Wei Yuan and China's Rediscovery of the Maritime World*. Cambridge, MA: Council on East Asian Studies, 1984.

Levenson, Joseph P. *Confucian China and Its Modern Fate: A Trilogy*. Berkeley, CA: University of California Press, 1968.

Levin, Richard. "Top of the Class: The Rise of Asia's Universities." *Foreign Affairs* 89, no. 3 (2010): 63–75.

Lewis, Mark. "Warring States Political History." In *The Cambridge History of Ancient China: from the Origins of Civilization to 221 BC*, edited by Michael Loewe and Edward L. Shaughnessy, 587–650. Cambridge: Cambridge University Press, 1999.

Li, Fengliang. "The Expansion of Higher Education and the Returns of Distance Education in China." *International Review of Research in Open and Distributed Learning* 19, no. 4 (2018): 242–255.

Li Gui 李圭. *Huanyou diqiu xinlu* 環遊地球新錄 [The new records of traveling around the world]. Changsha: Yuelu shushe, 1985.

Li Guojun 李國鈞, and Wang Bingzhao 王炳照. *Zhongguo jiaoyu zhidu tongshi* [中國教育制度通史 [A general history of Chinese educational system]. Jinan: Shandong Education Press, 2000.

Li Hongzhang 李鴻章. "Chouyi zhizao lunchuan weike caiche zhe" 籌議製造輪船未可裁撤折 [Memo on not abandoning the manufacture of ships] (20 June 1872). In *Li*

Hongzhang quanji, vol. 5 李鴻章全集第5冊 [Collected works of Li Hongzhang], edited by Gu Tinglong 顧廷龍 and Dai Yi 戴逸, 106–110. Hefei: Anhui Education Publishing House, 2008.

Li, Mei, and Rui Yang. *Governance Reforms in Higher Education: A Study of China*. Paris: International Institute for Educational Planning, UNESCO, 2014.

Li, Natasha. "Taiwan R&D Expenditure Ranked Third." *Taipei Times*, May 30, 2020.

Liang Shuming 梁漱溟. "Zhongguo wenhua yaoyi" 中國文化要義 [Substance of Chinese culture]. In *Liang Shuming quanji vol. 3* 梁漱溟全集卷3 [Collections of Liang Shuming vol. 3], edited by Academic Committee of Chinese Cultural Academy 中國文化書院學術委員會. Jinan: Shandong People's Press, 2005.

Lin, Xiaoqing. *Peking University: Chinese Scholarship and Intellectuals, 1918–1937*. Albany, NY: State University of New York Press, 2005.

Liu, Kwang-ching. "Early Christian Colleges in China." *The Journal of Asian Studies* 20, no. 1 (1960): 71–78.

Liu, Kwang-ching. *The Nineteenth Century: The Disintegration of the Old Order and the Impact of the West*. Chicago, IL: The University of Chicago Press, 1968.

Liu, Xu. "Institutional Governance in the Development of Private Universities in China." *Higher Education* 79, no. 2 (2020): 275–290.

Liu, Xu. "Institutional Governance of Chinese Private Universities: The Role of the Communist Party Committee." *Journal of Higher Education Policy and Management* 42, no. 1 (2020): 85–101.

Lo, Bobo. *How the Chinese See Russia*. Paris: ifri Russia/NIS Center, 2010.

Lockard, Craig A. "The Asian Resurgence in World History Perspective." *World History Connected* 9, no. 1 (2012): 1–23.

Lodwick, Kathleen L. *How Christianity Came to China: A Brief History*. Minneapolis, MN: Fortress Press, 2016.

Long, Xicheng. "Xu Zhihong: We Must Reform but Should Remain Steady as We Advance." *Chinese Education and Society* 37, no. 6 (2004): 48–54.

Lu Baoqian 陸寶千. *Guo Songtao xiansheng nianpu buzheng ji buyi* 郭嵩燾先生年譜補正及補遺 [Guo Songtao's chronicle: Corrections and amendments]. Taipei: Zhongyang yanjiuyuan jindaishi yanjiusuo, 2005.

Lu, Yongling, and Ruth Hayhoe. "Chinese Higher Learning: The Transition Process from Classical Knowledge Patterns to Modern Disciplines 1860–1910." In *Transnational Intellectual Networks: Forms of Academic Knowledge and the Search for Cultural Identities*, edited by Chrisophe Charle, Jürgen Schriewer, and Peter Wagner, 269–306. Frankfurt: Campus Verlag, 2004.

Luo Weier 羅威爾. *Xinan lianda de yichan* 西南聯大的遺產 [The great heritage of National Southwestern Associated University. Beijing: CITIC Press Corporation, 2018.

Lutz, Jessie Gregory. *China and the Christian Colleges, 1850–1950*. Ithaca, NY: Cornell University Press, 1971.

Mai, Jun. "Technology Key to China's Vision for the Future as a World Leading Power." *South China Morning Post*, March 6, 2021.

Mak, Ricardo K. S. "Introduction." In *Transmitting the Ideal of Enlightenment: Chinese Universities since the Late Nineteenth Century*, edited by Ricardo K. S. Mak, 1–11. Lanham, MD: University Press of America, 2009.

Makdisi, George. "Madrasa and University in the Middle Ages." *Studia Islamica* 32, no. 1 (1970): 255–264.

Mao Lirui 毛禮銳. *Zhongguo gudai jiaoyushi* 中國古代教育史 [History of ancient Chinese education]. Beijing: People's Publishing House, 1979.

Marginson, Simon. "The Anglo-American University at Its Global High Tide." *Minerva* 44, no. 1 (2006): 65–87.

Marginson, Simon. "Dynamics of National and Global Competition in Higher Education." *Higher Education* 52, no. 1 (2006): 1–39.

Marginson, Simon. "'Ideas of a University' for the Global Era." Keynote speech delivered to Positioning University in the Globalized World: Changing Governance and Coping Strategies in Asia, Centre of Asian Studies, The University of Hong Kong, Hong Kong, December 10, 2008.

Marginson, Simon. "Higher Education in the Global Knowledge Economy." *Procedia Social and Behavioral Sciences* 2, no. 5 (2010): 6962–6980.

Marginson, Simon. "Higher Education in East Asia and Singapore: Rise of the Confucian Model." *Higher Education* 61, no. 5 (2011): 587–611.

Marginson, Simon. "The West's Global HE Hegemony—Nothing Lasts Forever." *University World News*, March 28, 2014.

Marginson, Simon. "Is There a Chinese 'Idea of a University'?" Invited seminar delivered at Tsinghua University Institute of Education, Beijing, June 26, 2019.

Marginson, Simon. "Globalization of Higher Education: The Good, the Bad and the Ugly." *University World News*, May 15, 2021.

Marginson, Simon. "National Modernization and Global Science in China." *International Journal of Educational Development* 84, no. 12 (2021): 1–12.

Marginson, Simon, and Lili Yang. "Individual and Collective Outcomes of Higher Education: A Comparison of Anglo-American and Chinese Approaches." *Globalization, Societies and Education* 20, no. 1 (2022): 1–31.

Massy, William F., and Nigel J. French. "Teaching and Learning Quality Process Review: What the Program Has Achieved in Hong Kong." *Quality in Higher Education* 7, no. 1 (2001): 33–45.

Meade, Philip, and David Woodhouse. "Evaluating the Effectiveness of the New Zealand Academic Audit Unit: Review and Outcomes." *Quality in Higher Education* 6, no. 1 (2000): 19–29.

Medina, Leandro Rodriguez. *Centers and Peripheries in Knowledge Production*. New York: Routledge, 2013.

Meng Xianchang 孟憲承. *Zhongguo gudai jiaoyu wenxuan* 中國古代教育文選 [Selected ancient works on education]. Beijing: People's Education Press, 1996.

Miles, Matthew B., A. Michael Huberman, and Johnny Saldaña. *Qualitative Data Analysis: A Methods Source Book*. London: Sage, 2014.

Ministry of Education. *Education Statistics Digest 2017*. Singapore: Ministry of Education, 2017.

Ministry of Education. *Report of the Committee on University Education Pathways Beyond 2015*. Singapore: Ministry of Education, 2012.

Ministry of Science and Technology, Republic of China (Taiwan). *National Science and Technology Development Plan*. Taipei: Ministry of Science and Technology, 2017.

Minogue, Kenneth R. "The Collapse of the Academic in Britain." In *Buckingham at 25: Freeing the University from State Control*, edited by James Tooley, 86–100. London: The Institute of Economic Affairs, 2001.

Mohrman, Kathryn. "The Research University in Transition: The Emerging Global Model." *Higher Education Policy* 21, no. 1 (2008): 5–27.

Mohrman, Kathryn. "Sino-American Educational Exchange and the Drive to Create World-Class Universities." In *Bridging Minds across the Pacific: U.S.-China Educational Exchanges, 1978–2003*, edited by Cheng Li, 219–235. Lanham, MD: Lexington Books, 2005.

Mok, Ka Ho. "The Quest for World-Class University Status: Implications for Sustainable Development of Asian Universities." Working paper no. 8, September 2016, Centre for Global Higher Education, Oxford University.

Mora, José-Ginés. "Governance and Management in the New University." *Tertiary Education and Management* 7, no. 2 (2001): 95–110.

Morgan, John. "Sun Sets on Western Dominance as East Asian Confucian Model Takes Lead." *Times Higher Education*, February 24, 2011.

Mouat, Melissa. "The Establishment of the Tongwen Guan and the Fragile Sino-British Peace of the 1860s." *Journal of World History* 26, no. 4 (2015): 733–755.

Nakayama, Shigeru. "Independence and Choice: Western Impacts on Japanese Higher Education." *Higher Education* 18, no. 1 (1989): 31–48.

National Research Foundation. *Research Innovation and Enterprise Plan*. Singapore: Research, Innovation and Enterprise Secretariat, 2016.

National Research Foundation. *RIE 2025 Plan*. Singapore: Government of Singapore, 2020.

Newby, Howard, *Governance in UGC-Funded Higher Education Institutions in Hong Kong: Report of the University Grants Committee*. Hong Kong: University Grants Committee, 2015.

Ng, Tze Ming Peter. "Reimagining Christian Higher Education in China Today." *Christian Higher Education* 17, no. 4 (2018): 185–197.

Ng, Tze Ming Peter. "Resurgence of the Study of China's Christian Higher Education since 1980s." *Frontiers of Education in China* 14, no. 3 (2019): 364–386.

Normile, Dennis. "China Again Boosts R&D Spending by More Than 10%." *Science*, August 28, 2020. https://www.sciencemag.org/news/2020/08/china-again-boosts-rd-spending-more-10.

Odora Hoppers, Catherine A. "Education, Culture and Society in a Globalizing World: Implications for Comparative and International Education." *Compare: A Journal of Comparative and International Education* 39, no. 5 (2009): 601–614.

OECD. *The Knowledge-Based Economy: A Set of Facts and Figures*. Paris: OECD, 1999.

OECD. *Education at a Glance*. Paris: OECD, 2013.

Olds, Kris. "Global Assemblage: Singapore, Foreign Universities, and the Construction of a 'Global Education Hub.'" *World Development* 35, no. 6 (2007): 959–975.

O'Leary, Zina. *The Essential Guide to Doing Research*. London: Sage, 2004.

Orleans, Leo A. "Soviet Influence on China's Higher Education." In *China's Education and the Industrialized World: Studies in Cultural Transfer*, edited by Ruth Hayhoe and Marianne Bastid, 184–198. Armonk, NY: M. E. Sharpe, 1987.

Ortmann, Stephan. "Singapore: The Politics of Inventing National Identity." *Journal of Current Southeast Asian Affairs* 28, no. 4 (2009): 23–46.

Our Hong Kong Foundation. *Building the Technology Bridge for Scientific Breakthroughs: Developing an Innovation Hub of the Future.* Hong Kong: Our Hong Kong Foundation, 2020.

Paracka, Daniel J., Jr. "China's Three Teachings and the Relationship of Heaven, Earth and Humanity." *Worldviews* 16, no. 1 (2012): 73–98.

Pepper, Suzanne. *Radicalism and Education Reform in 20th-Century China: The Search for an Ideal Development Model.* New York: Cambridge University Press, 1996.

Perry, Elizabeth J., and Hang Tu. "Cultural Imperialism Redux? Reassessing the Christian Colleges of Republican China." In *China and the World—The World and China, Vol. 3, Transcultural Perspective,* edited by Barbara Mittler and Natascha Gentz, 69–87. Ostanien: Verlag, 2019.

Peters, Michael A. "Ancient Centers of Higher Learning: A Bias in the Comparative History of the University?" *Educational Philosophy and Theory* 51, no. 11 (2019): 1063–1072.

Petersen, Carole J., and Jan Currie. "Higher Education Restructuring and Academic Freedom in Hong Kong." *Policy Futures in Education* 6, no. 5 (2008): 589–600.

Platt, Stephen. "New Domestic and Global Challenges: 1792–1860." In *The Oxford Illustrated History of Modern China,* edited by Jeffrey N. Wasserstrom, 37–62. Oxford: Oxford University Press, 2016.

Poo, Mu-ming. "Innovation and Reform: China's 14th Five-Year Plan Unfolds." *National Science Review* 8, no. 1 (2021). https://academic.oup.com/nsr/article/8/1/nwaa294/6101717.

Punch, Keith F. *Introduction to Research Methods in Education.* London: Sage, 2009.

Punch, Keith F., and Alis Oancea. *Introduction to Research Methods in Education.* Thousand Oaks, CA: Sage, 2014.

Pye, Lucian W. "On Chinese Pragmatism in the 1980s." *The China Quarterly* 106 (June 1986): 207–234.

Queen, Sarah A. *From Chronicle to Canon: The Hermeneutics of the Spring and Autumn Annals according to Tung Chung-shu.* Cambridge: Cambridge University Press, 1996.

Qian, Zhixi. "A Study into the Incident of the Hongdumen Academy." *Frontiers of Literary Studies in China* 4, no. 4 (2010): 483–522.

Qiao Haofeng 喬浩風. *Zhongguo jindai daxue yanjiuyuansuo de fazhan jiqi zhineng yanjiu, 1902-1945* 中國近代大學研究院所的發展及其職能研究 (1902–1945) [A study of the development and functions of university research institutes in modern China (1902–1945)]. PhD diss., Soochow University, 2016.

Qiu, Jane. "China Goes Back to Basics on Research Funding." *Nature* 507 (2014): 148–149.

Qu Lihe 瞿立鶴. *Qingmo jiaoyu xichao: Zhongguo jiaoyu xiandaihua zhi mengya* [清末教育西潮：中國教育現代化之萌芽 [Western tides in education: The embryonic stage of China's educational modernization]. Taipei: National Institute for Compilation and Translation, 2002.

Rashdall, Hastings. *The Universities of Europe in the Middle Ages.* Oxford: Clarendon Press, 1895.

Reagan, Timothy. *Non-Western Educational Traditions: Alternative Approaches to Educational Thought and Practice.* Mahwah, NJ: Lawrence Erlbaum Associates, 2000.

Reischauer, Edwin O., and John K. Fairbank. *East Asia: The Great Tradition*. London: George Allen & Unwin, 1960.

Retna, Kala S., and Pak Tee Ng. "Singapore Principals' Understanding and Perceptions of the Challenges of 'Teach Less, Learn More' Policy." *International Journal of Educational Reform* 25, no. 4 (2016): 426–442.

Richey, Jeffrey L. *Confucius in East Asia: Confucianism's History in China, Korea, Japan, and Vietnam*. Ann Arbor, MI: Association for Asian Studies, 2013.

Rozman, Gilbert, ed. *The East Asian Region: Confucian Heritage and Its Modern Adaptation*. Princeton, NJ: Princeton University Press, 1991.

Rüegg, Walter. "Foreword. The University as a European Institution." In *A History of the University in Europe. Vol. 1: Universities in the Middle Ages*, edited by Hilde de Ridder-Symoens, xix–xxvii. Cambridge: Cambridge University Press, 1992.

Rüegg, Walter, ed. *A History of the University in Europe. Vol. III: Universities in the Nineteenth and Early Twentieth Centuries (1800–1945)*. Cambridge: Cambridge University Press, 2004.

Rüegg, Walter, ed. *A History of the University in Europe. Vol. IV: Universities since 1945*. Cambridge: Cambridge University Press, 2010.

Saravanan, Vanithamani. "'Thinking Schools, Learning Nations' Implementation of Curriculum Review in Singapore." *Educational Research for Policy and Practice* 4, no. 4–5 (2005): 97–113.

Schell, Orville, and John Delury. *Wealth and Power: China's Long March to the Twenty-First Century*. New York: Random House, 2013.

Schwehn, Mark R. *Exiles from Eden: Religion and Academic Vocation in America*. New York: Oxford University Press, 1993.

Schofer, Evan, and John W. Meyer. "The Worldwide Expansion of Higher Education in the Twentieth Century." *American Sociological Review* 70, no. 6 (2005): 898–920.

Scholars at Risk. *Obstacles to Excellence: Academic Freedom and China's Quest for World Class Universities*. New York: Scholars at Risk, 2019.

Schwarcz, Vera. *The Chinese Enlightenment: Intellectuals and the Legacy of the May Fourth Movement of 1919*. Berkeley, CA: University of California Press, 1986.

Scott, Peter. "The End of the European University?" *European Review* 6, no. 4 (1998): 441–457.

Selvaratnam, Viswanathan. "Higher Education Co-operation and Western Dominance of Knowledge Creation and Flows in Third World Countries." *Higher Education* 17, no. 1 (1988): 41–68.

Sharma, Yojana. "The Story of How Singapore Became a Research Nation." *University World News*, December 15, 2017.

Sharma, Yojana. "Minister Sets Limits to Academic Freedom in Yale-NUS Row." *University World News*, October 7, 2019.

Shen, Dingping, and Weifang Zhu. "Western Missionary Influence on the People's Republic of China: A Survey of Chinese Scholarly Opinion Between 1980 and 1990." *International Bulletin of Missionary Research* 22, no. 4 (1998): 154–158.

Shen, Zhihua, and Danhui Li. *After Leaning to One Side: China and Its Allies in the Cold War*. Stanford, CA: Stanford University Press, 2011.

Shils, Edward, and John Roberts. "The Diffusion of European Models outside Europe." In *A History of the University in Europe. Vol III: Universities in the Nineteenth and Early*

Twentieth Centuries (1800–1945), edited by Walter Rüegg, 163–230. Cambridge: Cambridge University Press, 2004.

Song Qiurong 宋秋蓉. "Sili daxue yu jindai Zhongguo de shehui zhuanxing" 私立大學與近代中國的社會轉型 [Private universities and China's modern social transformation]. *Journal of East China Normal University* 華東師範大學學報22, no. 1 (2004): 73–79.

Spence, Jonathan D. *The Search for Modern China*. New York: W. W. Norton & Company, 1990.

Stein, Sharon. "The Persistent Challenges of Addressing Epistemic Dominance in Higher Education: Considering the Case of Curriculum Internationalization." *Comparative Education Review* 61, S1 (2017): s25–s50.

Steinbauer, Anja. "Interview with Tu Wei-ming." *Philosophy Now* 23, Spring (1999): 28–31.

Su, Jie. "Seizing Opportunities, Hong Kong's Innovation and Technology Has a Bright Future." *Economic Review* (Bank of China) 11 (2017): 1–5.

Sun Hongan 孫宏安. "Zhongguo gudai jiaoyu tedian" 中國古代教育特點 [Features of ancient Chinese education]. *Journal of Liaoning Normal University* 遼寧師範大學學報 4 (1996): 26–29.

Sutherland, Stewart R. *Higher Education in Hong Kong: Report of the University Grants Committee*. Hong Kong: University Grants Committee, 2002.

Tan, Jason. "Recent Developments in Higher Education in Singapore." *International Higher Education* 14, Winter (1999): 15–17.

Tang, Winnie. "Singapore Is Committed to R&D Investment—What about Hong Kong?". *Harbor Times*, January 9, 2021.

Têng, Ssu-yü. "Chinese Influence on the Western Examination System." *Harvard Journal of Asiatic Studies* 7 (1942/1943): 267–312.

Têng, Ssu-yü, and John K. Fairbank. *China's Response to the West*. Cambridge, MA: Harvard University Press, 1954.

Third World Academy of Sciences. *Building Scientific Capacity: A TWAS Perspective*. Trieste, Italy: Third World Academy of Sciences, 2004.

Thompson, Larry Clinton. *William Scott Ament and the Boxer Rebellion: Heroism, Hubris, and the "Ideal Missionary"*. Jefferson, NC: McFarland Publishing Company, 2009.

Tian, Zhengping, and Taolan Chen. "A Textual Research on the First Private University in Modern China." *Frontiers of Education in China* 3, no. 4 (2008): 178–191.

Travers, Max. *Qualitative Research through Case Study*. London: Sage, 2001.

Trencher, Gregory, Masaru Yarime, Kes McCormick, Christopher N. H. Doll, and Steven Kraines. "Beyond the Third Mission: Exploring the Emerging University Function of Co-creation for Sustainability." *Science and Public Policy* 41, no. 2 (2014): 151–179.

Tsang, Yam-kuen Donald. *The 2009–2010 Policy Address*. Hong Kong: Government Printer, 2009.

Tsui, Lap-chee, and Rita Lun. *The Ecosystem of Innovation and Technology in Hong Kong*. Hong Kong: Our Hong Kong Foundation, 2015.

Tu, Weiming. "Beyond the Enlightenment Mentality." In *Confucianism and Ecology: The Interrelation of Heaven, Earth and Humans*, edited by Mary E. Tucker and John H. Berthwrong, 3–21. Cambridge, MA: Harvard University Press, 1998.

Tu, Wei-Ming. "Confucian Humanism as a Spiritual Resource for Global Ethics." *Peace and Conflict Studies* 16, no. 1 (2009): 1–8.

Tu Youguang 凃又光. *Zhongguo gaodeng jiaoyu shilun* 中國高等教育史論 [On the history of Chinese higher education]. Wuhan: Hubei Education Press, 1997.

Twitchett, Denis, and John K. Fairbank, eds. *The Cambridge History of China*. Cambridge: Cambridge University Press, 1978.

Underwood, Horace H. *Modern Education in Korea*. New York: International Press, 1926.

UNESCO. *World Education Report 1998*. Paris: UNESCO Publishing, 1998.

van Wyk, Berte, and Philip Higgs. "The Call for an African University: A Critical Reflection." *Higher Education Policy* 20, no. 1 (2007): 61–71.

Verger, Jacques. "Patterns." In *A History of the University in Europe*, vol. 1, *Universities in the Middle Ages*, edited by Hilde de Ridder-Symoens, 35–74. Cambridge: Cambridge University Press, 1992.

Wang, Dong. "The Discourse of Unequal Treaties in Modern China." *Pacific Affairs* 76, no. 3 (2003): 399–425.

Wang Tao 王韜. *Manyou suilu* 漫遊隨錄 [Casual notes made during the wander]. Changsha: Yuelu shushe, 1985.

Wang Xuezhen 王學珍. *Beijing daxue jishi 1898–1997* 北京大學紀事 1898–1997 [Chronicle of Peking University 1898–1997]. Beijing: Peking University Press, 2008.

Web of Science Group. *Highly Cited Researchers 2019*. London: Clarivate Analytics, 2019.

Welch, Anthony R. "Internationalization of Vietnamese Higher Education: Retrospect and Prospect." In *Reforming Higher Education in Vietnam. Higher Education Dynamics, Vol. 29*, edited by Grant Harman, Martin Hayden, and Pham Thanh Nghi, 197–213. Dordrecht: Springer, 2010.

Weston, Timothy B. *The Power of Position: Beijing University, Intellectuals, and Chinese Political Culture, 1898–1929*. Berkeley, CA: University of California Press, 2004.

Williams, Ross, and Anne Leahy. *U21 Ranking of National Higher Education Systems*. Melbourne: Applied Economic & Social Research, University of Melbourne, 2020.

Wilshire, Bruce. *The Moral Collapse of the University: Professionalism, Purity and Alienation*. Albany, NY: State University of New York Press, 1990.

Wong, Kam-Cheung. "Chinese Culture and Leadership." *International Journal of Leadership in Education* 4, no. 4 (2001): 309–319.

World Bank. *Higher Education Reform: A World Bank Country Study*. Washington, DC: World Bank, 1997.

Wright, Arthur F. "The Study of Chinese Civilization." *Journal of the History of Ideas* 21, no. 2 (1960): 233–255.

Wu, Weiping. "Managing and Incentivizing Research Commercialization in Chinese Universities." *Journal of Technology Transfer* 35, no. 2 (2010): 203–224.

Wu, Wen-Hsing, Shun-Fen Chen, and Chen-Tsou Wu. "The Development of Higher Education in Taiwan." *Higher Education* 18, no. 1 (1989): 117–136.

Xiao Chaoran 肖超然. *Beijing daxue xiaoshi* 北京大學校史 [History of Peking University]. Shanghai: Shanghai Educational Publishing House, 1981.

Xie, Qingnan, and Richard B. Freeman. "Bigger than You Thought: China's Contribution to Scientific Publications and Its Impact on the Global Economy." *China & World Economy* 27, no. 1 (2019): 1–27.

Xiong Mingan 熊明安. *Zhongguo gaodeng jiaoyu shi* 中國高等教育史 [History of Chinese higher education]. Chongqing: Chongqing Press, 1983.

Xiong Yuezhi 熊月之, and Zhou Wu 周武, eds. *Shengyuehan daxueshi* 聖約翰大學史 [History of St. John's University]. Shanghai: Shanghai renmin chubanshe, 2007.

Yang, Cheng-Cheng, and Yueh-Chun Huang. "Promoting Teaching Excellence of Universities in Taiwan: Policy Analysis with a Special Reference to Educational Equality." *International Education Studies* 5, no. 5 (2012): 129–140.

Yang, Huanyin. "Confucius." *Prospects: Quarterly Review of Comparative Education* 23, no. 1–2 (1993): 211–219.

Yang, Rui. "Internationalization, Indigenization and Educational Research in China." *Australian Journal of Education* 49, no. 1 (2005): 66–88.

Yang, Rui. "Enter the Dragon: China's Higher Education Returns to the World Community." In *Higher Education: Handbook of Theory and Practice*, edited by John C. Smart and William G. Tierney, 427–461. Dordrecht: Springer, 2009.

Yang, Rui. "Self and the Other in the Confucian Cultural Context: Implications of China's Higher Education Development for Comparative Studies." *International Review of Education* 57, no. 3–4 (2011): 337–355.

Yang, Rui. "Indigenizing the Western Concept of the University: Chinese Experience." *Asia Pacific Education Review* 14, no. 1 (2013): 85–92.

Yang, Rui. "Reassessing China's Higher Education Development: A Focus on Academic Culture." *Asia Pacific Education Review* 16, no. 4 (2015): 527–535.

Yang, Rui. "The Cultural Mission of China's Elite Universities: Examples from Peking and Tsinghua." *Studies in Higher Education* 42, no. 10 (2017): 1825–1838.

Yang, Rui. "Foil to the West? Interrogating Perspectives for Observing East Asian Higher Education." In *Researching Higher Education: History, Development and Future*, edited by Jisun Jung, Hugo Horta, and Akiyoshi Yonezawa, 37–50. Singapore: Springer, 2018.

Yang, Rui. "Transformations of Higher Education Institutions in the Chinese Tradition." In *Handbook of the Politics of Higher Education*, edited by Brendan Cantwell, Hamish Coates, and Roger King, 66–78. Cheltenham, UK: Edward Elgar, 2018.

Yang, Rui. "Emulating or Integrating? Modern Transformations of Chinese Higher Education." *Journal of Asian Public Policy* 12, no. 3 (2018): 294–311.

Yang, Rui. "The Cultural Experiment at East Asian Universities." In *Contesting Globalization and Internationalization of Higher Education: Discourse and Responses in the Asia Pacific Region*, edited by Deane E. Neubauer, Ka Ho Mok, and Sachi Edwards, 33–47. Gewerbestrasse, Switzerland: Palgrave Macmillan, 2019.

Yang, Rui. "Turning Scars into Stars: A Reconceptualized View of University Development in Beijing, Hong Kong, Taipei and Singapore." *Frontiers of Education in China* 14, no. 1 (2019): 1–32.

Yang, Rui. "Schooling in China." In *Routledge Handbook of Chinese Culture and Society*, edited by Kevin Latham, 34–49. London and New York: Routledge, 2020.

Yang, Rui. "Political Culture and Higher Education Governance in Chinese Societies: Some Reflections." *Frontiers of Education in China* 15, no. 2 (2020): 187–221.

Yang, Rui. "China's Higher Education during the COVID-19 Pandemic: Some Preliminary Observations." *Higher Education Research & Development* 39, no. 7 (2020): 1317–1321.

Yang, Rui. "World-Class Universities in China's Heroic Past." *International Higher Education* 107, Summer (2021): 18–19.

Yang, Rui. "Baby and Bathwater or Soup? Some Epistemological Considerations of How to Observe China and Chinese Education." *Globalization, Societies and Education* 20, no. 1 (2022): 49–55.

Yang, Rui, Meng Xie, and Wen Wen. "Pilgrimage to the West: Modern Transformations of Intellectual Formulation in Social Sciences." *Higher Education* 77, no. 4 (2019): 815–829.

Yao, Xinzhong. *The Encyclopedia of Confucianism*. London: Routledge, 2003.

Yonezawa, Akiyoshi, Akinari Hoshino, and Sae Shimauchi. "Inter- and Intraregional Dynamics on the Idea of Universities in East Asia: Perspectives from Japan." *Studies in Higher Education* 42, no. 10 (2017): 1839–1852.

Yu Ying-shih 余英時. *Zhongguo wenhua yu xiandai bianqian* 中國文化與現代變遷 [Chinese culture and its modern changes]. Taipei: Sanmin shuju, 1992.

Yuan, Zheng. "Local Government Schools in Sung China: A Reassessment." *History of Education Quarterly* 34, no. 2 (1994): 193–213.

Yun, Sa-Soon. "Confucian Thought and Korean Culture." In *Korean Cultural Heritage, Vol. II. Thought and Religion*, edited by Joung-won Kim, 108–113. Seoul: Samsung Moonhwa Printing Co., 1996.

Zapp, Mike, and Francisco O. Ramirez. "Beyond Internationalization and Isomorphism: The Construction of a Global Higher Education Regime." *Comparative Education* 55, no. 4 (2019): 473–493.

Zhang Deyi 張德彝. *Hanghai shuqi* 航海述奇 [My fantastic experiences during overseas voyages]. Changsha: Yuelu shushe, 1985.

Zhang Kaiyuan 章開沅, *Zhongxi wenhua yu jiaohui daxue* 中西文化與教會大學 [Chinese and Western cultures and missionary universities]. Wuhan: Hubei Education Publishing House, 1991.

Zhang Kaiyuan 章開沅. *Wenhua chuanbo yu jiaohui daxue* 文化傳播與教會大學 [Cultural communication and missionary universities]. Wuhan: Hubei Education Publishing House, 1996.

Zhang Yan 張雁. *Xifang daxue linian zai jingdai Zhongguo de chuanru yu yingxiang* 西方大學理念在近代中國的傳入與影響 [Western ideas of a university in China: Introduction and impact]. Hangzhou Zhejiang University Press, 2009.

Zhao Dachuan 趙大川. "Wanqing minuo shiqi de Zhejiang sili fazhenzhuanmen xuexiao" 晚清民國時期的浙江私立法政專門學校 [Zhejiang College of Law and Political Science during the late Qing and Republican era]. *Research on Rule of Law* 法治研究 3 (2007): 2.

Zhao, Zhenzhou, and Sun Yi. "Revisiting Religious Higher Education in China: Comparative Analysis of Furen University Narratives." *Asia Pacific Education Review* 21, no. 4 (2020): 629–638.

Zhejiang University. *Seeking Truth and Pursuing Innovation*. Hangzhou: Zhejiang University 2020.

Zhong Shuhe 鍾叔河. *Cong dongfang dao xifang* 從東方到西方 [From the East to the West]. Shanghai: Shanghai remin chubanshe, 1989.

Zhou Bangdao 周邦道. *Diyici Zhongguo jiaoyu nianjian* 第一次中國教育年鑒 [The first Chinese yearbook of education]. Shanghai: Kaiming Bookstore, 1934.

Zhou Chuan 周川, and Huang Xu 黃旭. *Bainian zhigong* 百年之功 [A hundred years of achievements]. Fuzhou: Fujian Education Press, 2005.

Zhou Yutong 周予同. *Zhongguo xuexiao zhidu* 中國學校制度 [School system in China]. Shanghai: Commercial Press, 1931.

Zhu, Xiaoyan, Bing Qin, Xiaodan Zhu, Ming Liu, and Longhua Qian. "Knowledge Graph and Semantic Computing: Knowledge Computing and Language Understanding." Paper presented at 4th China Conference, Communications in Computer and Information Science (CCKS) 2019, Hangzhou, China, August 24–27, 2019.

Zhu Ziqing 朱自清. "Lun xueshu de kongqi" 論學術的空氣 [On intellectual atmosphere]. In *Zhu Ziqing quanji* 朱自清全集 [The complete works of Zhu Ziqing], edited by Zhu Qiaosen 朱喬森, 490–495. Nanjing: Jiangsu Education Press, 1993.

Index

Academia-Industry Technological Alliance, 84
Academia Sinica, 83
academic audit, 88
academic community, 23, 111
academic culture, 97, 117
Academic Degrees Committee, 85
academic freedom, 3, 30, 48–49, 54–55, 58, 79, 95–96, 116–117, 124, 126
academic model, 1, 3–4, 8, 117, 120–121, 131–132, 134
academic nationalism, 61
academic system, 93, 104
academician, 95, 115
academies 書院, 13, 16–17, 21–22, 30, 34, 36, 38, 58, 62–63
Academy of Sciences of Hong Kong, 82
Act of the Parliament in 2000, 74
Act of University, 73
activity freedom, 96, 114
Altbach, Philip G., 2, 11, 13, 48, 57, 102–104, 113, 120, 132
American model, 39, 45, 98
Amoy (Xiamen) University, 51–52
Andersson, Bertil, 84
Arrangement of the Constitution of the Tianjin Chinese and Western School 擬設天津中西學堂章程稟, 41
Ashikaga Gakkō, 29
Asian model, 98
Asian system, 93
   See also Asian model
Asian values, 54

Aurora University 震旦大學, 51
Authorized School Regulation 欽定學堂章程, 34
autonomy, 3, 39, 48–49, 54–55, 58, 69, 71–74, 79, 86, 95–96, 116–117, 124, 128
   See also academic autonomy; institutional autonomy; operational autonomy; university autonomy

Beiyang University 北洋大學堂, 7, 31, 41
bicultural condition, 100
bicultural identity, 109
bicultural intellectual mind, 8, 110–113, 123
bicultural mind, 110, 128
   See also bicultural intellectual mind
bicultural situations, 111
   See also bicultural condition
Binchun 斌椿, 37
blended/experiential learning, 87
Board of Science & Technology, 83
Book of Han 漢書, 10
"Boston of the East," 75
brain drain, 85
British-American model, 39
   See also European and American models; European–North American model
British colony, 71, 101
"British lighthouse in the Orient," 70
British system, 94
   See also UK system
Building the Technology Bridge for Scientific Breakthroughs, 83

Cai Yuanpei 蔡元培, 49, 115
Canton Kwong Wah Medical College 私立
　廣東光華醫學院, 51
Celestial Empire, 32
Census and Statistics Department, 78
centralized administration, 73
century of humiliation, a, 百年國恥 32
Chang Hao 張灝, 59
Chen Yinke 陳寅恪, 10
Chengjun 成均, 10
Chern Shiing-Shen 陳省身, 52
Cheung Bing-leung 張炳良, 62–63
China Association for Science and
　Technology, 82
China's first modern school system (壬寅學
　制 in 1902 and its modified form 癸卯學
　制 in 1904), 13, 34
　　See also Presented School Regulation
China's intellectual tradition, 53
China's response to the West, 33
Chinese Academy of Sciences, 95, 115
Chinese and Western ideas of a university,
　2, 8, 100, 113, 116–117, 126, 128
Chinese and Western intellectual traditions,
　45–46, 50, 121
Chinese and Western traditions, 56–57, 94,
　101, 118, 121–122, 128
　　See also Chinese and Western
　　　intellectual traditions; indigenous
　　　and Western traditions
Chinese characteristics, 47, 94
Chinese civilization, 28–29, 32, 46, 62
Chinese Communist Party (CCP), 66, 69
Chinese culture, 12, 18, 27, 35, 53, 63,
　108–109, 114–115
　　See also indigenous cultures;
　　　traditional culture
Chinese idea, 1–2, 7–8, 53–54, 56–57,
　61–64, 113
Chinese idea of the university, 56, 61, 64
Chinese identity, 33, 49
Chinese intellectual tradition, 34, 60, 114,
　126
　　See also China's intellectual tradition;
　　　indigenous intellectual traditions

Chinese model, 7, 98
Chinese political administration 73
　　See also governmental intervention
Chinese power, 8, 67
Chinese societies, 1–4, 6–9, 45, 53–54, 59,
　63, 65–66, 71, 75, 81, 85, 91, 95–97,
　102–103, 105–110, 112–115, 117–118,
　120–124, 126–128
Chinese tradition, 3, 6, 10–29, 53, 57–59,
　62, 99, 103, 115, 126, 128
Chinese University of Hong Kong, 62, 70
Chinese values, 111, 118
Chongqing University, 48
Choson kingdom, 25
Choson period, 25
Chucai Xuetang 儲才學堂, 40
city-state, 75, 80
civil service examination system, 17, 21–22
CNKI 中國知網, 59
co-creation for sustainability, 99
colonial domination, 120
colonial history, 114
colonialism, 104, 119, 125
Confucian bureaucracy, 27
Confucian classics, 17, 24, 26–27
Confucian context, 3
Confucian ethics, 11, 18, 20
Confucian ideologies, 11, 21
Confucian learning, 25, 27
Confucian model, 7, 91
Confucian scholars, 16, 18–19, 29
Confucian sociocultural contexts, 7, 100
Confucian spirit, 111
Confucian-style, 117
Confucian traditions, 24, 26
Confucian values, 5, 25, 29, 114
Confucianism, 10–11, 16, 18–22, 24–29, 47,
　53, 64, 113
Confucius 孔子, 10–11, 17–20, 62–64
contemporary knowledge system, 112, 123
　　See also modern knowledge system
Contention of a Hundred Schools of
　Thought 百家爭鳴, 20
co-production of cultural and physical
　product, 97

corporate governance, 72
COVID-19, 1, 87–88
cultural beliefs, 90
cultural change, 3, 12, 23, 67, 108
cultural confidence, 101
cultural gene, 113
cultural heritage, 4, 24, 63, 100, 110, 117
    See also cultural gene; cultural roots;
    cultural traditions
cultural identity, 5, 7, 100, 103
cultural modernity, 122
    See also cultural change
cultural roots, 3, 100, 102, 114, 120
cultural sphere, 127
cultural traditions, 6–8, 12, 25, 28, 53, 57,
    101, 103, 107, 109, 114
cultural values, 3, 4, 25, 96, 99, 103, 117,
    123, 126
culturally hollow, 111

Dae-kwa or Mun-kwa, 25
Daigaku-ryō, 28–29
decentralization, 39, 68, 73, 79
    See also American model
Department of Cyber Security, 83
"dependent fiefdoms," 61
Deputy Shōgun Uesugi Norizane, 29
Director of Educational Affairs 管學大臣,
    43
Dong Zhongshu 董仲舒, 3, 14, 18, 21, 68
Dongmunhak, 26–27

East Asian cultural sphere or Sino sphere
    東亞文化圈, 24
Eastern Han period, 14
Eastern Zhou dynasty, 10
East-West integration, 70
education hub, 70, 75
educational paradigm, 112
e-learning experience, 87
emerging global model, 101
Emperor Huizong 宋徽宗, 15
Emperor Ping of Han, 14, 21
Emperor Renzong 宋仁宗, 15
Emperor Taixu of Northern Wei, 17

Emperor Tenji, 29
Emperor Wu of Han, 18–19
Emperor Wu of Jin, 14
Eurocentric knowledge system, 102, 123
    See also Western knowledge system
European and American models, 63
European form, 56, 127
"European institution par excellence, the"
    127
European intellectual traditions, 36
European–North American model, 38
European tradition, 6
    See also Western tradition

Fei Xiaotong 費孝通, 50
Feng Youlan 馮友蘭, 11–12
First Opium War, 1, 32, 108
First Sino-Japanese War, 41–42
Five-Year Plan, 76, 80, 82
flagship universities, 8, 90, 117, 126
French centralized system, 39
    See also French model; French
    system
French system, 94
Fu Jen Catholic University, 45
Fu Ssu-nien 傅斯年, 110
Fudan Gongxue 復旦公學, 51
Fudan University, 51, 68
Fukien Christian University, 47
funding system, 77, 79
fuqiang 富強, 33
fusion of cultures, 112
Fuzhou Chuanzheng Xuetang 福州船政學
    堂, 40

Gan Yang 甘陽, 61
Geng Zi 庚子, 1
Ginling Women's College, 45
Glanzer, Perry L., 119
"glass ceiling," 3, 57, 107
Global Competitiveness Report, 78
global knowledge system, 81, 104
global rankings, 91, 101, 115, 121
"Global Schoolhouse," 74
global university, 106, 127–128

globalization, 2, 5, 62, 97, 100–104, 113,
        122, 128
Gongche Shangshu 公車上書, 42
Gongsun Hong 公孫弘, 19
government-university relationship, 97
        See also civil service examination
        system
Gramscian hegemony, 127
Great Learning 大學, 31, 60
gross domestic expenditure on research and
        development (GERD), 78–79
Guangxi University, 48
Guangxu 光緒, 13, 38, 41
Guimao Educational System, 癸卯學制, 34
Gukhak, 25
Guo Bingwen 郭秉文, 47
Guo Qijia 郭齊家, 10
Guo Songtao 郭嵩燾, 37–39
guoxue 國學, 13
        See also xiangxue 鄉學
Guozijian 國子監, 15, 21, 58
Guozixue 國子學, 14–15

Han dynasty, 14, 16, 18, 21, 35
Hanlin Academy 翰林院, 39
hanlin xueshi 翰林學士, 39
        See also Hanlin Academy
Harvard and Yale Universities, 7, 41
Hayhoe, Ruth, 3, 7–8, 20–22, 31, 34, 36, 39,
        41, 49, 51, 53, 56–58, 67, 99, 102, 117,
        134
hegemony, 2, 91, 127
Henan University, 48
Higher Education Evaluation and
        Accreditation Council, 89
Higher Education Evaluation Center, 85
Higher Education Law of the People's
        Republic of China 中華人民共和國高等
        教育法, 68
higher education system, 2–3, 8–9, 24, 36,
        57, 65–66, 70, 72, 75, 84–85, 90, 92, 94,
        97, 100–103, 120, 123, 126
higher education tradition, 4, 59
higher learning institutions, 10, 20–21, 23,
        55–56, 73

higher learning tradition, 1, 24, 60, 64, 121
        See also higher education tradition
homogenization, 65, 128
        See also isomorphism
Hongdumen Academy 鴻都門學, 14
        See also Taixue
Hong Kong Institute of Education, 62, 70
Hong Kong Technical Colleges, 70
Hong Kong University of Science and
        Technology (HKUST), 4, 70
Hu Shi 胡適, 40
Huang Chun-chieh 黃俊傑, 64
Huang Qingcheng 黃慶澄, 37
human coexistence, 101
Hung, William 洪業, 47

idea of a university, 8–9, 36, 56, 64, 87, 115,
        123–126
ideas of higher education 高等教育理念, 59
"impact-response," 33
imperial China, 21, 24
imperial examination system 科舉, 21, 48
Imperial Tientsin University 天津北洋西學
        學堂, 7, 31, 41–43
        See also Beiyang University; Peiyang
        University
indigenization, 111
indigenous cultures, 113
indigenous intellectual traditions, 34–35
indigenous traditions, 7
individual freedom, 96, 114
Industrial and Scientific Revolutions, 112
information communication technology
        (ICT), 87, 89
Innovation and Technology Bureau, 82
Innovation and Technology Commission,
        82
Innovation and Technology Committee, 82
innovation and technology ecosystem,
        82–83
Innovation and Technology Fund, 82
innovation ecosystem, 83–84
        See also innovation and technology
        ecosystem
institutional autonomy. *See* autonomy

institutional management, 37, 72
intellectual mind, 34, 121
intellectual traditions, 44–45, 55, 115
inter-civilizational dialogue, 100
interference, 71, 120
internal governance, 69, 72
international benchmark, 94
    See also international norms;
      international standards
international financial hub, 78
international knowledge network, 104
international norms, 110
international practice, 43, 53, 56
international standards, 42, 92, 105, 107
isomorphism, 65

Japanese model, 39
Jiajing era, 16
Jin dynasty, 15
jing she 精舍, 16
jinshi 進士, 39, 42, 48, 58
Jixia Academy 稷下學宮, 20
juren 舉人, 39, 58

Kang Youwei 康有為, 42
Kangxi 康熙, 17
King Min of Qi 齊湣王, 20
King, Yeo-chi Ambrose 金耀基, 15, 61–62
knowledge-based economy, 75, 81
knowledge economy, 80, 100
knowledge society, 53, 84, 117
knowledge-transfer activities, 85
Koguryŏ kingdom, 25
Kokugaku, 29
Koryo kingdom, 25
Kwa-keo, 25

LASALLE College of the Arts, 73
latecomers, 7, 65, 98, 100
"Leaning to One Side," 66
Learn from the West to defend against the
    West 師夷長技以制夷, 40
learning-centered pedagogies, 91
Lee Kuan Yew 李光耀, 74
Levin, Richard, 3

Li Gui 李圭, 37–38
Li Hongzhang 李鴻章, 34, 38, 41, 58–59
Liang Qichao 梁啟超, 40, 43
Liang Shuming 梁漱溟, 110
Liao dynasty, 15
lifelong learning, 91
"loss of memory," 34, 62
Ly dynasty, 27

Mao Lirui 毛禮銳, 14–16
Mao Yisheng 茅以升, 42
Mao Zedong 毛澤東, 40, 66
Marginson, Simon, 2, 5, 7, 54, 57, 81–82, 91,
    101–102, 123
Massive Open Online Courses (MOOCs),
    87, 89
Matching Grant Scheme, 77
Mateer, Calvin Wilson, 31
medieval Europe, 55–56, 127
medieval universities, 2, 21, 23, 119–120,
    124–125, 127
Medium- and Long-Term Science and
    Technology Plan (2021–2035), 81
Mencius 孟子, 17, 63
Middle Ages, 112, 119
Ming dynasty, 15–16
Ministry of Education, 28, 51, 73, 76, 85–86,
    89–90, 105
Ministry of Science & Technology, 84
minority studies 土司學, 16
model of the European universities, 30
    See also European form
modern knowledge system, 101, 110, 121
modern universities, 1–4, 6–8, 16, 23,
    30–31, 35, 37, 41, 43, 47–50, 53, 56,
    58–59, 62, 64–67, 85, 95, 99, 109, 111,
    119–121, 127
modernization, 7, 27, 35, 40, 52, 57, 59, 63,
    70, 93, 100, 110, 122, 125
Morrison, Robert, 44
Mozi 墨子, 17
multi-source financing system, 75

Nankai University, 50–52
Nanyang Academy of Fine Arts, 73

Nanyang Gongxue 南洋公學, 51
Nanyang Technological University (NTU),
    4, 73, 75, 84, 90
Nanyang University, 73
National Applied Research Laboratories, 84
National Development Fund, 83
National Natural Science Foundation of
    China, 82
National Taiwan University (TU), 4, 64, 71,
    108, 111
National Tsing Hua University (THU), 4,
    94, 107–108
National University of Singapore (NUS), 4,
    73, 75, 84, 90, 93, 103, 106, 108
nation-building, 13, 39, 49–50, 102
Neo-Confucianism movement, 16
neoliberal ideologies and approaches, 72
New Daoism 玄學, 15
"no distinction between ruling and
    education, and officials as teachers" 治教
    無二，官師合一, 13–14
Nobel Prize, 107
non-Chinese societies, 102
non-European traditions, 56
    See also non-Western traditions
non-Western societies, 4, 8–9, 66, 99–100,
    102–104, 110, 115, 119, 122–125, 128
non-Western traditions, 56
Northern Wei, 14

official ideology, 11, 25
officials-as-teachers system, 14
one country, two systems, 71
opening-up policies, 67
Order of Dao 道統, 63
Order of Zheng 政統, 63

Paekche kingdom, 25
pedagogical traditions, 90
Peiyang University 北洋大學堂, 31
Peking University 北京大學, 4, 49–50, 56,
    61, 95–96, 107, 110–111, 115–117
Peking University 京師大學堂, 31, 43–44,
    48, 53
People's Republic of China, 42, 52, 71

Peters, Michael, 56
philosophical heritages, 126
phoenix, 1
political pragmatism, 24, 95
post catch-up stage, 84–85
Presented School Regulation 奏定學堂章程.
    See Guimao Educational System
    癸卯學制
Program for Promoting Teaching
    Excellence of Universities, 89

Qing dynasty, 13–14, 22, 31, 34, 39, 71
Quacquarelli Symonds (QS) World
    University Rankings, 71, 87
quality assurance, 85, 88, 101, 105
quasi-feudal empire, 33
Quốc Tử Giám, 27

"rectifying rightness without scheming for
    profit; enlightening his Way without
    calculating efficaciousness" 正其誼不謀
    其利，明其道不計其功, 19
Regulations for State and Private
    Universities, 51
Renaissance, the, 112
Research and Development (R&D), 8,
    76–84
Research Assessment Exercise, 94, 105
Research Grants Council, 4, 77
Research Innovation and Enterprise (RIE)
    plan, 80–81
Ricci, Matteo, 16, 120
Rüegg, Walter, 55

Samguksagi, 25
scholarly circles, 128
scholar-officials, 25–26, 35–36, 38, 48
science and technology (S&T), 76, 83–84
Scimago Journal & Country Rank, 83
Second Opium War, 40
Second Sino-Japanese War, 48
seeking truth, 22, 96, 112, 116
Self-Strengthening Movement, 35
Seongkyunkwan, 25
Shang dynasty, 10

Shantung Christian University, 45, 47
she 社, 15
    See also shexue 社學
Sheng Xuanhuai 盛宣懷, 41
shexue 社學, 15
Shoheiko, 29
Silhak, 26
Silla kingdom, 25
Singapore Institute of Technology, 73
Singapore Management University, 73–74
Singapore University of Technology, 73
Six Dynasties period, 14
"smart nation," 84
social and economic development, 63, 81,
    84, 102, 106, 127
social role of the university, 39
social transformation, 52, 121, 125
Soochow University, 45
Son of Heaven, 18–19
Song dynasty, 15–16, 22
Southeast University, 47
Southern Song period, 16
Soviet Union, 66–67, 120
speaking truth to power, 95
split personality, 111
Spring and Autumn, 14
St. John's University 聖約翰大學, 31, 45–46
St. Paul's College of Macau, 31
state-led governance, 72
state-led higher education institutions, 51
state-led universities, 50
    See also state-led higher education
        institutions
State Council, 68, 85
Sui dynasty, 14, 21
Sun Jianai 孫家鼐, 42–43, 48

Taehak, 25
Taihoku Imperial University, 71
    See also National Taiwan University
Taiwan Strait, 108, 112
Taixue 太學, 14–15, 18–21, 58, 61
Tang dynasty, 11, 14–16, 21–22, 25
Teaching and Learning Quality Process
    Reviews (TLQPRs), 88

technology-oriented universities, 93
Tengchow College 登州文會館, 31, 44
Tenney, Charles Daniel, 41
"Thinking School, Learning Nation," 91
third mission, 99
Three Kingdoms period, 25–26
Three Teachings of Confucianism,
    Buddhism, and Daoism, 10
Tianjin Anglo-Chinese College 天津中西
    書院, 41
Ti-yong 體用, 43
    See also Zhongti xiyong
Tokugawa Period, 29
Tongwen Guan 同文館, 40
traditional culture, 2–3, 57, 96, 109, 116
    See also indigenous cultures
traditional values, 111, 120–121
    See also Chinese values
Treaty of Shimonoseki 下關條約, 42
tribute students 貢生, 14
triple-helix model, 99
Tsinghua University 清華大學, 4, 50, 76, 96,
    107, 109, 111–112, 138
Tu Youguang 塗又光, 60
Tung Chee Hwa, 82
"twisted roots," 2, 57

unequal treaties, 32, 47
unified Silla kingdom, 25
University Grants Committee (UGC), 71,
    77, 87–88
University of Hong Kong (HKU), 4, 59, 70,
    104, 106, 114
University of Malaya, 73
University of Nanking, 45, 47
University of Twente, 88
University Organizational Law, 51
UK system, 93
US system, 93

Verger, Jacques, 119
virtual teaching and learning, 88

Wakon Kansai, 29
Wakon Yosai, 29

Wang Pengyun 王鵬運, 42
Wang Tao 王韜, 37
Wang Wenshao 王文韶, 41
Warring States periods, 14
Way, the, 63
Wei Yuan 魏源, 35, 40
West China Union University, 47
Western academic model, 3, 8, 117, 121
Western challenge, 108, 110
Western civilization, 7, 29–30, 42
Western concepts, 36, 62, 85
Western concept of a university, 35, 48, 59,
    114–115, 121–122
    See also Western idea of a university
Western efficiency and modernity, 111
Western experience, 2, 23, 34, 65, 121
Western idea of a university, 25, 31, 57,
    59–60, 95, 115, 120–121
Western knowledge, 7–8, 26, 29, 34–36, 41,
    100, 110, 112–113, 123–124, 126
    See also Western knowledge system
Western knowledge system, 13, 34, 129
Western learning, 7, 27, 43, 49, 62, 100–101,
    110, 112, 120, 122–123
Western management, 111
Western model, 1, 5, 36, 49, 58, 95, 100, 102,
    113–114, 120–121, 123, 126–128
Western powers, 26, 32–33, 35, 41, 65
Western-style, 3, 8, 38, 41–42, 45–46, 48,
    66, 71, 91
Western-style universities, 3, 41, 48, 71
Western supremacy, 126
Western systems, 66, 115
Western tradition, 97, 99, 101, 118, 122,
    128
Western values, 3–4, 44, 101, 107, 111–112,
    120, 128
Western Zhou period, 10
Westernization, 33, 112, 128
White Deer Grotto Academy 白鹿洞書院,
    16, 61
White Paper on Human Resource
    Development, 90
"working with (or even for) government,"
    95

world-class education, 47
    See also world-class higher education;
        world-class universities
Wong Fun 黃寬, 46
world-class higher education, 57
    See also world-class universities
world-class status, 85, 93–94, 96, 102, 109
world-class universities, 3, 4–6, 8, 75, 90, 94,
    107–108, 121, 126
World Economic Forum, 78
Wu Ta-You 吳大猷, 52
Wuchang Zhonghua University 武昌中華
    大學, 51

Xia dynasty, 10
Xiang 庠, 10
Xiao 校, 10
xiucai 秀才, 39, 58
Xu 序, 10
Xun Kuang, 17

yang 陽, 15–16, 19
    See also yin 陰
Yenching University 燕京大學, 45–47
Yingshi University 英士大學, 48
Yu period, 10
Yu Ying-shih 余英時, 11
Yuan dynasty, 15
Yung Wing 容閎, 46
yusaeng, 25

Zen, 107
Zeng Guofan 曾國藩, 35
Zhang Baixi 張百熙, 34
Zhang Deyi 張德彝, 37, 39
Zhang Zhidong 張之洞, 40, 43
Zhongguo Gongxue 中國公學, 51
Zhongti xiyong 中體西用, 43
Zhu Xi 朱熹, 61
Zhuangyuan 狀元, 48
Ziqiang Institute 自強學堂, 31, 40
Zongli Yamen 總理衙門, 38, 40
Zuo Zongtang 左宗棠, 40